PHOTOGRAPHERS ON THE ART OF PHOTOGRAPHY

In Conversation with Charles Moriarty

ACC ART BOOKS

ISBN: 9781788840880

British Library Cataloguing-in-Publication Data
A catalogue record for this book is available from the British
Library.

Design: Louise Brody

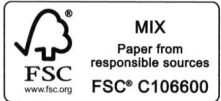

Printed in Slovenia
for ACC Art Books Ltd., Woodbridge, Suffolk, IP12 4SD, UK

www.accartbooks.com

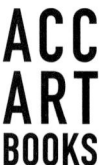

CONTENTS

INTRODUCTION

At a table with good friends, a conversation about the ever-evolving state of photography led to this book's birth. A book that in part asks why photography is important, but which also tries to discern what this art form brings to society, as it is so far removed from its basic origins as a means of documenting.

Being curious, and having been given the opportunity, I also wanted to ask questions that would relate to an individual's visual journey – and, more broadly, to the journey of life we are all on, in the modern image-saturated state of existence.

I'm not a journalist, or a writer. Though I have, with trepidation, started to carry the title of 'artist', I'm most comfortable with 'photographer'.

I began taking photographs when I was a teenager. I had a brief lesson with my art teacher about the darkroom and how to load a roll of film, and off I went. As a teenager, without much in the way of tutelage, my work was messy, but going on to study art history at university and being a massive cinephile really helped me understand things like composition and use of colour. For the longest time I had little regard for technicalities, and was more interested in finding or creating 'moments'. Photography wasn't something I took seriously – it was just another way of interacting with the people around me.

When I was 21 and finishing my first degree in London, I was asked by a friend to photograph a young up-and-coming singer she knew. That singer, Amy Winehouse, was working on an album and needed a cover. That one assignment led to the beginnings of my professional career. This moment would push me to move away from the film industry and into photography – so, without any real education, I pushed forward. Although I soon began to get a better handle on things, I did make mistakes – I still didn't know what an f-stop was.

Years later, when I finished a degree in photography (from the renowned institute, the London College of Communications) I still felt lost when it came to the medium. I spent most of my time working at a rowdy bar called The Florist in east London. I was also working on and off as a medical photographer, specialising in eyes. I was desperately trying to make ends meet. It would take several more years and false starts in the wrong direction before I could focus on making images, but eventually, I had to make a decision about who I was and who I wanted to be.

I think we all reach this fork in the road at some point in life. You have to make a decision about what's important to you. Photography had my heart.

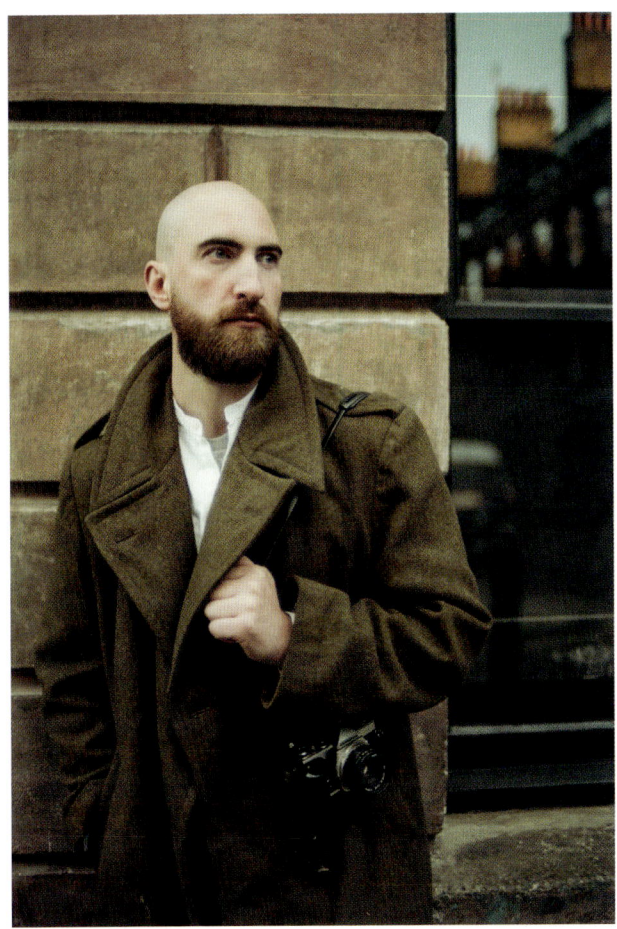

Charles Moriarty, © Fraser Rigg

lessons in how to live life as a photographer. It shows how everyone's path to success is different and, I think, inspiring.

Listening to and learning from the people in this book was a real joy. They come from all walks in life, and had so much to share. Sadly, since I started making the book, two of them have passed on: the great Terry O'Neill and the courageous Eva Sereny. It was a privilege to know both of them, even if only briefly. Neither will be forgotten.

It is somewhat ironic that so much of life can be captured in a still frame. Whether by happy accident or decided intent, photography continues to capture the ups and downs of life, from the street outside to scenes from around the world. Simple, intimate acts and grand, unending landscapes are delivered to our door each day via Instagram and other visual platforms, each image a window. I hope these interviews can also act as a window, bringing each reader into places new.

So, what lies before you? *Photographers on the Art of Photography* is a series of interviews (although some are more akin to conversations) with a diverse range of individuals about their own personal practice and experiences. It is not a technical how-to manual. Nobody here will guide you in the use of a camera, or tell you how to light for every occasion. But this book does share many

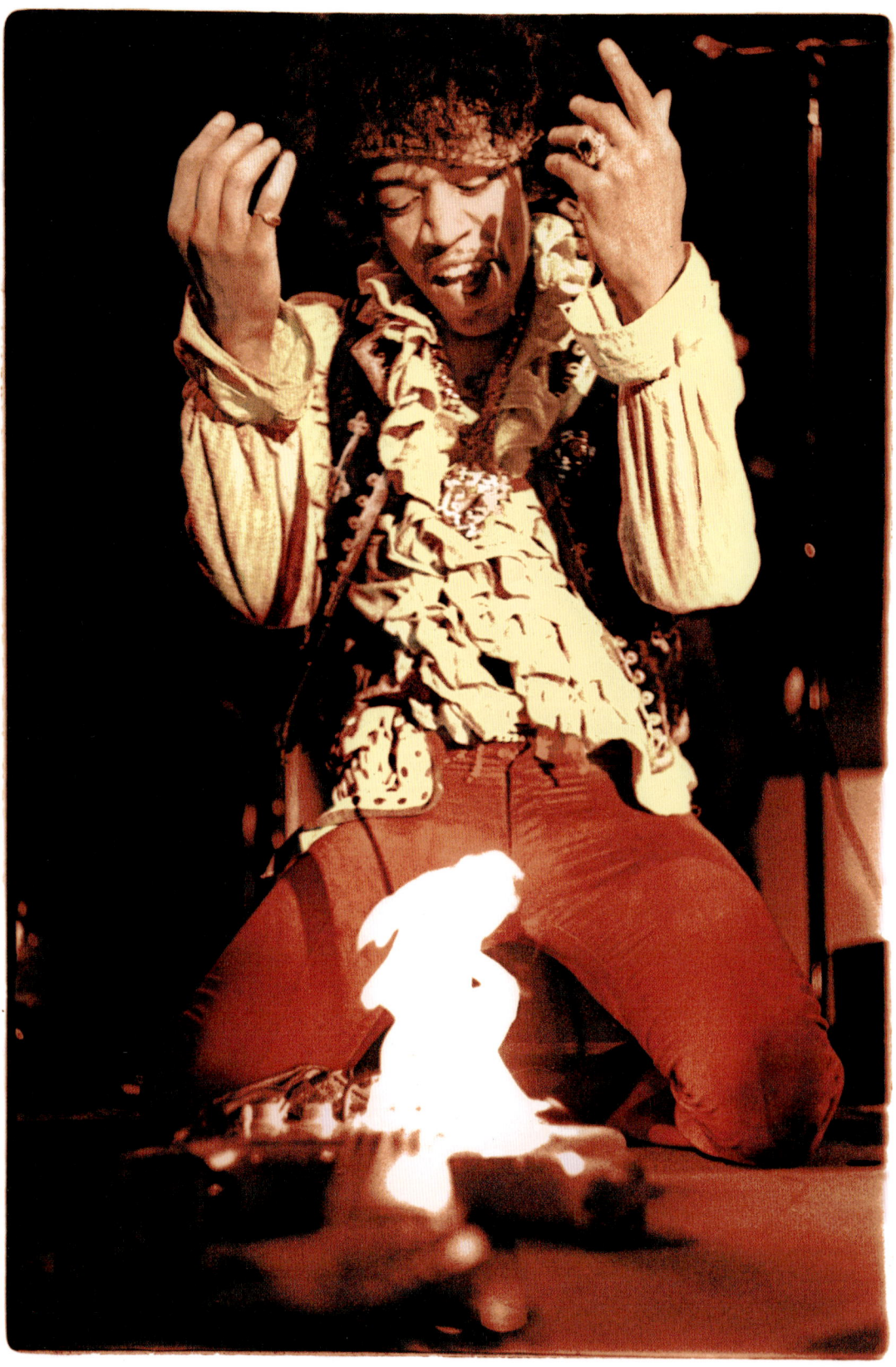

ED CARAEFF

I met Ed in a tiny taqueria in east
Los Angeles. It was the spring of 2019,
full of sun, palm trees and those Santa
Ana winds. Outside the restaurant sat
his midnight blue VW van, in which
he now mostly resides, journeying
across America. I wanted to talk to him
about his time as a photographer in LA,
starting out very young in the '60s,
then moving into the early '80s, when
he worked with some of the major
music icons of the time.

Ed Caraeff, Hendrix at Monterey, 1967
© Iconic images

Charles Moriarty:

How did it all kick off?

Ed Caraeff:

There was one photography teacher and I remember her to this day. She was younger than any [other] teacher.

She only wore black and her skin was real white, and she had black hair, you know? She was wacko. The kiddos liked that, you know? She had that style, and she was young, younger than most teachers. I thought... Well, I kind of had a crush on her. 'I'll take photography.' That was the reason.

CM:

For most teenage boys, it's a pretty good reason.

EC:

That was the reason. She was all business, no nonsense. I don't remember her laughing or joking, you know? Anything. [...] I kind of liked photography. I liked the concept of you having a light-sensitive material, whether it be film or paper or whatever, and you can control how much light gets on that through time and aperture. You know, the lens, and lenses. I liked the concept of it, and I loved working in the darkroom.

When I talk about it, I still smell the hypo smell. I wasn't really one to use the tongs. I put my hands right in there, you know? I liked photography and I took it again with her, Photography 2, Advanced. But during that semester my parents transferred me out of that school into a different one right near Los Angeles International Airport. When I got to the new school, they had a photography teacher, and he was like the coolest guy you'd ever met. To this day, he and his wife from back then are some of my best friends.

At this school I became the school photographer and he let me use the school's photography equipment any time I wanted, anywhere I wanted. He let me use the darkroom any time of day. [...] If

I skipped a class or whatever, I could work in the darkroom. Out of sight, out of mind was his attitude. Because that school was so close to Los Angeles International Airport, I started a career I never really knew existed, an occupation I never even considered – which was basically a rock-and-roll photographer. I'd photograph the models and comedians, lots of comedians, and bands arriving to Los Angeles.

I lived just miles from Hollywood so I spent all my time on Sunset Boulevard, Hollywood, offices. Big offices, little offices. Record companies, recording studios, parties in the Hollywood Hills. Hugh Hefner's penthouse parties before he moved to the mansion.

CM:

So, you were 15 when you started sneaking out?

EC:

I was about 15 and a half, which is too young to drive. But because I went to a school that was outside of my living district, I got a special permit, which was technically to drive to and from school. Not to drive around Hollywood at night. I still can't believe I never got caught doing that.

CM:

Do you remember what camera you started with?

EC:

I started with a plastic Brownie camera. It had a big button. You'd just rip film on paper, like a roll of film. It was made of plastic, Bakelite. I think it was called a Kodak Brownie camera. That was my first camera. From that I moved to the school's equipment, and after I sold my first photos, I bought a black Nikon F, with a sports finder, because I wear glasses when I photograph.

CM:

How did you get into venues to photograph at such an early age?

EC:

[...] Back in those days, you go to the airport, you could walk right down to where the plane gets next to the terminal. Different times. You'd bullshit your way in.

CM:

You've had three careers really. Do you still do much photography?

EC:

I have my camera [points to iPhone] right here. I love it. Nowadays my camera connects me to the internet. I can get phone calls and text messages with it. I love it. The editing and the things I can do, I used to pay tens of thousands of dollars and wait weeks for. [There were] two retouchers back in the day in this town. There were two people who could take out the bags under your eyes, whiten your eyes, take out that sign. There were only two people who could do that flawlessly in this town.

CM:

Who were they? Do you remember?

EC:

They were Charlie White and I can't remember the other person. Charlie White was my main go-to guy. This is very important; they could only do this magic on dye transfer prints, and there were only two people who made dye transfer prints. Bob DeSantas, I think was one. Do you know what a dye transfer print is?

[...] If you didn't print on a dye transfer, make a dye transfer print... [They were] very expensive, very specialised. If you didn't do that, the only way you could retouch was to add to the print, cover things with paint. But with a dye transfer print you could go in and bleach. Especially for all that smoothing stuff. But now I can do it with one hand as I eat.

CM:

What were your other careers?

EC:

My other career... hard to believe... I was an art director in New York City for five, six years. I started with CTI Records, a jazz label. They had an ad in *The New York Times* for an art director. They said, 'Are you calling about the art director job?'

I had already been art directing. I started as a photographer, just giving them the photos. Then I realised they were going to crop them square and create type and bleed around the sides. After seeing what they were doing with my photos, I started to realise that if the bands maybe were the same colour tone, it would be better. Then I started thinking about the lighting and the background. What is it about the name of the album or the band that relates to the photograph? Soon enough, the art directors would hire me and I'd deal with it.

CM:

So how long did you work as an art director? Did you stop taking pictures?

EC:

I stopped pretty much... By 1981 I was an art director. In 1980 I moved from California to Manhattan, to New York City

CM:

Going back to photography – you became infamous with the Hendrix image.

EC:

It took 20 years before people really saw that photo. There's actually a song about how you get famous when you're on the cover of *Rolling Stone*. [Dr Hook – 'The Cover of the *Rolling Stone*'] 20 years after the fact, Jann Wenner made [the Hendrix image]

famous when he called me and asked permission to put it on the cover – and in the same conversation, asked for permission to colourise it. That's when I was on my third career. I was a chef then.

CM:

I did wonder – was it originally black and white?

EC:

Black and white.

CM:

How did you feel about this happening 20 years later? Was that a great thing, or were you frustrated it took 20 years?

EC:

Well, when he told me on the phone, the way he framed it was that he was going to do a *Rolling Stone* issue on the best live shows of all time, the best live performance shows of all time. And he didn't hesitate. He said, 'I've got it down to two shots, but want to go with your shot of Jimi burning his guitar.'

I wasn't really one to use the tongs. I put my hands right in there, you know?

CM:

What was the other shot?

EC:

The other shot was Pete Townshend doing the windmill guitar thing that he does. I said, 'He does that every show.'

CM:

True. Were you more interested in shooting live music or did you prefer studio?

EC:

As soon as I could afford it, I had a Swiss-made strobe light set imported. It was this beautiful faded blue. Beautifully designed. I saw it in the best camera store in Hollywood. Seriously – I got it from Hollywood Boulevard, Chaffer Camera. I took it everywhere that I could plug it in.

My skills were that I developed all my own film [and] made all my own prints, including colour prints. And I did lighting. I mean, I knew the importance of lighting, lighting, lighting. They say restaurants are location, location. Well photography, let me tell you, it's lighting, lighting. It's a high 90 per cent lighting. Lighting, lighting, lighting. I had strobes and infrared strobes; I was totally into lighting.

CM:

You would like to think every photographer is.

EC:

I have a good story. Well, it's a lighting story [...] This is early '70s. But I'm really cooking now; I've got a nice unique home studio up in Beverly Hills. It's all happening. The phone rings early one morning. It was a Friday morning and it was the art director of Warner Bros. Records, Ed Thrasher. You know who he is? Really powerful guy. I worked with him because the acts would hire me. Most of my work came directly from the band. The record company would inherit me because they didn't want to piss the band off. So, that's how I knew Ed. He calls me and he's... I laugh when I think about it. He calls me and asks if I'm available at 5:00, you know? To go to the session where Frank Sinatra's recording and assist him with lighting it.

He's going to do the photography. But he's not a photographer. He said, 'Because Frank will only let people he knows photograph him, and he's comfortable with me photographing him.' Now, at the time, I wasn't into... I mean, I was into music. My mother was into Frank Sinatra, you know? So, I said thanks but no thanks, and I kind of regret that now.

But my point being, why I pivoted there was because... yeah. I mean who's going to light that? You know what you're going to get? You're going to get big hollowed-out eye sockets.

You can light it right. You can light it wrong. You can put a lot of your own attitude and style into how you light it. I had every effect and soft filter in the darkroom. I had stockings over knitting frames that I would move. I would print on number 6 Axford paper and get it so you pull it out just before it gets too contrast-y but not smoky, and keep it moving.

Right from the beginning, I would tilt the easel sometimes. Just put something under one end of like, a long thing, then crop it off or cut it off. I did that in my earliest high school work at 15. I was tilting the easel. And the texture screens – I mean right from the get-go. Sandwiching negatives was very popular with me. I would sandwich negatives and move them around a little bit. They would be on a strip, so you could move them and get a cloud.

CM:

Very surreal.

EC:

Oh, right from the beginning. Big influences, visual influences for me... this came later... but Magritte, mind blowing.

CM:

Who else were big influences for you?

EC:

Certain album covers, you know? In my family's stash of albums there was a comedy album by Lenny Bruce, where the cover is him alone having a picnic outdoors in a cemetery. Have you seen that one? [...] There was a photographer who I think actually photographed Magritte, named Duane Michals. He put a lot of motion in the photos and they were kind of surreal.

CM:

What was your set up like back then?

EC:

I had a studio, and another darkroom and another studio outside of my house. But I also had three people on the payroll and a partner, who was taking money of course. More bills meant I couldn't afford to miss a big payday.

I'd had a session scheduled for months with the Bee Gees. They had one afternoon where they were going to do a session, and that's a big billing job. That's all we need to say about that. And when they came to town, I was so sick. I had a high fever of – I think – 104. I remember the morning of the session before they came. I took an ice bath to get my fever down. That's how important it was to do that – and I did it.

The photos are iconic images. And you'd never know by looking at the photo that I was sick.

CM:

You've worked with quite a few iconic people. How often did you work with Dolly?

EC:

I think I did three or four covers. [...] Dolly was a country artist and I had her country albums. My musical case is very broad to this day. It's all over the place. I had Dolly's album at the time I got the phone call. [...] Dolly had, I believe, signed a new record deal with a new producer and a new manager. And the manager chose me and contacted me to, I quote, 'photograph Dolly and get her out of the country thing into a more contemporary setting.'

So, I was selected specifically for that purpose. I first met Dolly when I knocked on the door of a Beverly Hills hotel room. She opened the door and said, 'Come on in.' [...] I was driving her, she was coming in my car. I lived right up the road and I had a Volkswagen Beetle at the time. I said, 'What are you bringing?' Because that's super important, right? Especially with Dolly. Who knows what it's going to be? And she said, 'Well, come into my closet and you pick.'

That was that. So, I picked the shorts and the *Li'l Abner* polka dot. Well, I'll send you a photo. I picked the outfits and drove her up and photographed her. There was a store in Santa Monica called the Plastic Mart. They made everything out of plastic and they had rolls of plastic. You buy by the yard and they had black vinyl and red vinyl. And I had some of that and if you rolled it and hung it and then hit it with a strobe, it made a neat effect. So, I did some stuff with that plastic. I shot 35 but Hasselblad. I got Hasselblad as soon as I could afford that with Polaroid backs. I had two of them.

I mean, I was rocking and rolling. I had a motorised Hasselblad, regular Hasselblad. I had fish-eye lenses; I had Polaroid backs for them. I had a DISTO French tripod. I mean, I'm shooting squares *exact*. I need *exact*. I know exactly how much I need to bleed around the back. I need to see everything. I want it square. I want to use strobes; I want to see a Polaroid that I'll pop on the other back. It was great. That was my main way to jam, as soon as I could afford it.

I photographed Dolly and then drove her back to the hotel and then came back up the hill to my place to develop all the film, including the colour film. As soon as it was safe to look at it on my light box, I did the edit. This is the same day.

CM:

A very fast turnaround.

EC:

I did the edit and then I made a composite Cibachrome print. I had an idea where I put three of the shots together. The next day, I had an appointment to see Dolly and her new manager at his house in Bel Air, way up there. I had the whole set. I had a light box and loops. I took all the photos and my composite. I went up there and Sandy Gallin – he was a great guy – said, 'Follow me.' He took me to his bedroom suite and I remember he had exercise equipment. I had never seen anybody who had exercise equipment. It was like, 'Whoa. I want to be you badly.' He took me to the bedroom. The bed was made, and sitting on the bed, dressed, was Dolly. [...] My sister used to conduct business on a bed. Nothing out of the ordinary. It's a made bed. Meticulous, everything's meticulous. Bigger than this restaurant.

[Sandy] goes, 'How'd they come out?' So, I take out the composite print, which had [...] the logo on it, the one [Dolly] uses today. Which I art-directed someone doing. I picked the guy who had the style I wanted, named Mike Manoogian. Anyways – I laid it out. They never even looked at the other shots. That's how it went most of the time. They liked my edit. I printed it on a 10-and-a-half inch square because the paper didn't go big enough. So, they saw a little mini album cover. Years after, she came to my studio on Robertson, the second one, in a limousine, just to give me gold albums of it and hug me.

CM:

How did you end up working with Elton so much? You were at his Troubadour gig, all those years ago.

EC:

I met Elton in London, backstage at a show done by Three Dog Night. I was Three Dog Night's photographer. They took me to Europe for their first visit when they played the Marquee Club. I'm there with the band, who were friends of mine by then. Backstage after the gig, in the dressing room, Elton and Bernie [Taupin] came by, because Three Dog Night covered one of their songs on their album, 'Lady Samantha'.

Crosby, Stills & Nash's first album just came out that week. Elton and Bernie had a copy, and they said to us, 'You want to come back to listen to it in the control room on the speakers...?' So we all went back and we bonded, and that's how I met Elton and Bernie.

At that point I didn't know anything about any of them. They weren't famous. 'Your Song' hadn't hit yet. I met their art people. They didn't have a photographer, but they had art director people, friends who did their albums and graphics. We met them.

Then Elton comes for the first time to the Troubadour. I'm up at the hotel that afternoon when they arrive, and while I'm in his hotel room, I take a photo, which became the cover image for *Honky Château*.

CM:

It's a really nice photo of him. Tell me this – for people who are starting out in photography, what would you give as advice?

EC:

Good luck. I have no clue how you would do that. It's easy nowadays to get good photos. If you're going to monetise, I can't tell you how to do that.

CM:

That's the hard part. You never had an agent, or anything like that?

EC:

I didn't have a portfolio. I had nothing on the walls of my house or studio.

CM:

It was your relationships with the artists that led you to keep that all going?

EC:

And record companies, yeah. I didn't fuck anybody over, because I grew up in the offices of record company presidents yelling and screaming about album covers and waiting and deadlines, and 'I had to wait for the fucking lyrics and now I want this. How long is this going to take? Retouching? I don't have no time for...'

[...] I knew it wasn't me, so I didn't take it personally. I was always very professional.

CM:

How is your journey going?

EC:

I made a bucket list. What would I regret? Not going, doing, experiencing, saying something to somebody. Travelling. I've travelled to so many places. I regretted that I didn't do what some of my close friends did. Before they started college or whatever, they just drove around and... no reservations. Mostly New Mexico, California, Nevada. Well, I had a little practice before I decided to do this. I spent a year and a half renting campers. I was still cooking, but I would rent the camper and go out. Do I really want to live in 80 square feet? Luckily, I could rent a camper and try it. And I loved it. I got my house. I have everything right here. It's kind of nice.

CM:

In the end, everything has worked out.

EC:

It all comes out in the wash.

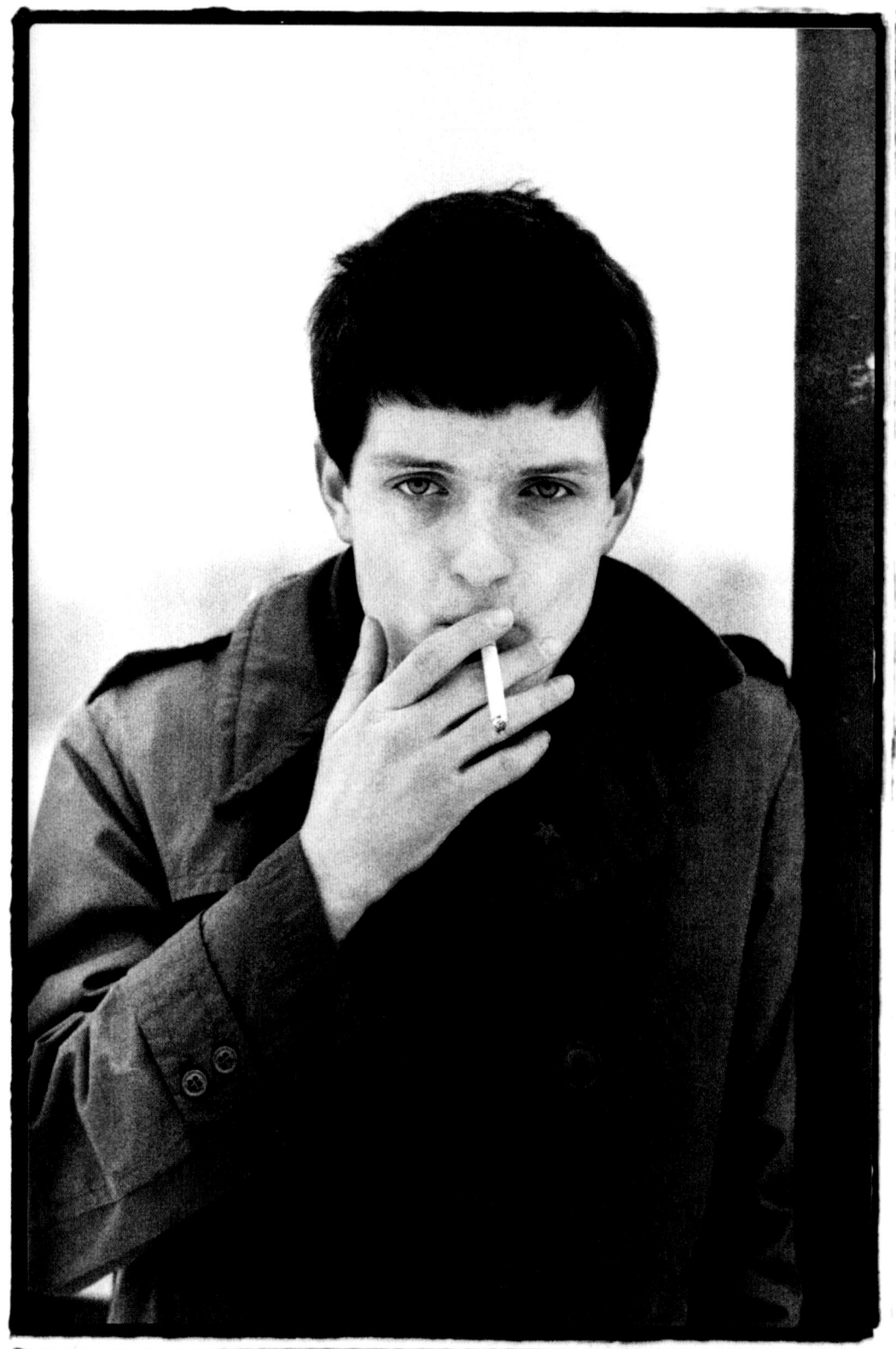

I've had the pleasure of knowing Kevin casually for a few years now. We crossed paths more often than not over a glass of wine in The French House on Dean Street, Soho. I've admired Kevin's work since I started reading *NME* and *The Face* as a teenager, but it wasn't until later in life, when his book on Joy Division was released, that I began to understand who Kevin really was. Kevin has captured the British and global music scene and brought them into our homes. I caught up with him over a pint in London at the start of autumn, 2019.

Singer Ian Curtis (1956-1980) of Manchester rock band Joy Division, Manchester, 6 January 1979. (Photo by Kevin Cummins/Getty Images)

Charles Moriarty:

I've probably been looking at your work without knowing it for decades. You were quite prolific on the Manchester music scene, and some of your work is instantly iconographic. You started taking photographs when you were quite young, right?

Kevin Cummins:

[...] I got a camera for my fifth or sixth birthday, and on a holiday to London I shot a roll of film. My dad showed me how to process and print it. I used to play around in the darkroom, making photograms and stuff like that. I got really into it and as a teenager it took over a bit. I was going to go to Warwick University, to do Russian-American Studies, and a friend said, 'Why don't you go to art school? It's more what you want to do. You don't want to be a teacher.' Much to my parents' annoyance, about three weeks before I was supposed to go to Warwick, I changed and studied photography and graphic design at Salford.

CM:

What was that like?

KC:

It wasn't great. I wanted to go to Manchester Poly, but because we lived in Salford, I couldn't get a grant to go to Manchester. I got a grant to go to Salford because I lived there; no choice was given. It was good in a way because it taught me a lot about composition and working with other people. [...] I think I learned more when I landed on my feet. When you leave education, you don't have four months to a project.

[...] I did work experience, I think, for a week with a fashion photographer in my final year, a guy in Manchester. I learned more about the industry in that week than my whole time at college, because he was quite lazy and he'd sit there with a bottle of red wine all day. Manchester is a big fashion-brand, catalogue place, and so there were several model agencies and a couple of fashion photographers who shot everything. This guy's name was Roger Alexander. I sat around watching him and chatted to models all week.

While I was there, he had one shoot. He showed me how he did it, and he was very engaging. I thought I would spend three months shooting something that was supposedly for a magazine so we could learn grid design and layout, how to tell a photo story – whereas he'd dick about all week and then...

CM:

Just snap away for a few hours and be done?

KC:

I understood then, that's kind of how it has to be. I learned. When I graduated college, I started shooting bands – punk had exploded in Manchester. But I also started teaching photography for a year, two days part time, twice a week at Salford, to first-year students. Mainly so I could have access to the darkroom and the equipment. I needed that at the time, because I only had one camera body with a standard lens.

CM:

What did you start with?

KC:

Pentax Spotmatic SP-500. They were the cameras we had at college, and we had all the lenses so there was no point in me buying a Nikon or anything else because I would have had to buy the whole kit. I also did two days a week printing for industrial photographers, about 10 miles outside [Manchester]...

CM:

When you say 'industrial', what do you mean?

KC:

They were photographing machinery and stuff like that. I was also doing PR things. They used to do a PR shoot with [people] shaking hands in front of a new bit of machinery. I'd have to do 200 prints of that, so I learned how to make 200 prints in an hour.

You have to use the developer at a lower temperature, because it warms up the more prints you put in. I'd do 50 at a time, using your hands always; you don't use tongs. So, by the time the 50th was in, which was maybe five minutes after the first one had gone in, the first one was ready to come out. And all the time you're moving the desk light. It really taught me very quickly how to print real amounts.

When I used to shoot a gig for the *NME* I'd have to stay completely sober because I was driving 10 miles outside Manchester after a gig. I'd stay up, talk to the band and all that stuff. Then I'd have to go back to Salford, process the negatives, dry them, contact sheet them, pick the best six prints, do those, dry them and then drive back into Manchester.

The only way you could get pictures to paper in those days was by putting them on the train, the Red Star Parcel service. I would go to Piccadilly in Manchester, put the pictures on the train and, hopefully, someone at the *NME* would pick them up at about 10 o'clock in the morning. I'd get home about 6:00 in the morning and I'd have to start work again at 8:00. I'd get £6.50 if they used a picture and it would cost me...

CM:

Way more than £6.50 was worth, I imagine.

KC:

14 hours, maybe.

CM:

Do you remember the first gig you shot?

KC:

I wanted to photograph Bowie when I was at college, so I went to see him at the Free Trade Hall in Manchester. I just took a camera with me. No one was bothered in those days, and not many people had a decent camera, obviously. Towards the end of the show, he did this mime to 'The Width of a Circle', the song. And there was a moment where I felt if I'd been stood in a different place, I'd have got a better shot, so I went to see him two weeks later in Leeds.

CM:

And stood in the right spot, I presume?

KC:

I waited for that moment and got the shot. I think that's when I learned never to be complacent and not to settle for the first picture, if you don't think it's the best one. Try and find another way of doing it.

I was on tour with Perry Farrell in the summer, and I think that the first gig was a bit of a nightmare because I didn't know anything. They'd already been touring in America, but I didn't know their stage set up. I spent half my time running around, trying to be in the places that I should've known to be in. MTV was a boon, because when you were able to watch bands on TV you could see whether that person held the microphone in their left hand or their right hand, or whether they looked at their guitarist a lot or they looked at their bass player a lot. You knew where to stand to get the best shot.

I'd always try and research it as much as possible and look at photos and music papers. See where I felt the best picture would come from, because in those days you didn't have a pit, so you didn't get anywhere. Once you'd chosen your spot you couldn't really move, you had to stay there.

CM:

I know you mentioned shooting Bowie when you were at college but was Joy Division your real big start into that world?

KC:

Buzzcocks were, really. Joy Division weren't big at all. Not until Ian died, and then maybe 10 years after that. I can tell by the print sale I have with agencies. I hardly sold any Joy Division until the 10th anniversary of Ian's death.

CM:

I'm expecting that to happen with Amy Winehouse a bit.

KC:

The problem you have with that is, lots of people photographed her. Whereas lots of people didn't photograph Joy Division, because there wasn't a platform. I could photograph any band out on the street and no one would give me a second glance, whereas these days with digital and with everybody carrying a camera around with them, it's very difficult.

I was photographing an actor on the bank of the Thames for the National Theatre. She had an ice cream and was licking her fingers, with the raspberry sauce in the ice cream and stuff, and she said, 'This is getting really difficult.' And I said, 'Why? Do you want another ice cream?' We had a big tub of ice cream. And she said, 'Have a look up there.' I looked up and there was about 600 people photographing me photographing her.

I always liken it to being almost like the new Victorians. When photography became something that wasn't just used by wealthy people, by photo studios or by priests and the clergy; once Kodak made it affordable to the masses, everybody got shoot cameras and they were out photographing their street. You find at the turn of the century you've got thousands of pictures of every street in Britain. They'd get them printed cheaply as postcards and send them to family.

We're like that now. We're photographing everything we do and not editing it, because people aren't taught how to edit; they don't understand how to edit.

You must get it? People sending you things all the time. One sentence about liking you, then, 'Will you look at my pictures? Will you have a look?' Then they send you 5000 pictures they've taken at a gig, one gig.

CM:

I would witness trigger-happy photographers regularly while working backstage at fashion week.

KC:

I said, 'Pick five you like.' 'I like them all.' Well, you can't like 5000 pictures.

You might as well have just shot a movie and taken some stills from it. When I shot a gig I would shoot, generally, one roll of film. I'd make it last, because I was paying for the film and also because it makes it easier to edit.

I shoot digital in the same way. I shoot it really sparingly and if I shoot theatre, I don't just keep my finger on the trigger and shoot a whole scene. I pick the shot and I wait for the right moment, and if I don't get it then it's tough luck.

[...] People just take pictures of absolutely anything, and bands do, as well. When I was working for the *NME*, when *NME* music press existed, we were building iconography. Now there's no iconography. There's no iconography because bands give too much information away. The reason those pictures of Joy Division are so valued is, firstly, because pictures of Ian are scarce. Secondly, because when I was photographing him in his raincoat, with a cigarette, I took maybe five frames. Now I'd take a hundred, but it wouldn't be as good.

When I'm shooting a portrait, I'm looking through the camera and I'm waiting for a moment. If I just stand there and press the trigger, I'm not going to ever get that. The other thing with portrait photography is, you've got to break the barrier of the camera down. They have to respond to you, and that's where the film plane is. If they're just looking at the lens, they're not responding to you. I think the reason people love some of my pictures is because there's a lot of trust in them.

CM:

The camera disappears, essentially.

KC:

The camera's gone, yeah, and that's the most important thing. I think when you're being commissioned by people at record labels, you're being commissioned by people who make good in their own field, but they don't understand that.

I've been on trips with bands – we used to get maybe five days in LA with a band for an *NME* feature. I'd maybe not shoot anything for two days. You want to get to know what the dynamic is, and that's what I want. And you've got a PR constantly nudging you in the ribs, saying, 'That's a good picture, why don't you take that?'

You take it, if you think it's that good. They don't let you do your job because they don't really understand what you're doing or why they're paying you when they could actually, they think, probably take it on their phones.

CM:

Sadly, that is often the thought in people's heads: 'I can just do that on my phone.'

KC:

And they do. And bands do it. Bands take pictures of themselves in the dressing room, just as they're going on stage. All sorts of stuff. Less is more. You don't want to know everything about a band. You want to imagine what they're doing. There's no mystery any more. I would've hated to think of David Bowie sitting down for breakfast. I wanted to think he'd be in a spaceship and have moon dust. Not that he'd just eaten the same standard stuff I've had.

> I think sometimes, if you go completely over the top and then rein it in, you'll get the shot you want.

CM:

When did you start at NME*?*

KC:

'77. I worked with them for 20 years. I moved to London in '87 so I could do more. I was doing everything I could in Manchester. I shoot a lot of theatre and I got to a point where I was shooting every theatre company and I was shooting all of the music stuff, as well. But you're never taken seriously if you don't live in London, unfortunately, so I had to move here. I'd come down to London every couple of weeks to show them I was still alive. And they'd wonder, 'Why don't you go and photograph acts?' And then if I sat in Manchester, I'd never get a phone call, so I'd have to come down again.

CM:

You were one of the founders of The Face. *It's probably one of the most iconic magazines of that whole period. It's one of the first magazines that I collected as a teenager.*

KC:

I've still got the first 100 issues.

CM:

Stacked somewhere in the house?

KC:

Yeah [...] It was interesting to do stuff for *The Face*, but I felt quite detached from it, being in Manchester. I used to have to come down, so I'd come down to London to go into the *NME* office, go into *The Face* office, get a commission and then get back on the train again.

CM:

Did the move to London land you with a very full schedule?

KC:

It made a massive difference. I could go to editorial meetings and I could be part of the decision making. When I moved down, it was just as the whole Manchester acid house thing started. It was all happening in Manchester – so I had to go back to Manchester about twice a week, having moved away. It's quite funny really, because I've lived here in London for 33 years and I still get people saying, 'Oh, have you just come down for the day? What time's your train?'

Even people I see at the weekends sometimes, when I go up for football, they'll start a conversation with you in the pub as if you've just been to the toilet, rather than not been in the pub for two weeks. It's like we're carrying on a conversation from two weeks ago. Then they'll say, 'Oh, when did you move down? When did you move to London? It's a shit hole isn't it?' [...] Most Man City fans – or most football fans – their idea of London is Euston Underground and a pub, so they don't really engage with the city.

CM:

You've got a decent scene in London for live music. What content did you start shooting after '87? Was it always music?

KC:

I concentrated mainly on music. I would obviously get commissions, because I'd photographed in the theatre scene for about 10 years in Manchester. I still have that link. I've done things at the Royal Court and the National Theatre and so on. I also shoot for Adidas. [...] A photograph of a person is a photograph of a person, whoever they are.

When the *NME* existed, I had a lot of freedom and I could do whatever I wanted. Luckily, because I'd built up a good reputation over the years, when I've shot things for the National Theatre or when I've shot stuff for Adidas, they just let me do what I want.

CM:

They have confidence.

KC:

Yeah, which is really nice, because otherwise you end up thinking, 'What am I? Am I a photo booth?' if you're being so heavily art directed you're just somebody who owns a camera bag.

CM:

Do you have a process?

KC:

I gave you the example earlier, where you could research how a band looked on stage and then make sure to be in the right place for that. I plan things a little bit. If I'm shooting something for a play, I'll read the text, obviously, so I get a sense of who, what it is and what they're doing. But quite often, you're given no time with anybody.

If you're shooting for a newspaper, for instance, you've got hardly any time. You've just got an actor in a hotel room and he's on an afternoon junket. He's doing five interviews and you've got to get a shot. My thinking with something like that is, I want to get the best picture out of the five people who are shooting. You give yourself a challenge, really.

When I had to photograph Javier Bardem, for instance, at The Dorchester, it was for the whole of Japan. It was for the Japanese distributors of his film and he wasn't going to do photos. He was just doing interviews. And they gave me five minutes for the whole of Japan, in a flowery hotel, for what was a gritty movie. I was sat talking to PR while one of the interviews was going on, and I said, 'I'm going to need him to go outside to do this shot.' 'He can't go outside.' So I said, 'I need him to step out of his room because this room is terrible.' 'He's not going outside the room.' So I said, 'Okay.'

When he turned up, I shook hands with him and I was having a chat and the PR said, '4 minutes, 20 seconds.' And I said, 'Okay.' I said, 'Can you come out in the corridor?' He said, 'Yeah, of course.'

They were going mad because I'd asked him to step into the corridor, after I'd been explicitly told not to do that. I thought, 'I've got to get the best shot.'

I shot him in the corridor, under a light on the wall, and exposed for that. And I got two people walking down the corridor and I shot it wide open so at 1.4 or 1.2, their silhouettes were in the background and then I couldn't get rid of the dark. I made it look like it was shot at an underpass. We came back in, after I'd taken these pictures, and he said, 'You got two minutes left.' And I said, 'Don't need them.'

Then they asked to see the pictures, and I went home and did them and sent them through. He'd just done a 20-grand shoot, the day before in Spain, and they scrapped the whole thing and bought mine.

I did that in 3 minutes and, well, 2 minutes 20 seconds actually. There's no point ever in complaining about the time you've been given, when you're doing a job like that. You've got to…

CM:

Work with what you have.

KC:

And also, you've got to sometimes go with an idea. If you know you're not going to get any time with anyone, or if a musician is notoriously late, I've always got two or three stock shots in my head that I can use. I think, 'Right, I can do this with them if this is the situation. I can shoot it like this.'

For instance, once we wanted to do an *NME* cover with Todd Terry, who's an acid house producer, and we wanted him to wear a smiley baseball cap. He hated the whole smiley scene. So I thought, 'If I ask him to wear a smiley baseball cap, he's not going to do it.'

There was a shop at the time at Covent Garden that sold all that gear and I bought about 50 quid's worth of smiley stuff. Bandanas, baseball cap, badges, everything. I had five minutes in the hotel with him and he was reluctant to even turn up. I said to him, 'Right, we've got five minutes. This is what I want you to do.' I said, 'Stand in front of that banner, with your bandana on with that, with the t-shirt.' And he said, 'I'm not doing that.' And I said, 'How about if you just put the baseball cap on?' And he was so relieved at not having to wear it all he puts on the baseball cap. I said, 'Do you want to hold the bandana a bit, as well?'

And so, I got the shot I wanted. I actually got more out of it than I wanted, but if I had just asked him to do it initially... I think sometimes, if you go completely over the top and then rein it in, you'll get the shot you want.

CM:

What's a nightmare scenario for you?

KC:

You can get to a point where everyone hates each other and there's absolutely no respect. That's always problematic. I always remember Derek Ridgers going to Australia to photograph Evan Dando. Evan Dando didn't get out of bed for three days. In the end, Derek convinced the record company that since he'd actually travelled to Sydney, he had to go home with something – so he said, 'I'll photograph him in the bed, since he won't get up.' And Dando said, 'Okay.' He agreed to do it. Derek walked into his bedroom and said, 'Well, just put a t-shirt on.' And he pulled this t-shirt on that was under his bed, and Derek said, 'I see the invention of the iron has passed you by.'

Derek would really wind people up because he didn't actually care. I'll never wind anyone up when I'm photographing them. I had a similar problem

with Duran Duran. All stayed in separate hotels, not getting out of bed, not coming down to...

CM:

Did they hate each other that much?

KC:

Yeah. Management would say it was for security reasons, but that was a lie, just a cover story. That was a nightmare. We were there for a week for a one-day shoot and I ended up shooting 18 frames. It was an impossible job. When you work for a music paper, you're not getting paid very much either. You're just getting repro; you're not getting a commission for it. So, if there are five people in London who might run it, you can do five individual shots.

At least it makes the job worthwhile, which is why I started shooting people like the New Order session, with three silhouettes and one lit in the foreground, because then I knew I'd get four pictures in rather than one. Obviously, aesthetically it's an interesting shot and I always felt they were very young and easy standing together anyway. It made it a more interesting shot to just put three silhouettes, then a light wall, make shapes with it, and then do four separate shots like that.

CM:

How do you feel about the disappearance of the NME*?*

KC:

Kids get their information from all sources, don't they? No one wants to wait a week for a record or a review. They just press a button and they can hear it straight away.

People around the world used to treat the *NME* as a bible almost. It was virtually impossible to get that information in countries like Chile or Eastern Europe. They'd wait months to read anything.

They'd finally get some underground copy of it, find something they liked, try and send off for it and hope it wasn't stopped at the border. And six months after the record had come out, they might actually get to hear it.

That's why I always felt we had a responsibility to our reader to, in a photograph, tell them what the band were going to be like. With Joy Division, on the bridge shot in the snow, you look at that and you know what their sound's going to be like.

I saw a photo, before the *NME* finished. It was a print edition. I saw a photo with The Strokes for a public feature, and it looked like the photographer was terrified of the band. He or she had taken the photograph from about 200 yards away. Hadn't even bothered talking to them. I couldn't see the point of the shot – it was taken from across the road or something, I don't know. I didn't get it. I didn't understand the picture.

CM:

You worked a lot with The Smiths. How was that?

KC:

Good. I've always got on with the people I photograph. It's rare that there's any antagonism, at all. The first photo I did of The Smiths was quite interesting. What normally happens with a young band when you're photographing them and they're not used to being photographed – it was the same with The Sway – they stand... What I normally do is, I say, 'Right, stand over there or stand here or whatever.' I move them around a bit, and they always stand in the same positions they stand on stage.

CM:

What I find really funny is when you ask them to stand together and have a bit of a laugh, to try and communicate some form of togetherness or joviality, they can't do it.

KC:

Quite often they stand as if they're waiting for a bus. I can move them around a bit. [...] Because I quite often used to shoot portraits with a 35mm lens – or even wider, 28 sometimes – I'm *this* close to them, and because it's quite difficult explaining what you want with people, I'd just be grabbing them and saying, 'Go like that.' I'd just move their face. So, I say, 'Look, I'm actually going to touch you a lot while I do this and I need you to understand that.'

It makes it easier. I did a session once, when Suede first started, and I felt that they were all quite uneasy in front of the camera, so I just said, 'Look, why don't you come back tomorrow and learn how to pose?' I put mirrors around the camera, full length mirrors. I said, 'I'm not going to put any film in but just watch yourselves when you're being photographed.' And I spent a couple of hours pretending to take pictures of them, so they could just get used to how it looked. Then when we did the session, it was great.

CM:

You've been lauded as having taken some of the greatest images in rock 'n' roll, particularly by people in the industry and musicians. But for you, what are the images that hold real importance and emotional value?

KC:

It's difficult, because I like pictures that remind me of certain moments. Quite a lot of people I photograph like that. So the pictures of Ian, prior to the first session I was commissioned to do for the *NME* – he died a month after I shot them. I was 23, and apart from my tortoise, I'd never know anyone die. It was quite a shock.

We'd also had a really brilliant time with Marc Bolan. We spent three days with him. He was a very, very lovely person. He just dragged us round the studio and around Manchester. We – Paul Morley and I – had a great time.

CM:

You've moved through a lot of musical changes and scenes. Do you have a favourite?

KC:

I like punk [...] I like glam because that's what I grew up liking. I liked punk because I liked the energy of it, and being part of that scene. I wasn't a punk but everyone I knew was, and we used to just really have a great time.

CM:

I read that Iggy threw a chair at you. Did he say sorry after?

KC:

He gave me his shirt, actually, as an apology. It had red make-up on it, like fake blood. It was in a drawer at my mother's and she said, 'I threw that old shirt out.'

CM:

She didn't.

KC:

She threw Iggy's shirt out.

CM:

No.

KC:

I know, I know, I know.

CM:

What are you shooting at the moment?

KC:

I'm doing a shoot for Adidas next week, actually. It's style stuff. It's a capsule range. I like it because, again, they let me do what I want.

CM:

Where do you see everything going?

KC:

That's a hell of a question. I'm lucky, I guess. I photographed music through its absolute heyday. I also photographed it when people couldn't afford to pay for it. Now it's very difficult. I get asked to do loads of stuff for no money. Sometimes you can do it – for instance, if New Order need something Joy Division-like for merch or for their stage, I can do it because I've done well out of my archive. But when you're being asked to shoot someone new and being told it's good for exposure, I'd say fuck exposure.

Sometimes I don't even mind helping out young bands. I just did a shoot, actually, in the Czech Republic, in Prague, for a band there whose manager absolutely loves Joy Division. He wanted to know if I could do it and so I said, 'Yeah, why not?' The shots are nice and they're very much my style. Because I was going over to Prague to photograph this band, I did a piece on national TV of why I was there. I did interviews for three different magazines. They were excited I was coming over to photograph one of their bands.

CM:

Do you have photographers that influenced you?

KC:

Because I studied photography, I studied Diane Arbus and Bill Brandt and August Sander. I really liked Snowdon and thought he was very underrated.

I felt his portraits were very, very engaging. But what I learned from Snowdon [Antony Armstrong-

Jones, 1st Earl of Snowdon] was, he understood that you couldn't just get the royal family together and say, 'Right, now shall we go over there? Shan't go over there. Let's just have a walk round and see.' You've got to have the idea ready. He would prep it the day before with his assistants and friends and he'd shoot that picture and get the shot exactly right, and then he would say to the royal family, 'Right, you go here.' And he'd do it in 20 minutes. And I thought that was a brilliant, brilliant idea.

That's why I always felt we had a responsibility to our reader to, in a photograph, tell them what the band were going to be like.

I took that and used it right from the start when I was working with people, like when I photographed New Order. The silhouette shots, and others, but particularly those. I spent 12 hours, the day before, doing the shoot. Trying different angles, trying different ways of lighting it, different backgrounds. I had a colour lab directly behind my studio in Manchester. I'd send off to get a clip test, look at it. I worked the whole shot out, and then when New

Order turned up, it took 10 minutes to take six rolls of film, with a band shot and then four individual portraits, four lots of pictures. To this day, they think that shot took 10 minutes. They have no idea I spent hours doing it. And they don't need to. It's not their business.

Similarly, if I was going to New York to photograph a band, I'd work out exactly where I wanted to take it. I take a picture with a press officer or with my assistant and I'd have the shot ready and I'd know where I was going to shoot it from, how I wanted it to work, what the shutter speed was going to be, everything down to the finest detail. The only problem you've got then is when the musicians say, 'Oh, I don't want to do that.' And you've spent half a day doing it.

CM:

Have you had that often?

KC:

I've had it a couple of times. But generally, the main problem you've got working with musicians is that there's only one 10 o'clock in a day.

CM:

It tends to be the one where there's no light left.

KC:

You've also got to have absolute, supreme patience. I say to people my job is 90 per cent sitting in hotel lobbies waiting for people to turn up and 10 per cent photography. I can do a very nice book of hotel lobbies, if anyone's interested.

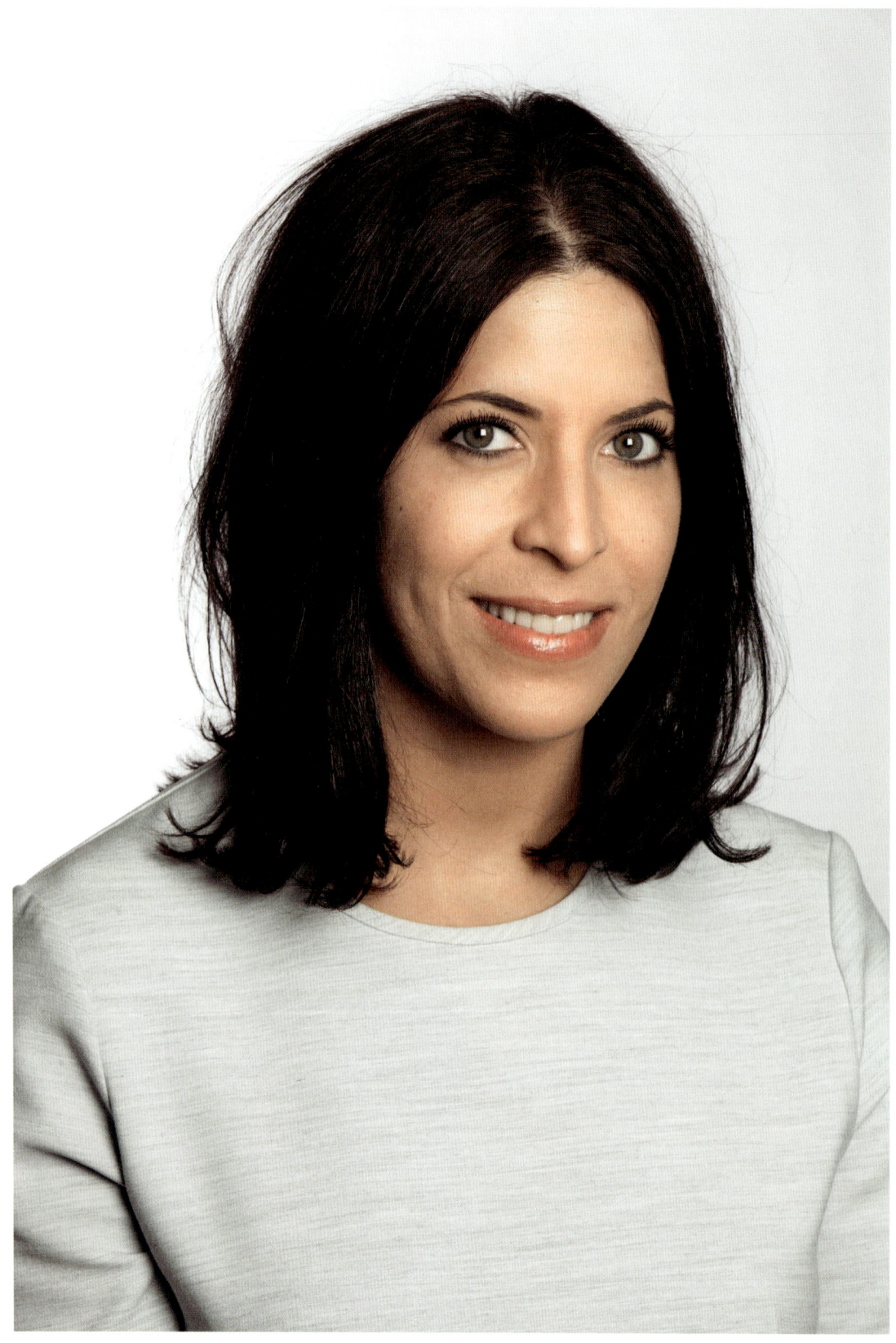

BRANDEI ESTES

I first met Brandei at an event in Soho for acclaimed photographer Tony McGee. We talked briefly about photography but would later reconnect at the *Masculinities* exhibition at the Barbican, over works by Peter Hujar, Richard Avedon, Robert Mapplethorpe, Sunil Gupta and many more. We hopped on the phone on a Saturday in London's second lockdown, November 2020, to talk about photography and the art of selling, buying and collecting it.

Charles Moriarty, Brandei Estes, 2021
© Charles Moriarty

Charles Moriarty:

Brandei, could you please introduce yourself?

Brandei Estes:

I'm the head of photographs at Sotheby's in London, and I've been here just over seven years. My background has always been in photography. I worked for almost 11 years in galleries, so I worked in the primary market before I went to Sotheby's. When I worked in the galleries of London and Paris, I was always focused on photography, but I also worked in a contemporary gallery when I first moved to Paris, and I studied history of art and Italian at university. So, my background has always been in the arts. At university I studied High Renaissance arts — completely different from what I do now. In my role as head of photographs at Sotheby's here in London, I look after all the sales, all the consignments and photographs.

Every time you see a photo at Sotheby's, I have looked at it, approved it, put a value on it and checked it. My main work is client facing: going out and meeting clients, and finding works, particularly high-value lots. I also do selling [...] but the harder part is finding pieces, and finding real gems, sourcing them and then negotiating deals and contracts.

[...] I like to be either with the photograph, or with the person, or both. I like research, but I'm more of a people person. For my job, I usually travel every 10 days; I'm on a plane going somewhere, looking at a work, meeting a client, going to a photo fair or festival. I also teach collecting photography. I guest lecture, and I nominate and judge photo competitions. [...] It's my – I don't want to say my dream job, but it's pretty close. I'm pretty happy, and lucky, and I count my blessings every day.

CM:

Where did you grow up?

BE:

I was born in the States. I first came to London in the early '80s, as a child with my family. I grew up mainly here, and in Hong Kong and Singapore. I never lived [in the States] as an adult. I spent a very small part of my childhood there, but my family are still there, so I go back often [to see them], and also for work. I'm in the States a lot.

CM:

When did photography start to emerge as something you were interested in?

BE:

When I left university, I started working for David Gill, who is a design curator and gallerist. When I arrived to work for him, I quickly fell in love with his photography collection. I hadn't studied photography at all. I went to UCL here in London, and I think the latest class I took was [on art from] around 1860. So, I didn't study the Impressionists, modern, or contemporary art. I missed photography at university. Well, I say miss, but in a way...

CM:

It was hardly there.

BE:

Exactly. But I feel like I had a really good, solid foundation of the typical canon that youth study in a Western university. I enjoyed that. Then it was so nice to discover something completely different in my professional life. After David Gill, I met Michael Hoppen, and that's when I focused solely on photography. But my first foray into it was [David Gill's] incredible photography collection; it really got me into it.

I thought after university, I would go and be a

conservationist. I was really into conservationism, and painting, and was all set to go to Florence and study there – but then I got offered a job, and I never looked back.

CM:

When studying art history, I found an interconnected-ness between the lighting in Renaissance paintings and photography, which I really enjoy.

BE:

Yes, absolutely. [...] Also, when you see compositions in photographs, that mathematical component comes through with the shapes, and you think, 'Okay, that reminds me of the perspective in that painting' and the golden rule and all that.

And of course, there's all the instruments they used. [...] It was da Vinci, wasn't it? He was so industrious, using glass and instruments in a photographic way to help him with his art.

So yes, I think there is a lot of crossover. I also think more and more that there's such a common ground between photography and sculpture, which I find so interesting. I love artists who explore those common synergies.

CM:

Were there particular photographers who drew you in?

BE:

When I first started working for David Gill, I didn't know much about photography besides the big names. I was really struck by what he had in his collection. It sounds so dated now – this is going to put my age to this – but he had a lot of Vanessa Beecroft's work, and I just found it so fresh. I hadn't been exposed to anything like it before.

Then when I went to work for Michael Hoppen, I really fell in love with vintage photography, more because of the techniques. Michael's such a great

ambassador and champion of photography. That was a real learning moment for me. In my early days, when I started with him, I fell in love with the work of Lucien Hervé. He was a French photographer, not very well known or famous now, but he shot some of the most extraordinary architectural shots. Also Ellen Bene, who teaches [photography]. She's French, but lives in London. [...] Just – the scale of some of her works. They're hand prints, silver prints. Just the compositions, and the light.

Those two were my first big 'wow' photographers. I think you can go on and on about the genius of Cartier-Bresson and Irving Penn. And don't get me wrong, I'm still wowed by them, but it's nice to discover people who aren't so well known.

CM:

Do you spend a lot of time searching for hidden or overlooked archives?

BE:

Sometimes. It depends. [...] Often, when I do panel discussions, people in the audience will say, 'Oh, how come you only sell big names? What about more unknown photographers?' I often get the women question – 'You don't sell very many women photographers?' My answer is always, 'Well, I'm not a museum.' I'm not an educational point. I have a bottom line: I work for a company, and we have to make a profit. So, these unknown archives... For me, it's not my only prerogative, and it's not that I'm just going in with my commercial hat on either – but that is my day job, right? I have to think, 'Can I sell this?'

[...] Often selling entire archives is hard. We do sell collections of photographers, usually owned by one person, so we call them single owner sales – but it's hard to find an unusual archive and then just sell it. That would normally be a private sale. Even then, people come to Sotheby's and look for recognisable names. Someone they couldn't buy in a gallery, maybe because the edition was sold out. [...] So, it's hard for me to launch new works, new careers, new artists, because people are coming to me for recognisable names.

CM:

When you sit down with a photograph and assign it a particular value, what are the things you look for?

BE:

There is no cookie-cutter rule for every photographer, but there are basics you can go by. Is the work signed? When was the work made? Is it a vintage print, close to the negative date, or is it a later print? You're looking at the paper, the condition and the surface.

For me, the big thing is the signature. There are photographers who didn't sign their work, and there are photographers who didn't at first, and did later on when their work was commercialised. You see that with a lot of Cartier-Bresson. He usually stamped his work in the '40s, '50s, '60s. Then obviously, in the '80s, when he started working with galleries, he signed his work in black ink in the lower right margin. All his works are the same format and the same quality, and I like that consistency in a market print.

Sometimes people think older vintage is better. Not always. It depends on what people are looking for. For me, when I'm sitting down, I'm looking at authentication – I guess that's how you would classify the signature, the stamp. That tells me if [the photograph] is real or not. The paper, too. [...] If I think of someone like Rodchenko, I find it challenging to date his work, because...

CM:

Russia.

BE:

It's hard to know if it's vintage, or did his son or grandson just use that vintage paper and print it in the '60s, and so forth. You have to be a bit of a detective, but the physical work — that's your evidence. That's the crime scene. You just have to learn how to read it.

That's what makes it hard in these days of not being able to travel, because you just see a JPEG. It looks real. It looks good, kosher, and then it arrives and you're like, 'Holy shit'. Then the client will say, 'But I've just spent 300 euros shipping it from Italy'. You have to see things with your eyes. You have to touch them. Sometimes – it sounds weird – but you have to smell it.

[...] Recently I've seen quite a few fakes, which is kind of flattering for a distributor. 'Oh, someone has bothered to make a fake Newton'. It means you're doing well.

But people are looking at the prices and looking to take advantage of the market. It's potentially very dangerous. [...] When you have small regional auction houses where there's a specialist for prints, photographs, contemporary art, they're jack-of-all-trades. They have to be really careful to make sure they know what they're looking at. That's what's good about the big auction houses. There's one person who is an expert in one field. Whereas these smaller houses, you have an expert in so many different areas. I've seen things come up and I think, 'That's fake. That's not right.'

It's not their fault; they just don't know as much. They haven't gone as deep, because they're looking over so many different departments – but equally, it's dangerous with these fakes coming around.

Often you can immediately see it from the paper, if it's an inkjet print. I saw this Helmut Newton recently – it was a shitty inkjet print and the format was wrong. It was triple signed, which Newton never did.

Again, it's about being a detective, and really just knowing what to look for. The only way you learn that is through experience. Physical, hands-on experience with your eyes and hands. You can't learn that from a computer. You can relay that to someone and tell them what to look for, but experience is best when it's first hand.

CM:

Do you find counterfeit is on the way up?

BE:

It is, particularly with the big names like Avedon. This year, I've seen a fake Avedon and a fake Penn. We don't often see many, but this season, we've seen a number of fakes.

CM:

When you curate a photography exhibition at Sotheby's, what's your starting point?

BE:

Honestly, it depends on what people are selling, and what we have. One year, I had tons of fashion photography. This must've been about five years ago. A journalist interviewed me and said, 'So, how did you curate this?' I said, 'It was just luck that everyone wanted to sell their fashion photographs, and it worked out.' You are at the mercy of what people want to sell.

We have our main sale, but we also do an erotic photograph sale in February. We have a very successful biannual sale called Made in Britain, which is British photography. Things come in, and you can filter them off if there's a thematic sale that's appropriate. But in my main sale, I do like to have a bit of everything, if I can.

Very rarely do we have 19th-century sales – [...] the clients are just not looking for that. Also, a lot of great 19th-century photography has already been sold, and is in collections. That's obviously a finite market, and it's hard to come across a real gem now. We do better with post-war to contemporary pieces in London. New York and Paris are quite good with 19th-century photographs – you cater not just to the people consigning, but your buying market. There has been a long-standing tradition of 19th-century photographs being bought in Paris, so I don't mess with that.

In our main sale I try and have a bit of everything, a nice smorgasbord of gems. I try and keep it well mixed – not every work is a masterpiece with a 50 grand price tag. You want to have the odd little unknowns. And that's where you can have a big name with an image that isn't so known, which has a surprisingly low estimate. That for me is the best kind of gem – as opposed to a completely random artist. [...] As I said before, people are not necessarily coming to me to discover a brand new name, but maybe a brand new work from a known name.

CM:

What's your advice on collecting?

BE:

To start, it's so easy to do your homework, do your research. First of all, make friends with all of the auction house specialists and the galleries. They're much more approachable than contemporary market people. Because our market is still so small and growing, everyone who's in it is passionate about it, and happy to share information. There seems to be a lot more transparency, and because it's small, we all know each other. There's a lot of accountability, and it's easy to infiltrate.

Always go to a good gallery and a good auction house. You can trust the work that comes out of those places, because they've done the homework for you. Know what your tastes are. You'd be surprised how many people go, 'Oh, send me some photos. I don't know what I like.' People are really lazy, and spoon-fed, and everything is given to you on a plate, which is so boring.

CM:

Do you think that's because people are trying to follow a trend?

BE:

I do, but people have become lazy. It's so much fun to discover something and go down the rabbit hole, but most people can't be bothered. They'd rather other people did it for them. Again, it's annoying. It's like – no, if you want something on your wall and you're going to live with it, do the research. Find out what you like.

[...] And if you're spending more than, I would say £3,000 to £5,000, make *sure*. Look the work up on Artnet – has that artist sold before? If they haven't, have they been in museum shows, or are they with a good gallery? You shouldn't buy for investment. You shouldn't buy thinking you're going to flip it. But if you are spending a lot of money, you should be careful about where you're putting it. Make sure the work is signed and you have a certificate, if the artist sells his work with certificates. Some people don't. Just the usual stuff.

But equally, go to a flea market and find a gem of a work that's unsigned, because you love it, and it's 50 quid. Buy it, frame it, put it on your wall – but don't expect that to sell for £100,000 at Sotheby's in five years.

I think this whole 'artist support pledge' thing is problematic too. I'm a little on the fence about it,

because on the one hand, it's a great initiative, and great for artists to be making some money and so forth. It's super well priced and accessible, but a lot of these – and I'm just talking about photographs – but these schemes that were started to raise money for BLM, or for food charities and so forth...

Know what your tastes are. You'd be surprised how many people go, 'Oh, send me some photos. I don't know what I like.' People are really lazy, and spoon-fed, and everything is given to you on a plate, which is so boring.

CM:

I had a piece in one of them.

BE:

A lot of those photographers didn't sign the work, right?

CM:

No.

BE:

I get that it's not editioned, fine. But you need a signature. I get again that we are in lockdown. But if you're sending it out, add on an extra £10 to have that picture sent from the lab to the photographer to sign. I'm worried that in a few years, we are going to have people going, 'Hang on, I bought this for £100 from Charles, and I saw his work just sold for £5,000. What do you mean, mine is not worth £10,000 now?'

I'm worried that a lot of the public, and younger collectors who are just beginning, don't understand that. [...] Just make a point of, 'You can also buy my amazing work that's signed and editioned, but this is something extra,' as opposed to, 'This is what I do'. I feel like a lot of my friends are like, 'Wow, it's so cheap to buy photographs. You never told me.' I'm like, 'No, it isn't. It isn't.'

CM:

It really isn't. Photography continues to get more expensive by the year, particularly if it's getting noticed. What are your thoughts on paper for printing? A lot of work printed digitally is a C-type on Fuji Crystal Archive paper. Do you prefer an inkjet Giclée, on a Hahnemühle? What's your preference?

BE:

It depends what the work is, right? With black-and-white photography, I personally prefer hand prints, silver prints. I like them on fibre-based paper. I'm not a resin coated fan. For colour work, I don't love this matte Hahnemühle thing. That doesn't turn me on. I love glossy or semi-glossy photographs. I love Fuji Crystal Archive paper. [...] It depends on the work, on the image, but I like things that are tactile. I like photographs to look like photographs. I find

sometimes on this Hahnemühle paper, depending on the work... I saw something recently and I was like, 'Fuck, it's like a watercolour.' That's my personal taste. It just turns me off.

CM:

There is often crossover between painting and photography. Sometimes painters try to make work more photographic, and vice versa.

BE:

I love the idea of painting on a photograph. I love collage, and stitching, and all of that great stuff: that intervention and playing with [the medium]. I love photographers who really push the concept of what a photograph is. It doesn't have to be two dimensional – like that piece of Adam Jeppesen's work we had in our sale, the cyanotype on silk. Suspended in oil, in a glass box. I mean, how fucking sexy was that? I love it. It's a sculpture but it's also a photograph. Artists like Jeppesen really get me going.

But I don't like photographs that look like paintings. I think paper can play into that, and of course framing and presentation is key. I would definitely tell anyone starting out to ask the photographer how they want [their work] to be framed. That's so important. Ask the gallery, ask the photographer, because I think it's important to the integrity of the work and the artist. Don't mess around with their vision, but if it's something high-value, an artist who has a good secondary market history, you want to resell it the way that people are used to. That's their standard; don't mess with it.

CM:

Do you have certain artists that you personally want to collect, or see as the most collectible?

BE:

Gosh, every day it changes. I just want everything and everyone. I'm so greedy. Who would I say? I would love to have a Mapplethorpe one day. That's a big name. And kind of anything, you know? It could be a dye transfer flower, it could be a silver print, it could be a flower, it could be a sexy nude. I would be happy with anything.

Then – oh my God, Peter Hujar. Anything, again. Anything he's put his hand on, I'll take it.

Then contemporary-wise – Clare Strand. She's amazing, and there are so many works of hers I would love to own. So, I would probably say her as a contemporary artist. I don't have a lot of colour; I'm looking around my flat as I'm talking to you. I'm kind of getting into colour, but it's more that I just really like black and white, and hand prints, silver prints.

CM:

What about Eggleston for colour?

BE:

Yeah, I love [William] Eggleston. There are a few images of his that I would kill for. Not all of them. Francesca Woodman – I'd love to have some of her work. Ana Mendieta – we had two lots of her work in our sale this year, in October, which was huge. I don't often see her work, or that of Helena Almeida. She's someone who I would probably get over Mapplethorpe. I would love a big piece by her, if I could afford it.

In my day job, I get to sit with these pieces. I had a real moment in the summer; I had to schlep to our warehouse and catalogue some works. I just sat there with this vintage Ana Mendieta, and I got really emotional. I was like, 'Fuck. How lucky am I?'

I admire her, and I imagine her life. I imagine how she lived. Everything she did, and saw, what she went through – and I'm sitting there holding a piece that she made. What an honour.

CM:

It's amazing when you can connect with a work like that. I saw [Wolfgang] Tillmans' work sold super well in the recent show. Do you watch those trends? Are they important to you?

BE:

We do watch them and follow them. Tillmans – I think I'm correct in saying he's the living photographer who's had the most solo exhibitions at Tate Modern. He's definitely had two, maybe three. After his last show, there was a big movement in his market, and it's still there, a few years on. Fashion photography has been on the rise. When I started my career, people were snobby about it – 'people' being collectors. It wasn't as collected. This is 18 years ago, so prices were still really affordable then, whereas now they are really expensive.

We live in such a contemporary world. It's so interesting to see what people are doing, and young artists. I personally like the trend of looking back to old techniques with cyanotypes, tintypes, etc. There was a great show at Foam [Fotografiemuseum Amsterdam] a few years ago called *Back to the Future*, and it was all contemporary photographers using old techniques. I feel like that type of craftsmanship is more appealing and sought after now by collectors. They're not looking for a massive, two-metre [Andreas] Gursky print, you know? They're looking for something small, intimate, handmade. I feel like that's coming back again.

CM:

As someone who shot film, and then felt like I had to move into digital, I now feel like I don't want to shoot digital anymore. I only want to shoot film, and I'd like to go back to the darkroom. When I look at an artist like Sally Mann, and the craftsmanship that goes into creating a single print, it's such a high standard, and the process is long. As an audience, it's no longer just the photograph you're engaging with, but the process too.

BE:

Definitely, and I think that's what the general public, or people starting out who don't know these techniques, need to really understand. These are techniques that can take years to master. One of my best friends, she recently bought a colour print that was made by hand. She was like, 'Oh, it's a little expensive.' And I shook her and I was like, 'You don't understand how hard it is to make this in the darkroom.' A colour print in the darkroom is impossible.

I told her, 'It's so much better that you're buying a couture piece.' She was like, 'Oh, now I get it.' When I put it in fashion words, she understood. Again, that's why I say do your homework, find out. Don't just assume. I just feel like we've become so lazy because everything is given to us. No; learn about this!

[…] That's why there are master printers who are not photographers, and many photographers are not great printers: because they're two different crafts in themselves. When you combine them, it's fucking gold, you know?

CM:

If someone wanted to get into the world of Sotheby's, or the world of buying and selling photography, what would be your advice to them?

BE:

I'm biased because it's my personal experience, but I like the fact that I started in the primary market and went to secondary. There are many people who do it the other way around, many people who bounce back and forth, but I think a strong grounding in art history is important. It doesn't mean you have to have studied that as your BA or MA, but you should have a good grasp and knowledge of as much of art history as you can, because that's informed where we are today with photography.

Everything relates. Knowledge is key. I think you can tell. I mean, I've been looking at photographs for a long time […] you can look at people and see if they've studied art history or not. For example, right before he became super well known, I met Erik Madigan Heck. We had commissioned him at Sotheby's to do our Sotheby's diamonds campaign. I found his work fascinating and so painterly. We did a panel discussion together, and he explained how he had studied painting, and was influenced by the Impressionists. That's what's so enriching in his work, but it also kind of validates it.

If someone wants to come into this industry, it's so hard now to get a job in the arts. When I started, it was really easy because there's not a lot of money in it, so you don't come in thinking you're going to be rich. Not rich financially at least, right?

So, when I started there were jobs left, right and centre in the arts world, because most of my friends were off being lawyers and bankers. I like the route I took.

[…] You don't have to, but definitely study art history. You can do courses online if you've studied something else. Of course, there are transferable skills. I feel like half the time, I should have an honorary psychology degree, because I am constantly managing my client's expectations. How do we feel about selling this? How do we feel when it doesn't sell? But of course, do internships, and get your foot in the door.

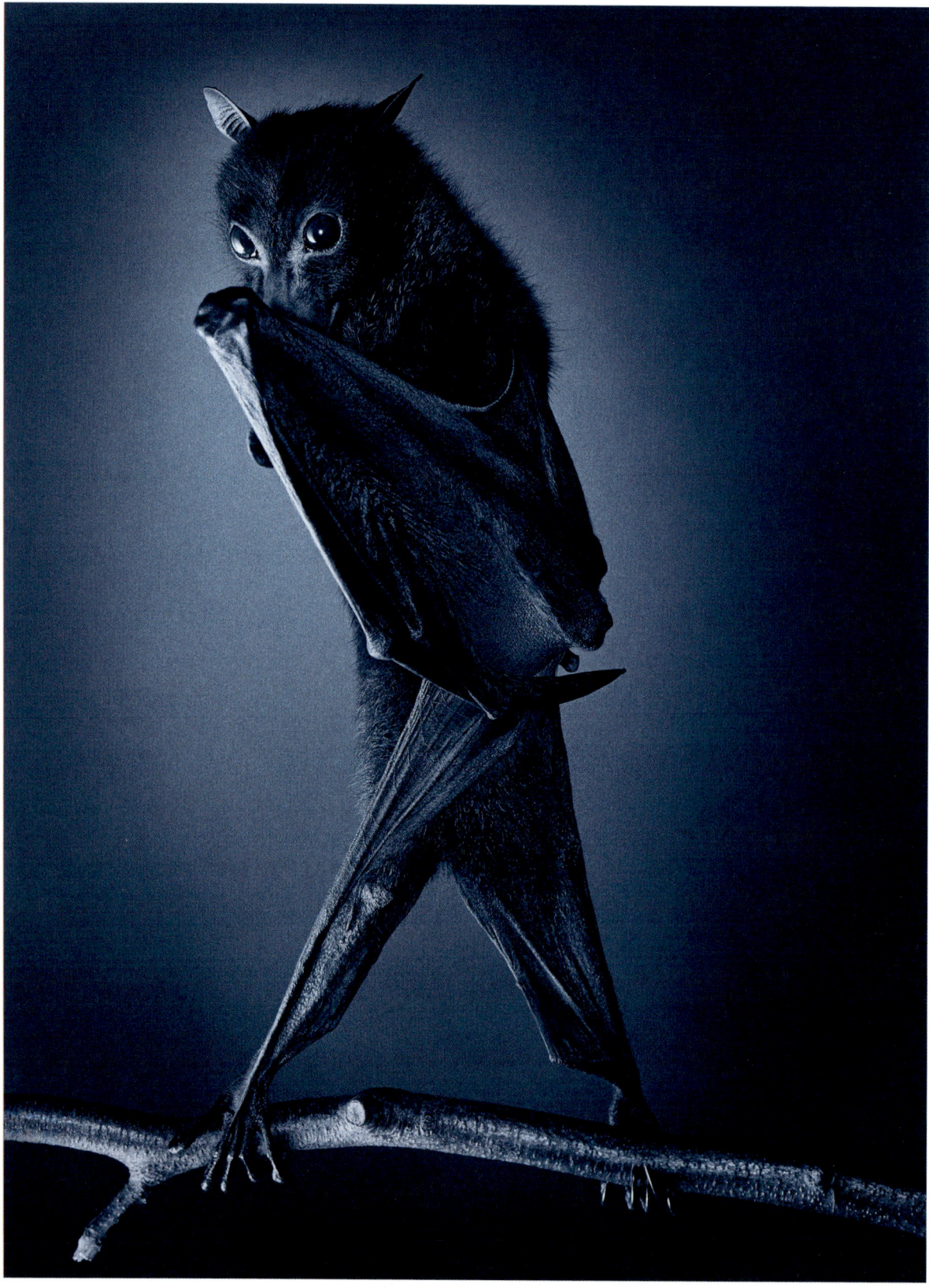

On 10 October 2019 in London, I visited Tim Flach in his Shoreditch studio, which I have walked past for many years and never even known was there. I first met Tim a few years ago, after his book *Equus* had been released, when he was working on *More Than Human*. However, we'd never sat down seriously to discuss his practice. Tim has been photographing animals for more than a decade and often comes at his subject matter with fresh ways of thinking and understanding. He is, I believe, a conservationist at heart, and uses his work to bring us all closer to the incredible and very much in danger Holocene and its animal inhabitants.

Tim Flach, Opera Bat, 2011
© Tim Flach

Charles Moriarty:

Hi Tim. Maybe you could start by introducing yourself?

Tim Flach:

My name is Tim Flach. I'm based here in Shoreditch, London. I spent quite a few years specialising in animals – perhaps not what you might describe as 'traditional' wildlife photography, more looking at how animal portraits can evoke such things as empathy and thereby perhaps provide conservation support.

CM:

Where did you begin?

TF:

I spent most of my childhood in the country, much of it in Cornwall. I went and lived in a place called Fowey and went to school in Launceston, which is not far away, still in Cornwall. So I spent much of my time rambling along coastlines.

CM:

Did you have photography around you at an early age?

TF:

No, I think it's interesting how some of us go in different directions in life. Sometimes your inabilities help guide you to where you find you're more naturally suited. It was quite evident early on that I didn't do word things particularly well and that I was more suited to the visual. So, I spent quite a lot of time drawing, painting and observing as a child. And maybe that's really helped formulate a sort of visual vocabulary or a kind of sensibility.

CM:

Was your relationship to animals something that came later as well?

TF:

I was definitely somebody who wandered off, not by the coast, but into the woods. I spent a lot of time in nature and affectedly that must've shaped things. But maybe that's because I've always been fascinated in particular with animals, about the spatial relationship. Our relationship to those animals and what divides us from other sentient beings – I think that intrigues me, as well as how we transform images to meaning. But in terms of my early childhood, I think a lot of it was spent where I was. Though I had a brother, I was the only child. My brother was with my father and stepmother, and I was with my mother and stepfather. So effectively, I was on my own.

CM:

I know you studied painting in London. Talk to me about those early years.

TF:

I studied at Saint Martin's School of Art, now Central Saint Martins, part of the University of Arts, London. I did what I felt I could do naturally, which is paint, but in a way everything I was doing was visual, and I think even that informed what I do today.

CM:

What kind of painter were you?

TF:

I was fairly figurative – and yet not very figurative. [...] I wasn't doing abstract expressionism or anything, but I was doing some sculptural work with re-found graffiti on corrugated iron, making structures. So, in one way it was kind of installation work.

CM:

Contemporary?

TF:

You could argue that. Yes.

CM:

When did you pick up a camera?

TF:

I didn't have a camera growing up at all. I think I might've once pressed my mother's happy snap camera and taken a picture of her. When I came to London, I did a foundation course in art and design, which in those days – 1976 – was probably something many of us did. You went to a course that gave you an indication of your potential in aspects of the arts, and you were introduced to all these different areas such as ceramics and 3D design. The foundation course gave you time to

> Our relationship to animals and what divides us from other sentient beings – I think that intrigues me, as well as how we transform images to meaning.

get a folio together. So, I did a foundation course when I was 18 and they had one week where you picked up a camera and they made you do certain exercises. Ironically, that was at the London Zoo, a place I then ended up working closely with on my last book, 30-something years later.

The first project involved photographing the animals at the zoo with the use of compositional exercises: do a symmetrical picture, do an asymmetrical picture, etc. I remember my tutors immediately saying 'You've got something there with photography'. When I was applying, they were quite keen for me to... I realised I might have something.

CM:

After you finished your degree at Saint Martins, did you move straight into photography? Did you assist?

TF:

I had a very informal assisting role. I had a friend who'd worked for this press photographer. It was a job in PR press really, and I went there straight after I'd finished my undergrad. He had just enough room in his studio at one end to get a Colorama across it, and a lot of the job was going out and doing retirements and whatever. He offered me the chance to assist him and print in the darkroom. Within about a year of that, I went back to do my postgraduate at Saint Martins.

CM:

Did you do the postgraduate in photography?

TF:

It wasn't really photography – it was painted structures. They call it 'painted photography and structures', but [...] I basically painted, but they obviously liked my painted structures and my photography more. So, they gave me my postgraduate in painting structures and photography.

CM:

After completing your postgrad, what next?

TF:

I didn't have a trust fund and I didn't have parents who were going to back me in any way. Having already worked in hotels at night to fund my way through my painting course and pay the fees as well, I then took my folio of corrugated iron structures and a few pictures I'd taken, and I tried to persuade PR departments or marketing departments of corporate companies to give me work. Sometimes they said, 'We'll do a few portraits, and if we like them we'll pay you'.

But they did pay me and they did invite me back, and gradually I started getting more and more corporate work. I also worked for annual reports when they had just started to become a thing that was important. That started giving me some kind of income so I could buy my cameras. At the same time, I carried on working at night in hotels for at least a year.

CM:

Do you remember the first cameras that you started with?

TF:

I had someone who could loan me a Rolleiflex, and as soon as I could buy myself a Hasselblad, which took me about a year or two to save up for, I went out and bought one. I had nothing much else, but I wanted this camera. I felt I needed it.

CM:

You still shoot on the Hasselblad now, don't you?

TF:

I do, but I also use Canon quite a lot because they've got the 5DS, 50 megapixel capture, and a lot of my subjects, particularly in my last book, were a long way away. I use Canon more than I used to.

CM:

What made you move into the world of animals, away from the corporate gigs?

TF:

As a person I was always aspiring to something more. I wanted to do other things in the medium, but I had to make a living. As I didn't have anything to fall back on, I had no option.

But having said that, before the animals I began working creatively with friends who were actors in the theatre. I would do posters for their shows, and then when everyone ripped them off of the venue walls to take home, I thought, 'Maybe that worked'. Working with friends and helping them create material that then obviously worked and was successful.

With respect to the animals, there was a particular point where I was doing a commercial job where I had to get a python – I think it was a 20-foot python – and a vulture into the studio. It turned out the guy who had these also owned big cats. And I asked him, how much would it be to get a panther into a studio? If you want to lead the direction of your work, you've got to initiate things. You've got to say, 'Well actually, let's see what happens,' and get a panther in a studio.

It was at the very beginning of stock photography, when it was moving from a cottage industry into a serious business. And I was thinking, 'Gosh, I'm winning all these awards for these things; I'm doing this, but I barely still make any profit'. I heard from somebody who was making something weekly that gave them a base from stock. So, I went to Getty, and they were looking for more visual people. It gave me a bit of financial space to create images where I could pick what I wanted, but maybe get the cost of the panther paid for.

CM:

So the enlargement of the stock industry helped you create your studio?

TF:

It did in the sense that I didn't do very many happy people on beaches, so it wasn't like I was driving that. I was just saying, 'I want to shoot these animals'. If I get the animals in, then I can find an avenue by which those costs are paid for. It gave me flexibility.

CM:

How old were you at that point?

TF:

I was about nine years into my career. I had previously got quite a lot of commissions and was busy; within about three years I was shooting almost every day. Not on big shoots, but in a small way. It could've been work for marketing departments or even property brochures, nothing terribly glamorous.

CM:

But continuous.

TF:

Gradually, I ended up working with an award-winning, design-led group, and from there I moved into advertising. I ended up doing a global campaign. I moved up through the various tiers, as my work was successful.

CM:

Equus *put you on the map as one of the foremost horse photographers in the world. How did that come about?*

TF:

I wanted to do something that was more personal. I think even when the pressure's on to make a living, it's really important to give yourself space, because otherwise you could ask why you're doing this career in the first place. I'm sure there are easier ways of making a living. And so, I'd already done quite a few personal projects, from the very beginning when I had very little. Often, that would be to help friends out. They would cover material costs; that's what I had been used to. With Getty, we were used to gambling and funding, and I was also retouching the work. I had quite a lot of autonomy in the way I practised. I wasn't a Getty photographer full-time; I just did it as one avenue of revenue. I always had commissions.

I got confident enough to know how to initiate my own projects without there being a commercial demand. I think it's quite important, for photographers to build up their own creative thoughts and ideas and then generate that as a body of work. So, *Equus* was something that came about because I did quite well in various awards. I started doing shoots in America, commissions and working with agents in New York, and they asked me to submit to some of the awards at the time. It was the easiest form of advertising across the gap, because I'd submit and get my work in, and then it would end up being the cover of these awards or annual PDN [Photo Annual competition] or whatever, communication arts or APG [Aperture Photography Group].

CM:

Would you say participating in those awards is one of the most important things photographers can do to get their work seen?

TF:

I think it's important... It depends, because each platform changes each decade, and I suspect there are other ways. It was a way of getting your work out there. But the reason it links back to the book is that the PDN ran the front cover with one of my images.

CM:

What's PDN?

TF:

Photo District News. They run an award in New York, which is quite respected, and a number of other bodies. They often ran my images. Now, a publisher [...] saw that work and approached me about doing *Equus*.

CM:

What was the image on the cover of the PDN?

TF:

It was a horse against a black background, shaking. It was a series that got me various awards. The awards [...] It was the window. And that publisher – I asked him, does he ever work with photographers that approach him? He said, 'No, I always like to approach photographers.'

CM:

When you set out to do Equus, *did the publisher give you a certain amount of financing?*

TF:

I think it was about 2005–2006, when the book publishing world was still healthy, so the advance for my very first book was – I think – over a hundred thousand pounds. They were quite happy to fly me out to China with my assistant to press it. Today, they wouldn't even do that because the industry is different. There's not the money, and of course printing has got better as well. Colour management is better.

CM:

Can you talk about how you approach photographing horses or any other animals?

TF:

I think I've naturally always wanted to bring out the personality and character of the animals. I didn't ever see myself as a wildlife photographer, even though I've obviously spent time in the Galapagos, in the Arctic, and for my last book, I went to all sorts of different locations, because the animals were not going to come into my studio. I couldn't bring a gorilla into my studio and it wouldn't be appropriate either.

So, when it came down to photographing animals, in or out of the studio, I'd always been interested in this idea of creating a sense of empathy with the animals, a connection. And

it's something that I've developed further as I've looked into co-publishing papers with academics, and looking at how certain images create empathy and thereby potentially conservation support. This is where my interest lies now – but in the past, I was really trying to get stylised images of animals. I just liked that sense of the character, the personality, and also almost removing them from their context, so you concentrated on what the animal was about.

Though *Equus* was an exploration of the horse, it wasn't about humans and horses. I never had an Arab holding a horse or cowboy holding a horse. It was actually more about exploring how we shape the animal, how we have different breeds around the world.

There was the heritage of that, and also an exploration into what photography can do. Photography has certain qualities that it innately does well, like capturing high-speed micro shots, just freezing something that you couldn't see normally. I really liked that opportunity [...] and I think I started with my horse project doing horses jumping, shaking.

CM:

Can you recount a favourite image from Equus*?*

TF:

The embryo is particularly striking. You're looking at something that just throws you into a different space. I always think the images have this slippage. They move in association – so maybe somebody had an abortion or they had a miscarriage, and suddenly a horse image you think has nothing to do with it slips into that process and creates unease.

CM:

Reminding us that we all come from a similar start in life.

TF:

Yes. I think that some people have done research into the development of embryos and how there's a similarity with certain mammals.

CM:

Was moving from Equus *to your second book,* More Than Human, *a natural progression?*

TF:

I wanted to do something that was close to home, and I was interested in the human connection with animals. How do I make that interesting? How do I curate 200 images for that? I wanted to show the diversity, but also take abstraction and landscapes and different types of forms, so that it kept the book moving along. In pagination we call that the pace.

More Than Human was actually more an exploration into how we shape animals, how we use animals. For instance, it might be that they're developing some goats that they put a gene from a spider in, and from that they produce milk and extract a protein that then produces a bulletproof vest, and mad things like that. I thought that was pretty interesting: how we do that, or how we shaped certain breeds of animal, or the relationship between the symbolism of the animal and us. The panda being something cute, and a diplomatic tool. [...]

It was really interesting, looking at that interface between us and animals. Like how we shape, how we form, how we create some cattle that have different muscling because the rump steaks are worth more than the other part of the body. How we actually...

CM:

How we utilise them?

TF:

Yes. And how that changes. How pigs can have more teats because we bred them that way, and all this kind of thing. I find that really fascinating.

There was one image that stood out for me, which is a featherless chicken. It's another image that can be disturbing, because you look at this chicken going across the stage like a ballerina and you're questioning, 'Did the photographer pluck the chicken?' I think my point here is that when you get ambiguity in a picture, where you're left with a question and some anxiety, that is not necessarily always a bad thing.

Maybe it's not the photographer, it's the person who owns the tech company who makes the money.

The research I've been doing with my images recently has shown that you need a certain anxiety to actually create the kind of empathy that then creates action. It's quite an interesting thing. The featherless chicken is interesting because it throws up that questioning.

There was a dog that looks like a mop, for example. You're questioning, 'Is it frozen there? Is it jumping?' And I think that's another area that I find really interesting.

CM:

Can you talk a little bit about how you compose, and how you work with light to create the movement for the eye?

TF:

I think it's a really interesting area: how does our brain work, and how we make meaning out of pictures. Artists have explored this for a long time, but perhaps it's something they feel they should emphasise in the magic of their work, the concepts, the ideas, [because they] don't discuss it so much. There's a lot of evidence that many of the significant artists and photographers who've emerged from our societies often do have a grasp of these areas.

One of the things I'm really interested in, particularly with portraiture, is... There are certain ways in which we have a tendency to do things. It's not that there are rules, because ultimately, we just have to feel something, we have to respond to it. It's never one-dimensional. But there are certainly things that we have a tendency to do collectively, and to understand that helps make pictures potentially more powerful.

CM:

You moved into the highly commercial realm of dogs. Was this a commercial decision?

TF:

There are several different sides to that. My publisher wanted me to do this. When you work on anything, you're working on relationships with agents and publishers. You have a relationship with your publisher and you obviously have to listen to them.

A lot of my commissions involved dogs, and I obviously love my dogs as well. I thought it would firm up my business, so there is a commercial side. But I also think I was well placed to do that kind of project. You get two sides to this: it meant I could explore the dog as a book in a particular way. But *Dogs: Gods* is slightly different to my *More*

Photography has certain qualities that it innately does well, like capturing high-speed micro shots, just freezing something that you couldn't see normally.

Than Human book, which is a commitment to something not very commercial. Ironically, going forward, *Endangered* [Tim's fourth book] was something I had to fund personally and expected to lose financially on, because I care, and we are all becoming more collectively aware that we live in very unique times.

[...] When I spoke to my publisher, my *Dogs* book, which took me the least amount of time and was the least amount of pages, had outsold any of the other books. But this is how it is. I think it was true for Elliott Erwitt and for many other photographers who share the same experiences. In a way, this firms up the possibility of oscillating between these types of projects.

I'm now doing a bird project, which I will enjoy doing. I want to do really well and produce something that has no equivalent in photography. Maybe that sounds a bit overconfident, but you've got to go in with that commitment, certainly in visual terms. […] And then I want to, after that, just concentrate on soil quality and insects, which is less sexy. I'm going from profit-making to loss-making, to a profit, to a loss.

CM:

What are the biggest challenges that you find when you're shooting with animals?

TF:

If you're very prescriptive and you have a commission where someone says, 'I want this particular behaviour', and it's a behaviour that doesn't suit the context of the studio. For example, a dog will go into the studio, and if it's used to being shown, it will spark up and go bright-eyed and think, 'Gosh, this is exciting'. It will respond to its owner, who's also excited because it's a shoot. But then if you want it to go to sleep or do something more passive, or to do something that's not conducive to that situation, then that's quite difficult.

If you want an animal to feel a bit more alert, then the studio might facilitate that. But for example, tomorrow I have an oscillated turkey in. It's an amazing wild turkey and very bright. We have two birds in. And they may display, but when you ask me the question about what is difficult, then what's really difficult is, I think, when you have some specific behaviour that doesn't complement the circumstance of the photo shoot. If you're chasing that, then it's harder.

CM:

It's been a long time since Equus *was published in 2008. Do you feel there is a big difference now with animals and awareness, thanks to this type of photographic conservationism?*

TF:

What's more important to look at is the underlying value systems that are changing. […] The idea that nature is vulnerable, is something that's only entered into the collective consciousness fairly recently. As a consequence, if nature's vulnerable, we're more exposed. In a sense, that shift is one that I think is shaping the way we think about the world. And I hope it does, because we do need to respond.

I've gone down with that journey. It isn't that I started out thinking a lot of these ideas. What you do is, you go on a journey, like a book project, and you trip over things and you meet people, and you can't undo what you see.

CM:

What images remain important to you on your journey?

TF:

It's really hard, that. Imagery, particularly where I work, is often about its relevance to what you're dealing with. A photographer can take a picture and then find himself moving away from its relevance – not that it's technically bad or anything, just it's not so relevant today. They might take some pictures of their local area and subtly, 50 or 40 years later, realise this is the only document of the shops that were once there.

They'd never even thought about it. And suddenly that takes on huge significance in historical portraits.

With the kind of work I've done, there are images I still feel close to that go back a couple of decades. For example, the bat images, where we flipped them upside down. There are certain images that still stay with me and there are other images I've moved away from.

CM:

Where do you see the photography industry going?

TF:

For me personally, that's one thing. For everyone else, I think that as someone who's been involved in all different aspects of the industry... I mean, just to put some perspective, today I sell prints, I direct commercials, I produce books, I give talks on conservation. And for all of us, we've had this kind of slippage, where the role of photography has meant it's not just waiting for a phone call, turning up somewhere, taking some pictures, going through the contacts, delivering the prints.

Just as we have shopping centres closing down in the North of England and the whole high street changing because of the digital age, you could argue that in all these things, the macro affects the micro. In our case, many of my contemporaries are going to struggle to get much usage out of editorial features or things that traditionally supported them. So much has moved online, and that, for our generation, has made it much harder to commoditise. That's not to say there isn't an opportunity. But maybe it's not the photographer, it's the person who owns the tech company who makes the money.

CM:

You're saying you have to be multifaceted at this point. Being just a photographer isn't enough?

TF:

I think you've always had to be responsive. But I do feel that photography didn't really change for much of the last century, and suddenly, with the digital revolution, it had to go through fundamental shifts. What we're seeing is, essentially, shifts in the very way we make a living, at a time when there are more graduates of photography. I've heard figures bandied about of 10,000 plus a year. If that's the case, I don't think anyone expects 10,000 new photographers to enter the workplace.

We're moving towards a more image-based culture. [Photography] has a bigger role to play, societally speaking, and training people up to be visually conscious is not a bad thing. But they may not become fashion photographers, or whatever they thought they were going to be, and make a living in the realm of Nick Knight or whatever. That's probably less likely for this generation: that they can run studios or do things as the previous generation did. It just changes.

I've been very lucky in the sense to have that kind of autonomy; that ability to say, 'I want to do a book', or 'I want to concentrate on issues that I care about'. That comes partly from having a financial buffer. As I said, when I started out, I didn't have anyone giving me that buffer. I had to do whatever would pay the bills, whether it was working for property brochures or whatever. As the years passed, I earned more freedom. But then I'm just over 60, and for someone [...] just starting out from university, I think that whatever they do, how they make a living, is going to be quite a contrast to what I would have done back in the day.

CM:

Do you know what your book about birds is going to be called?

TF:

I don't at the moment, no.

CM:

The project to follow is going to be about insects and soil. Are you going to try and tackle the soil crisis that lies ahead of us?

TF:

I think so. And I know it's not a sexy subject matter.

CM:

It's a scary subject.

TF:

A very scary subject. Like I said, scary and important doesn't often pay bills. What you end up finding is that the more commercial projects tend to pay the bills, and they often don't touch on any real issues.

CM:

How long have you been in the studio here?

TF:

Twenty-one years.

CM:

So you got in just before it got bad.

TF:

Yeah, but now the rates are so high I feel like most of my profit goes into paying the council. There are not many of us left in the area. Not many photographers can afford a studio.

CM:

A lot of people have cleared out. A lot of the art studios have become multipurpose commercial outlets.

TF:

Yes. I mean, there's another side to it: you can take your studio anywhere. You can take some mobile flash and make someone's home into one. In a way, there isn't a necessity to have someone at a desk answering the phone, because people would rather have a mobile number now.

CM:

When you work on location, do you normally have a large set-up, or do you try and keep it as small as possible?

TF:

When I'm gallivanting in the rainforest or chasing down gorillas, then I'm no lights, just long lens. I tend to tailor it to the circumstances and the control.

CM:

Did you actually chase gorillas?

TF:

I went up and down rivers, tracking western gorillas for two weeks, and tracking tigers in Russia, then on to diving for hammerhead sharks.

CM:

Any close calls?

TF:

A few. I got thrown up on the rocks on the Galapagos Islands, and I wasn't the best diver. With respect to the animals, I take the philosophy that you should get people who know what they're doing. Then at least you've got a better chance than otherwise.

SUE FLOOD

I took a train north to meet Sue near her home in Wales, where we talked about the magical world we live in and its wildlife. I first came across Sue through her love of penguins, which sent me down a rabbit hole of discovery.

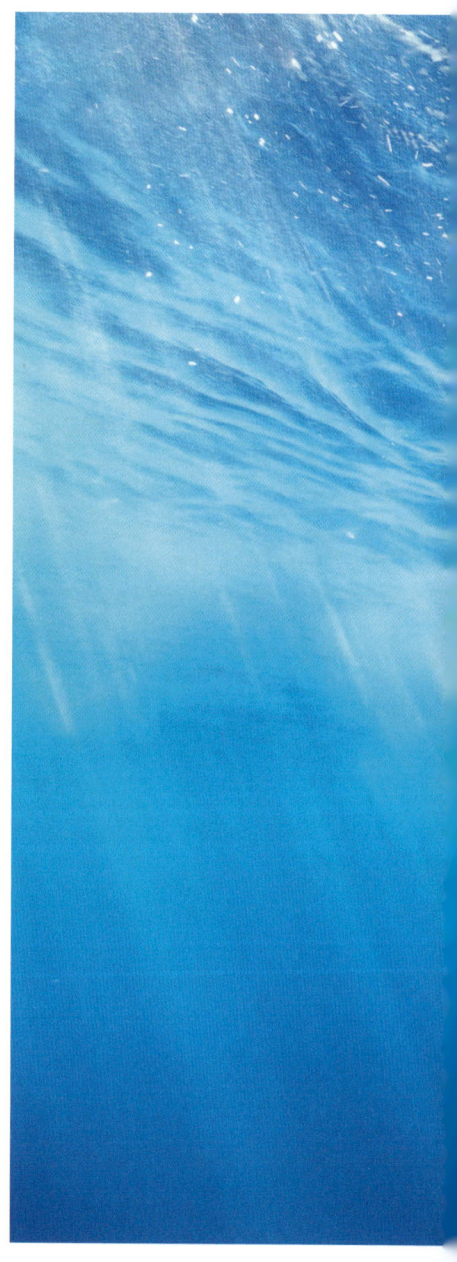

Sue Flood, Shark, 2002
© Sue Flood

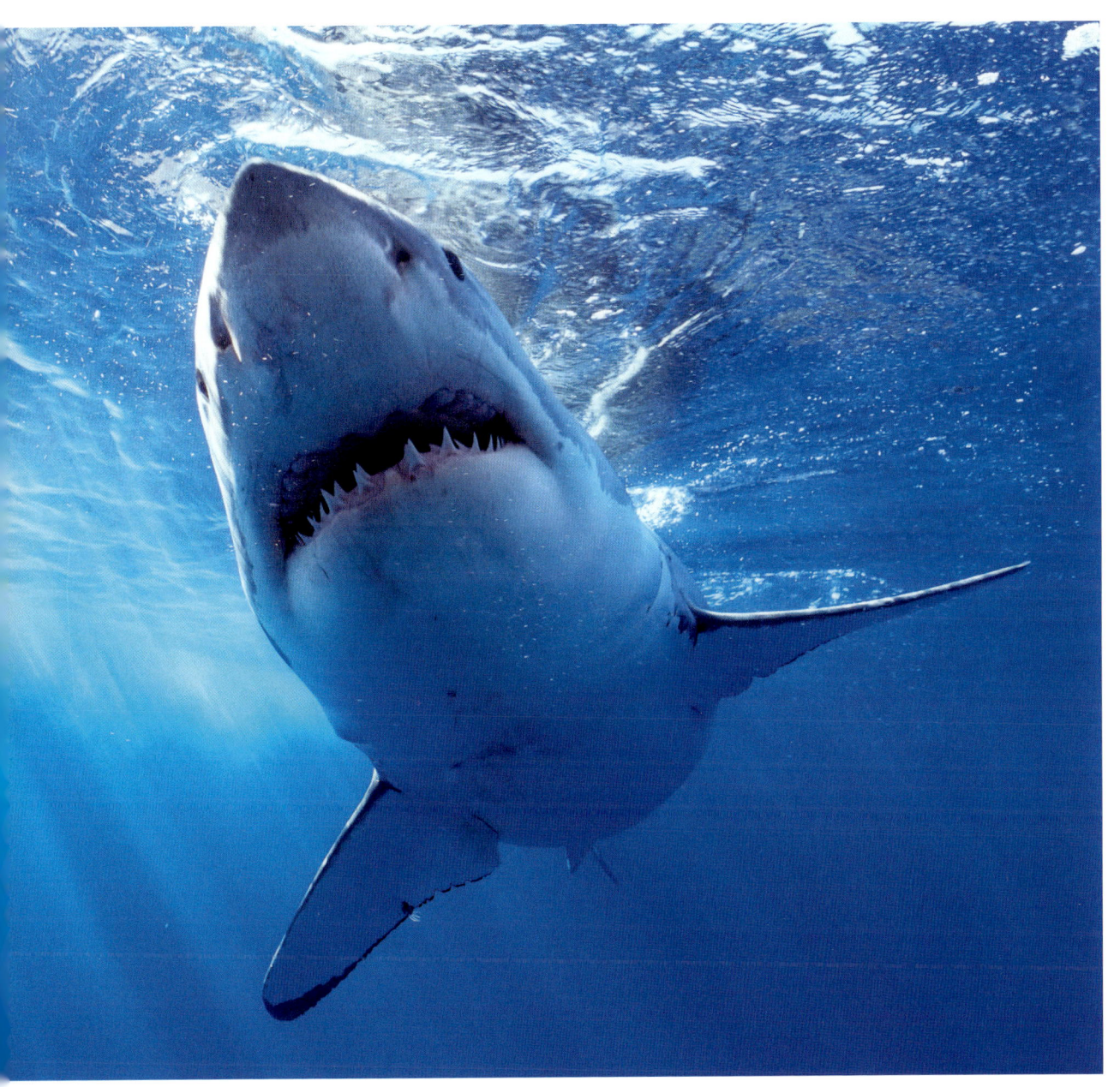

Charles Moriarty:

Did wildlife or photography become a part of your life very early on?

Sue Flood:

I was interested in photography, vaguely. I mean, as a child my dad and my grandad were in the local camera club, so I grew up seeing people take photos. But I was always into wildlife. There were two people who really influenced me when I was growing up. One was my dad, because he'd been in the Merchant Navy. I was a kid growing up in this little village in North Wales and I would be hearing stories from him, 'When I was in Rangoon. When I was in Shanghai. When I was in Japan.'

He has a camphor wood chest and it's just like a treasure chest, with head-hunters' swords from Borneo, kimonos from Japan, and these beautiful woven hats from Indonesia. I was allowed to play with this stuff, even the swords. And it just really lit my imagination.

As for other influences, my mum and dad loved watching documentaries, so I was watching David Attenborough on the TV. Also, the old *Time LIFE* magazines. I would sit and flick through those. They had a series of encyclopaedias on different topics, a bit like *National Geographic*. I'd look at these things, whether it was your Kalahari bushmen, or out in Australia, or in the Arctic, whatever it was. I'd just sit and pore over these, every night. I suppose it was that feeling of a world beyond North Wales.

Certainly, while I was at primary school I was an avid reader. Then when I was at secondary school in Chester I would devour nature documentaries. At 15, the teacher said, 'What would you like to do when you leave school?' And I said, 'I want to make wildlife films with David Attenborough.' But they said, 'No-one gets to do that. How about domestic science?'

CM:

Why do they never say, 'Go for it'?

SF:

About three years ago I got asked to go back to give a speech on prize-giving day on the subject of my choice. I spoke about following my dreams. I stood there in Chester Cathedral and told this story about what I wanted to do, and that I did it despite them. [...] I was very interested specifically in making documentaries with David Attenborough. That was my dream job.

I went and studied zoology at university. While there, I started writing to the BBC: 'I would like to work with David Attenborough.' And a kindly producer, Mike Salisbury, he basically gave me some very good advice, which was, 'Look, we get so many letters from people wanting to do this. You've got to stick something on your CV to make us take a second look at you. Because you've got to stand out from the crowd.'

[...] Have you heard of something called Raleigh International? It used to be called Operation Raleigh, and it got going about 35 years ago [started 1984].

[...] My friend said, 'Let's apply.' I said, 'There's no way I'll get on that. We'll never get on it.' We applied and I did manage to get on. I had to raise... Such a long time ago, this is 1986. I had to raise two-and-a-half-thousand quid.

It was a lot of money then. It's a lot of money now. I went off and worked for the National Parks and Wildlife Service in Australia. You can imagine, going from this little village, I'd only been abroad with my mum and dad on a holiday. It was brilliant. It changed my life.

CM:

Where were you in Australia?

SF:

In Queensland.

CM:

Does the current crisis with the fires scare you?

SF:

Yeah. I did a wildlife trip to Tasmania in November, which was brilliant – just seeing all the fantastic wildlife, like Tasmanian devils, wombats, kangaroos and wallabies. The current situation is overwhelming. It's so fantastic David Attenborough came out and talked about the climate changing. How can you not think climate change is happening?

CM:

I think the only people who are trying to say that climate change isn't happening are the people who are going to lose money. How long in 1986 were you in Australia for?

SF:

Five months in total. Three months doing this work, then I went and backpacked around Australia, as you do. It was fantastic. My mum was so mad because I wanted to stay on, and that didn't go down terribly well.

When I was at university, I had the same question: 'What do you want to do when you leave university?' I replied the same as before, 'I want to make wildlife films with David Attenborough. So now I'm going to get a zoology degree, hopefully.' And they said, 'Well, that's something nice to aim for, but quite a tough job. How about accountancy?'

[…] No one seemed to think I could do it. School says no, University says no. I thought, 'Oh dear, perhaps I'd better try and get a job.' I got an accountancy job and I hated every single minute of it. I also went from earning no money whatsoever to earning a lot. No amount of money on the planet would have made me enjoy accounting. This is one of my big rules: never do anything for the money.

I handed in my notice after a year of being asleep at this job to go and volunteer in Bermuda at a place called Bermuda Biological Station. It was a marine biology research facility and I worked for nothing, except I had my food and my board paid for.

I was working with the scientists, diving, doing first aid courses, and helping them with their experiments. It was brilliant, and that was what gave me the experience I needed for my CV.

CM:

For the BBC to notice?

SF:

Instead of not getting even an interview, I got an interview. I got to the last five but I just missed the job. I was in the top two, but there was only one position. The guy who was interviewing me said, 'Look, if you'd had TV experience, you would have got it.'

The man doing the interview said to me, 'If you're in Bristol, let us know and come for a coffee.' So, I pretended I was in Bristol. Got a bus from Chester to Bristol, with the National Express coach. We got a coffee, and he said, 'What have you been up to since we last saw you? Are you still wanting to be a researcher? What are you into at the moment?' And I said, 'Oh, well, I'm just waiting for this temping job to start.' And he said, 'I was about to have a new researcher start today, but she's dropped out. I don't suppose you've got any time?' I said 'Yes.' He said, 'When could you start?' I said, 'Now.'

I got a three-day contract and then I got another three-day contract, and then a three-month contract. I was there for 11 years. That was my big break. That was in '93 and my first 'proper job', as it were. It was on a series called *Wildlife*, presented by Sir David Attenborough. I got to be the researcher on that series, and it was like winning the lottery.

CM:

You must have felt very triumphant.

SF:

Yes, that's me. After that series finished, a cameraman friend – who later became my other half, who I got married to and divorced from – said, 'Hey, they're doing this new series on the oceans. [...] You should try and get a job.' I said, 'Oh God, I won't be able to get that, I just got my foot in the door.' But because I'd been doing all the diving and I was a dive instructor... I got the job as the researcher on it. The working title was *Ocean*, which became *The Blue Planet*. It really was like winning the lottery. I was on that series for five years and it changed my life, it really did.

CM:

What does being a researcher on these projects entail?

SF:

Another researcher and I spend a year trying to find stories for the series and map out scripts. We devise how the programmes are going to be divided: the coral reefs, the deep ocean, the polar seas and that sort of thing. What would be good sequences to have in there? When does it happen? Where do we go? What's the best time?

CM:

Essentially, you were a big part of pre-production and production.

SF:

I was very much on the production side. The career progression from researcher would be assistant producer to producer, which is the way I went. You're researching the stories, you're deciding where to go and when. Of course, for some of these wildlife things, that's very tricky, especially with these big television series, because there may be something no one's ever filmed before. So how the hell are you going to go about that?

But I loved the logistics and the organisation. I still do. It was a perfect job for me. On *Blue Planet*, the brilliant thing was to be working with world-class cameramen. On that series I think it was all men, but people who are really good at their job. I was taking stills behind the scenes, still on production but working with these fantastic people. I was picking up tips from them. I certainly wasn't employed as a photographer. I was employed as the researcher.

CM:

You were just having fun, capturing the moment?

SF:

Exactly.

CM:

What year was this?

SF:

I started on *Blue Planet* in '96. During the filming of *Blue Planet* there was this unusual situation where killer whales were hunting grey whales. No one had filmed it before, and I managed to get a series of shots, which led to an article in *BBC Wildlife*. That was the first time my work was published. Then we got another really unusual thing, which was something called a sassat. These beluga whales were caught in a hole in the ice. The last time the Inuit had seen this was 1967.

We heard about it and Doug and I had to fly up there with 24 hours notice. Doug was by then my other half. The moment we captured with the belugas became one of the main sequences in *Blue Planet*. He was filming and I was taking the stills. Those were two things I'd photographed that had never been captured before.

CM:

You must've felt impassioned and elated to be there. With photography I've thought – and think even more so now, after talking to so many people in this industry – that there is a certain amount of luck and timing in what you do.

SF:

I think that with wildlife filmmaking there is always an element of luck, but in doing the research you're trying to improve your chances, effectively. Research tells you how close you can get and where it is. How long does it take to get to the site? Some of these bits of behaviour might only happen on a day or a couple of days, until next year.

I was getting really good chances to photograph wildlife at work and to subsequently get published. Doug and I had gone on a holiday, and I photographed a great white; I was about as close as I am to you when I took it [roughly a metre]. And that ended up on the cover of *BBC Wildlife* magazine and on the cover of *National Geographic* kids' magazine. That was like, 'Oh my God, my picture is on the cover of a magazine!'

I remember standing in WHSmith in Bristol. I was so excited. I'd never thought of being a photographer, but someone was paying to use my photos. I remember Hugh Maynard, who's a really fantastic cameraman, wrote to me and said, 'I've just seen this photo. It's fantastic.' People who I admired were telling me my photos were good.

Then a photo ended up on the back of *National Geographic*. I was slowly getting closer to the front cover. It was all giving me the confidence to want to do these things.

By now I'd finished *Blue Planet* and a lot of other things in the Arctic. I really loved working in the Arctic with the Inuit, and working in the cold. My ex-husband used to work for the British Antarctic Survey, so we ended up doing lots of stuff in the cold together. And then I managed to get the job on *Planet Earth* and we had a completely different experience – we went to Tonga to film humpback whales. We were there for 65 days of filming and I mean, none of these are cropped [Sue shows me images of the humpbacks]. This is a 45-foot-long whale.

CM:

What's your lens on this?

SF:

24/105. 24/78.

CM:

You were really close.

SF:

I literally had to put my hand out on her side, because the current was pushing me into her. I was in the water with them for about two and a half hours and it was a mum and her calf.

Shortly after this, a fellow photographer friend suggested that I start entering competitions, which I did, and I started having some luck with that. Do you know the Lucie Awards? I'm still amazed by this. I ended up being one of the eight finalists, winning one of the eight categories. I won what was called the Special Award for Travel and Tourism for my work in the Antarctic. Then I won a silver medal from the Royal Photographic Society.

CM:

What year was this?

SF:

2008. I had done 11 years with the BBC, and I'd worked with David Attenborough on *Blue Planet* and *Planet Earth*. I'd also done some documentaries and I thought, 'You know what, I'm actually going to see if I can make a go with my photography'. I handed in my notice at work. People thought I was nuts. And then the very next day…

I was so lucky. Mind you, I say you make your own luck.

Somebody asked if I would go on their ship to the North Pole. It was an icebreaker. I was asked to go talk about photography and polar bears. [...] At the same time, a photographer who was with Getty had seen my shark photo, and he emailed me saying, 'Getty is local, you should have a word with them'. I called Getty in London and of course, never got an answer. I persisted and then got an answer from somebody in New York saying, 'If you can see us, I'll give you half an hour'. I flew to New York and saw this woman, Sarah Foster, and they gave me a contract. That was just after I left the BBC. I was really fortunate. I was with Getty until very recently.

CM:

It was probably a good time to go with Getty. Was this journey on the icebreaker for people who paid for a cruise to the North?

SF:

Yes, people who were paying guests on expensive trips. It's difficult to get a job even working on those ships. And I certainly couldn't afford to go as a passenger. So, it was a really good opportunity. The company, who curated the expeditions, were well respected in that industry of expedition shipping. They'd been working the poles for decades.

Then they asked me if I would like to join this icebreaker in the Antarctic for three months, which gave me my first sighting of emperor penguins. The Antarctic is just a life-changing destination.

CM:

You must be pretty up on your kit. What do you work with?

SF:

I shoot Canon. And I've just bought a 600mm – oh my God, it was more expensive than my car. But it's so beautiful. I've got everything from a 15mm fisheye through to a 600mm, depending on where I'm going and what I'm doing. I'm about to head to the Antarctic in just over a week, and I'll be photographing everything from whales to penguins.

Some friends have chartered a ship. It's the husband's big birthday and they're taking their family and some friends. They asked me to come along and document it, so I'm photographing the whole trip and making a book.

Shortly after I left the BBC, I started being asked to photograph private trips to the Antarctic, which has been a really wonderful experience. The first time I went and did this it was my first full-blown photography job, which was in 2007. So that was a very fortunate thing, being asked to go and talk with the client and his family, which led to me being asked to go and do a lot more of that sort of thing, where I was going as a photographer.

You know, I said, 'Don't do things for the money'. My other rule is, do not work with or for people you don't like. But I have been really lucky and worked for some extremely nice and wonderful people. There's a lovely niche; I've been doing all sorts of expeditions where I'm going on holidays and teaching people.

CM:

Do you give a lot of educational talks on those trips?

SF:

I was helping people learn about photography, so I gave a couple of photo talks. If people wanted to talk about it, they could; if they didn't, never mind. I was talking about wildlife. It's a bit of everything. Because I've got a zoology degree, I can really talk about the animals. So, I've got this lovely niche where I do a lot of guiding for a couple of really good, well-respected agencies. There's a company called Steppes Travel. They have been around for 30 years and they do really good adventure wildlife conservation holidays.

Shortly after I started doing these expeditions I got asked if I would have a meeting at Canon. Canon said, 'Would you be interested in having a solo exhibition at the Getty gallery?'

CM:

In Los Angeles or in London?

SF:

The one in London, which now is associated with Nikon, so I guess they paid them more money. I nearly fell off my chair. That was my first solo exhibition, and it was at the Getty Images Gallery.

At the same time, I had been interested in the idea of trying to do a book, but I didn't know how to go about it. Luckily, one of my friends is an extremely good editor with the BBC, and then another friend was a designer with *BBC Wildlife* and other magazines. I thought, 'There's no way if I try and find a publisher that I can get this going before the exhibition'. So, I put my money where my mouth was and I funded my book, *Cold Places*, so I could have it in the Getty gallery.

Simon, the book's designer, was great because he had contacts with the printers. I got the photos

and he happened to live next door to the book editor. We were all minutes apart in Bristol.

I had the exhibition at the Getty gallery and that got a lot of PR. Shortly after the exhibition, I was working on a ship in Vietnam and I received an email. 'Dear Miss Flood, are you aware you've been invited to meet Her Majesty The Queen at Buckingham Palace at a reception for adventurers and explorers?' My first thought was this was one of my friends winding me up. But they'd sent the invitation to my old house, because by now I'd moved back to North Wales. My dad wasn't very well. They sent the invitation to the old address and I was on a ship for two months. Somebody in Buckingham Palace had heard about my photography.

When I arrived, I thought, 'What the hell am I doing here?' I'm at the palace in this room and there's David Attenborough and Michael Palin. All these people who I had admired for decades in some instances and who had really impressed me. Ellen MacArthur, the yachtswoman; Reinhold Messner, who was a mountaineer. Ranulph Fiennes – I mean, just all these incredible people, and me thinking there's been a mistake.

I remember putting my coat in at the cloakroom and standing there and seeing this group in the corridor in front of me and just thinking, 'You've got to remember this'. It was so surreal.

CM:

What year was that?

SF:

2011. I had full-blown imposter syndrome.

CM:

When you work in the wild, what does that entail in terms of the journey? How do you get to your destinations?

SF:

There's quite a lot of diversity when it comes to finding locations. In the space of the last year, I've been on some multi-millionaire, billionaire's boat through to... I've been camping with Nenets reindeer herders in a tent for a week where there's no loo and nowhere to wash, and the whole family and the dogs are in a tent. There's no one day like another, which is brilliant.

CM:

Photographically, is working in the wild with animals a case of patience and understanding through experience how these animals work, how they move, and where they're roughly going to be?

SF:

In terms of photography, my mum always used to say, 'How come you're so patient with wildlife and not with people?' If I'm waiting for an animal to do something, I can wait, and wait, and wait, and wait some more. I'd be happy to wait for weeks for it to do something. I'm trying to anticipate what's going to happen. Of course that's where it's so useful to have the zoology, because if you've got an understanding of that animal's behaviour, you can hopefully anticipate what's going to happen.

I go a lot to Zambia in the South Luangwa Valley, which is a fantastic wildlife hotspot. I've spent maybe 10 years going there now. Being able to watch, for example leopards, you almost start to think like the leopard. You see a group of impalas grazing up here. You know the leopard, even if you can't see it, is probably lurking in the foliage, and it's maybe going to come out of the trees and use one of the gullies to sneak up on the gazelle. You try to put yourself in the mindset of the animal.

If a polar bear's walking towards you, is it curious? Does it look aggressive? Does it look timid? It's hard not to anthropomorphise. It's a bit like if you see a dog. If you walk into a room and there's a dog there, is it something like a friendly looking Labrador that comes up wagging its tail?

CM:

Have you had any dangerous encounters?

SF:

I have. It's funny, people will often think of a dangerous animal or something. I would say the danger is either to do with vehicles or people. I hate helicopters. Unfortunately, I've had several friends get in helicopter accidents.

I have had a few wildlife things. One when we were photographing the polar bear that was trying to capture these beluga whales. They couldn't catch one. As time went on, the hole was getting bigger and bigger, so it was finding it more difficult to catch one. It started walking towards us. Normally what you'd do, you'd fire a shot and that would frighten it off, but it didn't, it just kept walking. Of course, you don't want to shoot a bear. It ended up getting close enough that we actually used pepper spray. Luckily, that worked.

Another one, where I was diving with local seals in the Antarctic. When there were two of us in the water, it was fine. She was swimming around. They're really big seals, maybe 12 foot long or something. The person I was with got out and as soon as I was on my own, she completely changed her behaviour. She was swimming up and doing this big threat posture with her jaws. I remember looking down her throat, thinking, 'I could fit my whole head in her mouth.'

I stuck my head above water. My friends were on this yacht watching. It was just awful, because I heard them saying, 'Okay. We think probably time to get out,' and you could hear them trying to sound like everything was under control when it obviously wasn't. This leopard seal was basically dive-bombing at me all the way back to the boat.

The other one was actually... Where we had camped overnight, the ice had broken around our tent. We had about six hours waiting for a helicopter, because we were in the middle of nowhere. I truthfully thought I was going to die. While we were on there, Doug said, 'If we get rescued, will you marry me?' We both thought we'd had it.

CM:

Did you think the ice was going to melt and you were going to have nowhere to go, or did you think something was going to come and have you for lunch?

SF:

The former. It's feasible that a polar bear might swim there, but very unlikely.

CM:

Do you have big photographic influencers, or people who you look to and learn from?

SF:

When I was younger, I remember I'd sit and pour over *The Face*. I used to love some of the photography in *The Face*. Then, Annie Leibovitz. Now there are people who've ripped off her ideas, but I thought her portraiture was so fantastic. Things that are now so familiar, like Lance Armstrong on the bike, or Whoopi Goldberg in the bath of milk, or whatever else. I just haven't really seen anyone photograph people like her before, and also there's a woman doing this job in a very male-dominated industry.

CM:

Do you find being a woman in this job problematic?

SF:

I actually don't. I actually find it's been, funnily enough, really useful, because it's helped me stand out from the crowd. People are so surprised to see a woman in some of the environments I'm working in. I guess there's a tendency for people to underestimate me.

You have to show people how interesting [wildlife] is, for them to want to protect it.

I feel very comfortable in the cold. That's definitely my environment, more than the tropics. But I love working all over the place. Natural history filmmaking is a small world. Polar natural history filmmaking is a *really* small world. There are not many women who spend a lot of time working in the Arctic or Antarctic. I work on all seven continents, but certainly I've spent a lot of time in the polar regions. I guess having a name like Flood has come in handy.

CM:

In 2020, climate emergency is becoming a very standardised headline. Do you consider your work to be at the forefront of helping people understand this situation?

SF:

I wouldn't like to put it in such an egotistical way. What I would say is, the thing that drives me is trying to get people interested in the natural world and its conservation. Paraphrasing David Attenborough, you have to show people how beautiful something is for them to want to protect it.

No matter how much I would love people to watch some of the hard-hitting environmental issues on television, most people turn off. We know that. It's very difficult to look at. Some of the images coming out of Australia at the moment are heartbreaking. I can't... I'm watching them in tears. I'm making myself watch them. I know that lots of people can't do that.

But if you show someone a picture of a baby koala or a baby wombat, they won't turn away from that, though they know they're being lost. I think that trying to get people engaged with wildlife images is definitely something that drives me, as opposed to, 'Let's just take a pretty picture of something.'

When I was in Svalbard last time, a year and a bit ago, I was lecturing on the trip. As well as photographing bears, walruses, Arctic foxes and glaciers, I was also photographing plastic pollution and so on. We have a responsibility, I think, to not just show pristine habitats. We should be, need to be, documenting everything.

CM:

I saw that beautiful picture of you with the two polar bear cubs in your arms. That must have been a special moment.

SF:

That was definitely one of the happiest moments of my life. I was making a film about polar bears for the BBC with David Attenborough and I was working with scientists. There's a wonderful man called Ian Stirling who is the world's leading expert on polar bears, and I had the massive, massive privilege... That's the word that always comes up out of my job, 'privilege', because you are getting to do things that I would give my right arm to go and do, and I get paid to go and do them. How lucky am I, to get to experience the natural world like this?

I think this was part of the world's longest running polar bear study in Hudson Bay. They were going to tag the mums and cubs, so they darted the mum, who was tranquilised, and they were going to take a blood sample from the bears. It's a brilliant project. They weigh the cubs, and they can see how they're doing, who's related to who, how many cubs does this mum have, and how long do they survive. They've been able to see that on average the sea ice is breaking up a couple of weeks earlier than it was, the cubs are lighter, the females need food.

They said, 'Look, we're going to pick them up to take a blood sample. Do you want to hold them when we take the sample?' So of course, I said 'Yes.'

CM:

When people come out with statistics about animals and insects that have gone extinct in the last hundred years, what's your reaction to that?

SF:

I guess it spurs me on to want to keep documenting things. It's easier to get people interested in saving certain species because of what they look like, unfortunately, than it is to save some insects.

It's hard not to get depressed about the state of things with, say, rhino poaching or panda poaching or elephant poaching. It's depressing that, sadly, there are individuals for whom the fact these animals are getting rarer is a good thing, because they're making money out of it. But you can't be put off; you just have to try.

You have to show people how interesting it is, for them to want to protect it. As a result of some of the tours we've done in Zambia, people who were poachers are now being paid to guard the wildlife.

CM:

Do you think lack of education is the problem? Or is it society as a whole that needs to change?

SF:

I think education is part of it, for sure. And I think programmes like *The Blue Planet* and other wildlife documentaries have helped grab people's attention. I mean, the reaction in *Blue Planet* to plastics…

CM:

The plastics episode was so important. What does photography mean to you?

SF:

That's a very simple question, but it's actually very profound, isn't it? And no one's ever asked me that before. It seems odd to say I haven't even thought of it like that. But what does it mean to me?

It's what makes me get up in the morning. I feel like I finally found the thing that I was meant to do, that's given me a purpose in life. You know, I was never the brightest or the hardest working or the best at anything, but [photography is] the thing I know I'm good at, and I know that I love doing, and that other people react to. I guess it's the ability to feel like you're part of something that can actually make a difference, and to have been part of *The Blue Planet* and *Planet Earth* and work with David Attenborough and do things that you know have influenced people to want to make a difference themselves.

I guess what photography means to me is… Especially because wildlife photography is a way of life, it's very hard to switch off from. I mean, photography generally is, isn't it? Because you're sitting here thinking in images the whole time. I'm sitting here talking to you and I'm sort of framing it with birds. You can't help but do it. It's an all-consuming passion. It's certainly what drives me, but you have to want to do it more than…

Someone asked me this recently. I'd given a talk in Chester and someone came up to me and said, 'What would your advice be for my daughter, because she wants to be a wildlife photographer?' I said, 'You've got to want to do it more than anything else on the planet, because it takes over your whole life.' I mean, I don't have kids, but I wouldn't be able to have this kind of lifestyle if I had kids.

I was invited to give a talk at this amazing gathering of people in March last year. In the room you've got various Microsoft billionaires, you've got world-famous musicians, you've got world-famous actors, directors. It was like being in a dream. I had to stand up on stage and speak to these people, some of whom I've admired for decades. I said, 'Look, there's some incredibly cool people in the room who I've admired for decades, but I'll tell you this – I'm the one in the room who got the best job.' That's how I feel.

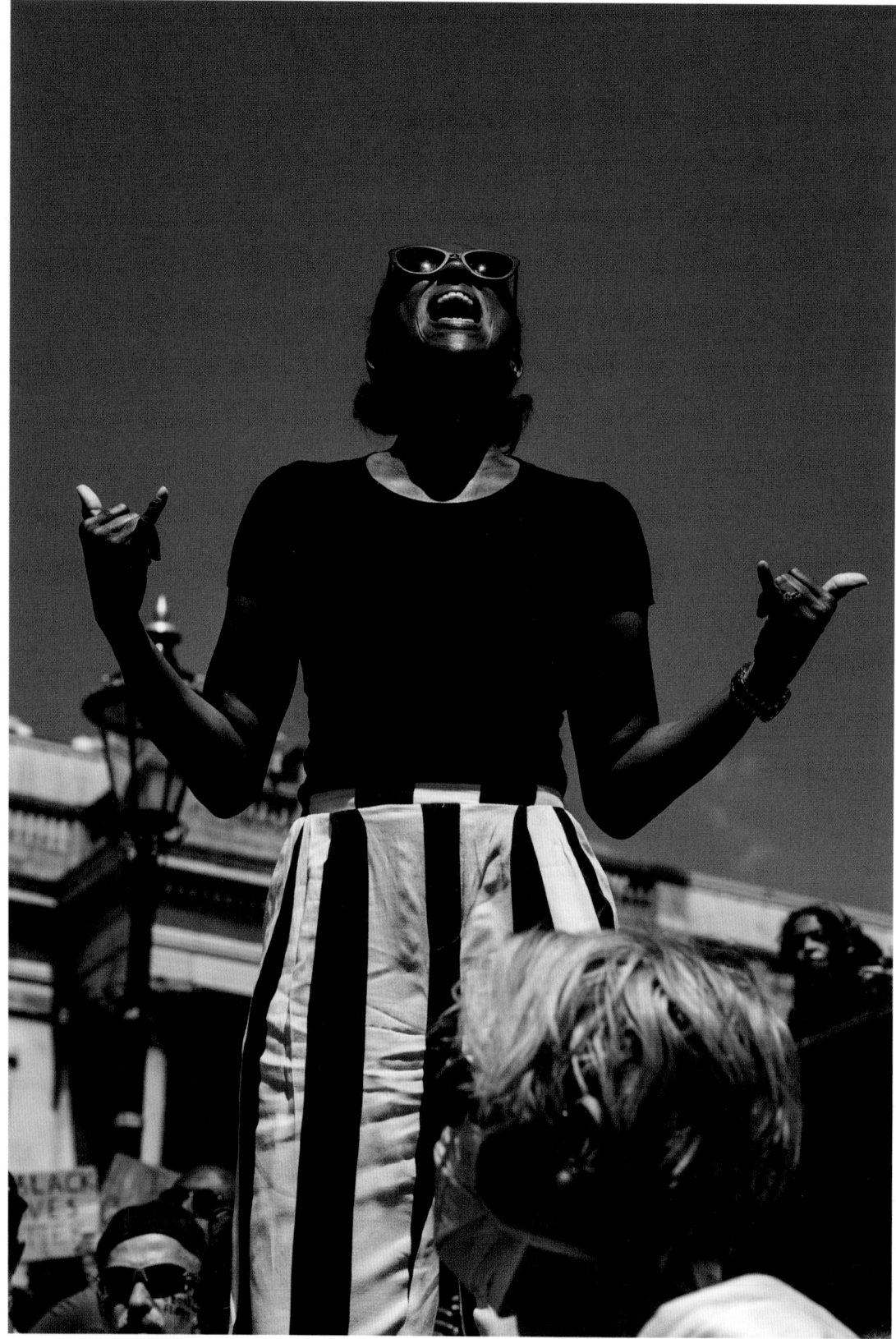

MISAN HARRIMAN

The first time I met Misan Harriman, we were sharing a table with Iconic Images at an award ceremony. The great Terry O'Neill was being awarded posthumously for his life's work. Move on several months, and the entire world was being introduced to Misan. I caught up with him over Zoom shortly after the publication of his now infamous cover for the September 2020 issue of British *Vogue*.

Misan Harriman, The Beating Heart of London, 2020
© Misan Harriman

Charles Moriarty:

2020. How's it going?

Misan Harriman:

My wife's amazing, otherwise it would be completely overwhelming. It's still surreal. I mean, the last I saw you, I was just figuring out what to do with my pictures, and it's just gone –

CM:

Now you have too many places to put them.

MH:

Yeah. I haven't processed everything that's happened.

CM:

You probably won't for a while.

MH:

I would guess so, but now I'm just putting in the work and trying to choose projects correctly and remember why I got into this in the first place – not get lost in any BS and just get on with it, you know what I mean? And also, to use whatever platform I have been put onto, to help people who deserve to be seen and heard.

CM:

There's a certain amount of responsibility, particularly now, as we see things both fall apart and come together for persons in power or those who stand centre stage.

MH:

Yeah, absolutely. I hopefully always had that message. It's just been massively expedited. And life, you know how it is, people are very fickle. But also, I mean, I go to all the marches and I see a bunch of guys with cameras, and it's interesting when I see them – they're like, 'Oh, it's you?' And I'm like, 'Yeah, it's me. It's just me. I'm like you, with a camera, taking pictures. There's no difference, really.'

CM:

Do they expect you to have an entourage?

MH:

I don't know. I've never been a press guy. I've never done that thing. I think sometimes they just don't know... You see a lot of people with cameras, and you don't know who's who, because you can usually figure out who the press guys are. I think it takes a while for them to think, 'Oh, he actually knows what he's doing.' You know what I mean? It's very difficult. What I've managed to pull off is some of the most difficult photography, because it's fast moving, in shitty lighting conditions, with no second take.

I've seen a lot of celebrity photographers who have huge followings online, who earn a fortune. They've gone out, particularly in America, and taken their pictures and then they're just not... Some of these guys, I think, are used to having phase one cameras in a perfectly lit studio with seven assistants. That's a different thing from getting your backpack and going out into the wild.

CM:

You're relatively new to the world of photography.

MH:

I properly started three years ago.

CM:

Was it a fascination beforehand or a hobby?

MH:

It was more than a fascination. I've been obsessed with film and music and photography to a pretty uniquely nerdy level since I was a kid. I think when most kids were talking about footballers, I was talking about the lighting of Stanley Kubrick's *Barry Lyndon*.

CM:

When did you actually pick up a camera for the first time? Do you remember?

MH:

My wife got me one about three [years ago]... I mean, over the years, like a gym membership, I've had shitty point and shoots that I never used. But a real camera, my wife got me a Fuji [Fujifilm] I think, and I just started using it and I liked how it wasn't very complicated. I just kept shooting. I'm completely self-taught. I used tutorials online and got out there. I guess I had a natural eye, compositionally.

It's weird. I truly think it's very odd, but I kept making quite big jumps in quality, relative to how long I've been shooting. Then I got really into lens research. I only shoot with primes. [...] I never shoot with zooms, but I also never shoot with lit scenarios. I always shoot with available light. So, I really got to get to understand how to look for light and to expose properly. And then I started getting a few Leica cameras and I loved how they shot.

Obviously, they added to the quality of what I was putting out. Then I just... People were posting stuff on Instagram that went viral really quickly, but it wasn't up until these Black Lives Matter images that it just went absolutely crazy.

CM:

We had dinner in February. Then the marches first started in March or April?

MH:

I think in April. I can't remember the dates, to be honest with you, but it was in the middle of lockdown.

CM:

Was your work from the marches something that all of a sudden you were recognised for? They really captured the moment.

MH:

I don't know why, but different people started using my work, I guess, to make statements. Even Martin Luther King's son himself. He used one of my images to make a statement. So did the Mayor of London, Puff Daddy, 50 Cent, Sarah Jessica Parker... Lewis Hamilton kindly made a very big statement with my image. And when people with that level of reach put your pictures out there, people respond. The editor-in-chief of British *Vogue* saw them and reached out, saying, 'I love how you shoot story and the honesty of what you're seeing out there on the streets. And we'd love to collaborate with you.' That's how the cover for *Vogue* started.

CM:

What words would you use to describe your style?

MH:

It's reportage, but [...] some of them are shot in medium format. Some of them are shot using 110mm primes to shoot marchers, which I think gives a look that you just don't... The average press photographer is not running around with basically a cinema lens. That's why some of the images are quite punchy. There's a lot of tonality and there's a huge amount of depth of field in some of the shots that I take.

I would say that's part of the story. The other part is, I love black and white, but I think a lot of people don't shoot black and white very well. I've spent a lot of time working on contrast and skin tones and making sure they pop. The third thing is, as a Black photographer, when I'm shooting a lot of Black people who have gone through a lot of the same life experiences as me, maybe there's a trust when they see me, because they give that 10 per cent, 5 per cent, whatever it is: more of themselves in the image.

Maybe the combination of those things makes these images stand out. The truth is, I don't know the answer, but people certainly are responding to them.

CM:

What's it like to be the first Black photographer to shoot the cover of Vogue *UK?*

MH:

I knew it'd be a big story, but I didn't know it'd be anything as big. I mean, when Christiane Amanpour wants to interview you to talk about pictures, you're like... I grew up watching her interviewing world leaders. That's when I knew this wasn't just another gig. But I've wept a lot. I've cried a lot because I've seen so many kids who would never have cared really about *Vogue* or this whole movement without feeling that they were included. When you get videos of people queuing up in the Co-op with their pocket money to buy the magazine you shot, it matters.

CM:

That's a beautiful thing.

MH:

It really, really matters. From the historian in me, if you look up September issues of British *Vogue* – I mean, obviously it's one thing shooting a cover, but it's another thing shooting the September issue. I think it's a really rarefied space in terms of the club that you're in, with photographers. I think the last one was Peter Lindbergh and it was the last thing he did with Meghan Markle. Before that, it was Nick Knight. It just goes on and on and on. If you go back a little bit further, it's a real who's who, from Irving Penn to Norman Parkinson to David Bailey. So, to be in that club is pretty special.

CM:

As a Black man, looking at representation – which I guess is what a lot of these kids now must be feeling, picking up a copy of Vogue *– do you see it as something that's changing in the photography world?*

MH:

I mean, you saw Nikon the other day announce their South African ambassadors. And they had no Black people. There'll be a lot of tokenism going on and [...] the difference is at the top. Edward Enninful is at the top. He runs British *Vogue*. So, it's a trickle-down effect.

In all industries, if you have a diverse group of board members to shape things, people will be more accepting. It has to be top-down though. There is a myriad of people, women and men from diverse backgrounds, who have the talent – but if decision makers don't ever breathe the same air space as them, of course it's wishful thinking. This is why the *Vogue* story resonates so much, because it's not like Edward knew me. He came across my work and he decided, 'This is good enough for the most important cover of the year.'

That kind of power to empower others... It's one thing having the influence; it's another thing to wield it in the way this man has done. And if you and I ever get into positions like that, we should just remember to cast the net as far as possible and give people who are good a chance. No one's asking for handouts. Trust me, if Edward thought my stuff was shite...

CM:

You don't get in the door if your work isn't up to standard.

MH:

I think photography is a funny thing as well. Because of Instagram, people can... There are influencers who talk about cameras, but they aren't really photographers. So, you get people with millions of followers who can barely take a picture – but they talk about photography, and they have a ton of followers. And then you get photographers who are just focused on what they do. They're really good at what they do, but they kind of miss the memo, re: building a reputation online. That breaks my heart. They don't get the work they deserve or the reach they deserve, and that's got nothing to do with the colour of their skin; it's just got to do with the internet today. There really is a lot going on.

CM:

Would you like to go into fashion?

MH:

If I go into fashion, I'm going to go into fashion my own way, in terms of shooting and style. It has to look like my work, which isn't such an impossible feat. Lindbergh shot mainly in black and white and didn't process his images, or very little. And that's similar to what I would like to do in fashion. I'm not interested in having glossy, glossy, shiny, super-retouched, over-the-limit stuff.

CM:

Airbrushed to death.

MH:

Yeah, that's not me. If brands or magazines want to work with me, they have to do what Edward did. Anyone who looks at that picture will say, 'Yep, that's Misan. That's how he shoots.' Even on that shoot, I did not use any external lighting. I relied on daylight.

CM:

How was the shoot itself?

MH:

It was one day in Manchester, in Marcus' garden. We had awful weather. It was actually raining, and we just hustled. It was a guerrilla shoot. Real photographers should be excited by that kind of thing. Again, it was the furthest thing away from a two-day studio shoot with a million opportunities to get the right shot. You've got a limited time frame, and you better nail it, regardless of the conditions Mother Nature is throwing at you.

CM:

Did you feel the pressure?

MH:

Mate, yeah. Come on. It's a healthy thing. You know your way around image making and you've been given an opportunity. I remember my wife saying, 'Misan, just have fun. When you have fun, the images will come to you,' and she was right. But I'll tell you a funny story. On the train to Manchester, I switched on my camera and it switched on for one second and both batteries just went red and it died. I hadn't brought a charger, but luckily some of the newer cameras have USB-C charging. So, I had a power bank. Thankfully, it's quite a long journey from London to Manchester, so I charged it.

Then when I finished the shoot, because it was a loaned camera, I didn't really know my way around it. Usually, when I do important things, I have two SD cards, one that is a backup. In case one is corrupted, right?

When I shot the most important shoot of my life, I didn't realise that it was set up to not back up, but just when one card is full, the next one starts. I finish the shoot and I put the first SD card into the reader and I put that into the computer and it says, no files. I was like, 'Okay, fine, fine. Maybe it's corrupted, but I have a backup.' So I put the next SD card in and it says, no files.

Everybody was clearing up saying, 'Hey, well done. High five, Misan. Nice to meet you.' I'm thinking, there's no shoot. There's no shoot. I kept my cool and said, 'I hope this SD card reader has a fault.' I had a spare SD card reader, and I put it in and of course, all the images were still there. But mate...

Some of these guys, I think, are used to having phase one cameras in a perfectly lit studio with seven assistants. That's a different thing from getting your backpack and going out into the wild.

CM:

Oh God... Where do you see yourself going now?

MH:

I'm going to keep finding the truth with a lens. I'm also going to get into filmmaking. I have a few documentary projects I'm going to get started, and I have a short film that I'm just finishing writing. I've got something on domestic violence survivors that I'm planning to do, and quite a few things linked to the film industry as well. The portraiture that people know me for is going to be a range of celebrity portraiture, all the way to being the tip of the spear, if you like, in civil rights. Not just BLM. I've shot a huge amount of Extinction Rebellion, a huge amount of climate strikes. I did both Trump marches last year. My general civil rights, civil protest imagery work is growing to be well over 10,000 images.

CM:

Do you think that's what's at your core?

MH:

I'm a multi-discipline. I think my work shooting festivals is as strong as protest, as is my work shooting engagement pictures of Princess Beatrice, or portraits of Meghan Markle or Liam Neeson. It's all part of the same thing: looking for the truth with the lens that we have.

I very much want to follow in the footsteps of Gordon Parks, who did it all. He directed films like *Shaft* and shot the most powerful reportage documentary for *Life* magazine, and then was shooting Audrey Hepburn and Ingrid Bergman on the other side. I want to have that full range of image-making ability and see where it takes me.

CM:

Would you impress anything upon people wanting to get into photography nowadays, as someone who's self-taught?

MH:

I think it's an incredible time to get into photography. Camera phones have made a lot of people lazy, but nothing can replace a camera with a real lens and looking into some kind of viewfinder. To me, it's that process of composing, understanding the relationship between shot, speed, aperture: all of those basic things. It's not the same as pulling out an iPhone and pressing 'burst'.

Some of my favourite photographs have been taken on the iPhone, because it's so convenient and portrait mode is very good, but mirrorless cameras have got very affordable. You can get a decent one for a couple of hundred quid with a kit lens that covers the focal distances you initially need to get into it, and then Bob's your uncle, just go for it.

Then you have this thing called the internet to put out your work. You never know who will see your work, as I am living proof. When you and me met, Charles, if you were going to tell me then in February that I would literally make history and would be interviewed by Enninful and the rest of them, I would have laughed, literally laughed at your face. That's the age of photography today, how quickly things can change with your images being put out there.

CM:

Do you have quiet moments where you laugh to yourself about the whole situation?

MH:

Every day I'm just like, 'Wow, this is kind of crazy.' But I'm 42 years old. My wife thinks this is what I've actually been looking to do my whole life. It's just found me now. I'm at the stage in my life with two young kids, and luckily married and settled, living out in the countryside where I'm in the right head space to handle the attention and the madness that comes with all of this. If I was 21 and this happened, oh my God. So it has happened at the right time in my life and it's important for me to use this in the right way. Not just commercially, but to really help people – creative, talented people from all backgrounds. For me, if you're talented, you deserve a shot.

CM:

Did you speak to Tyler Mitchell at all?

MH:

No, I don't know Tyler. I met him very briefly years ago in Miami, but I'm sure we're going to end up having a conversation. We are definitely kindred spirits now. I'm sure we'll have a lot of notes to share. I think he's New York based. When I'm next able to get out to the States, I'll definitely look out for a coffee with the great Tyler.

CM:

We're existing in a rather strange world. Final words?

MH:

I think for all of us, men and women who try and write poetry with lenses, the world has turned upside down, which means we've got work to do. It's as simple as that. We are living history in a way that I never thought would happen in my lifetime. All of us, whether it's a pandemic, what's happening politically in North America and in Europe, or the biggest human rights movement in regards to racism, ever. There is a lot to tell, and we have work to do. So, let's do it.

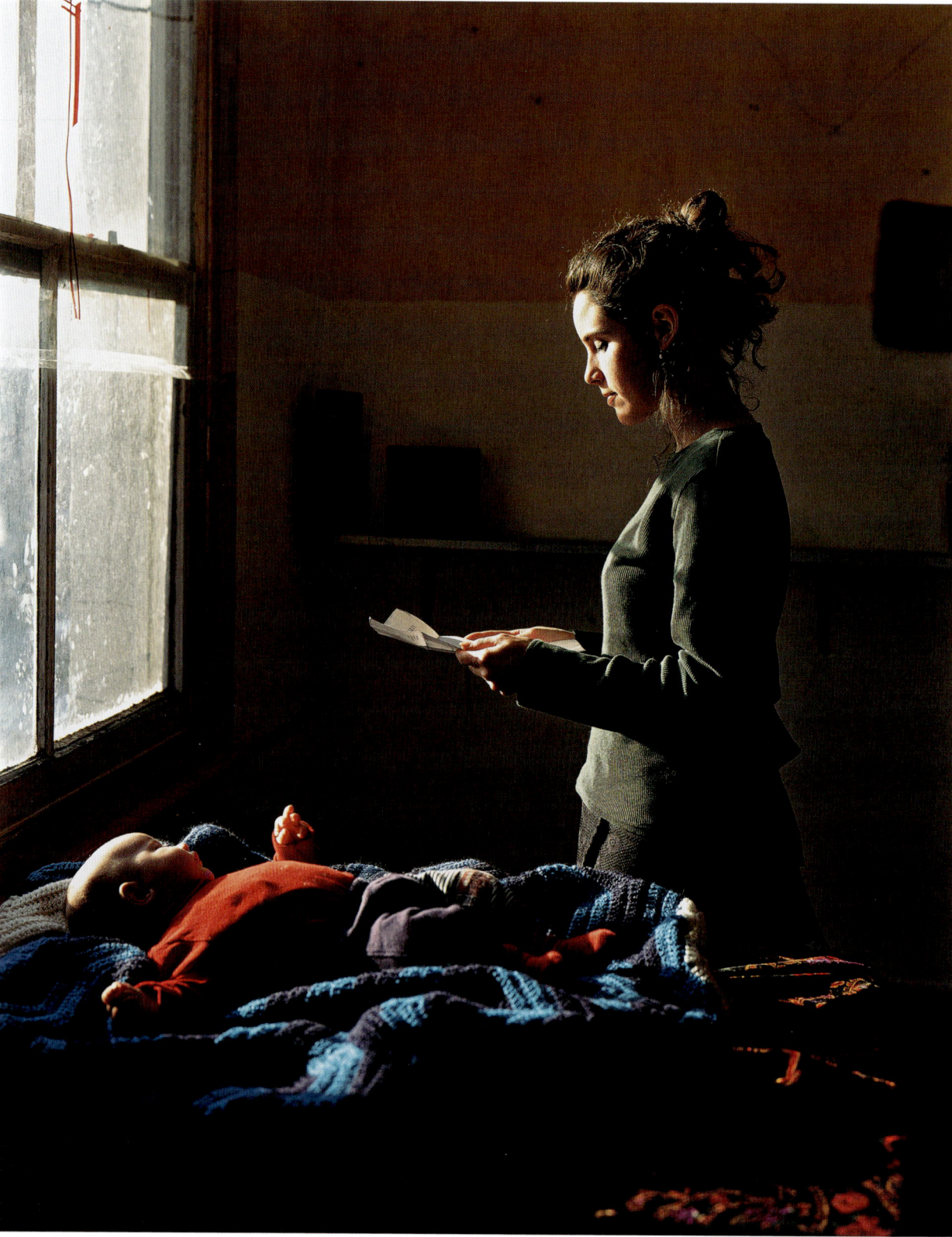

TOM HUNTER

Tom Hunter's work has been a significant part of my adult journey of discovery with photography and art. He won the Taylor Wessing prize at the National Portrait Gallery, then later showed at the National Gallery – the first photographer ever to achieve this accomplishment. I met Tom initially when he was one of the tutors at LCC [London College of Communication], where I studied photography. We spent some time talking over Zoom in lockdown.

Tom Hunter, Woman Reading Possession Order, 1997
© Tom Hunter

Charles Moriarty:

You were born in Dorset. Were arts and photography part of your youth?

Tom Hunter:

It was around. My dad was an art teacher later on in my life. When I was growing up, he was a carpenter and a builder. When I was in my teenage years, he retrained and became an art teacher. He had a darkroom in our garden shed and was really interested in photography. I used to go into it as a kid. It was quite a magical place to go: a very strange world with chemicals, red light, his papers. It definitely had an effect on me, seeing that. Photography was very much something you did by yourself and it was inspiring that you could do it in your own garden.

CM:

You worked in the forestry industry. Did that also come from your dad?

TH:

I seem to love trees. I love being outdoors. I did carpentry and then, where I lived in Dorset, I was in the middle of a forest really. I thought I'd really want to do the outdoor life. I didn't want to be in an office.

[...]. When I left school at 15 it seemed very exciting to work in a forest, but it was very boring actually. You were just planting trees day after day after day, 1,500 trees a day.

CM:

Was there a clear point in your life where you thought, 'I actually want to be a photographer. Enough with the trees!' Or was it always in the back of your mind?

TH:

It was in the back of my mind for a long time. I bought myself a Pentax 35mm SLR, which I was experimenting with, but I didn't know how you went from a young guy with no qualifications in a small village in the middle of nowhere to becoming a photographer. I couldn't connect how you would make that leap. I bought a ticket to America and hitched around for a few months. I eventually went to Puerto Rico and worked for the forestry service there. After I left, I was hitching around America and I thought, 'You've got to make asserted decisions about where you want to take your life, rather than just taking up something that becomes available like forestry, or whatever things come up.'

I decided I was going to make an effort in photography or the arts. I wanted to do that. Photography seemed to be the one that I had the most creation with. I went by myself to America, and although I met lots of people, it was a period of finding myself. I was totally free and I really wanted to just change my whole life. I wanted to completely rewrite myself.

CM:

Your work has been very reflective of your social circumstances and the people surrounding you, which you then punctuate with nods to painting, both contemporary and historical masterpieces. What led you to that duality?

TH:

My mum's a painter. She went to art college and I grew up in a very small village where all my friends were very working class. You worked on a farm, which I did, or you worked in forestry, or you worked in a factory. There wasn't really any culture there and I really enjoyed all that side of it. But there was the art and culture side from my parents, which I really enjoyed as well.

I think in some way I've always wanted to marry those two things up. I wanted to be connected with what was going on around me, the realities of working life and social interactions, but then also find this other element with culture and music and art and painting. I wanted to connect those things.

My mum always said I felt a little bit out of place in this very small village, where everyone was just talking about the shopping, the WI meeting and football. Mum used to drag me up to the Tate or National Gallery or to talks about high art. I always had that, mixed with reality.

I really wanted to talk about all the deprivation and unemployment and inequalities of life around me in Hackney in the '80s and in the '90s. I had no relationship to the reality of what was going on, but I really wanted to talk about it and put it in an art context so people could think about it in a different way; take it out of its own reality and make a new reality.

CM:

Was there a point in your life when you reconnected with the art institutions your mum had taken you to?

TH:

When I moved to London, I lived in squats and the people that I was meeting would quite often be art students who were doing degrees, and they were talking about these places, which I'd completely forgotten about.

I started visiting them again and the world opened up for me. Later on, I went to the LCP – LCC, as it is right now – where I teach.

Education was very inspirational for me: talking about different cultures, different art movements, different ways our history came into it. It got me excited for wider cultural issues, but also from my own history of remembering the pictures I saw as a kid, which I had rejected. […] Education reawakened the cultural heritage I had in my family from my

childhood, and let me think about the world in a much wider way.

CM:

Who were your early photography influencers?

TH:

When I went to LCC, it was magazine work by Diane Arbus, and I was just blown away by that because that's what I always wanted to do. When I came back from travelling, I thought, 'I'll just be a commercial photographer; I'll take pictures for magazines.' When I looked at the commercial work that she produced, it was made in such a way that it's high art. You know all its references are to the art world, but it speaks about day-to-day reality, on a much higher level. It transports you to another world. I was really inspired by her black-and-white photography.

Then, later on, Jeff Wall came into it. The way he reconstructed scenes, set up scenarios and staged photography was very important. Nan Goldin, because of the way she documented the AIDS epidemic in New York with the gay scene and the club scene, and the alternative culture she was surrounded by. She really made me realise 'Wow,' that I was part of a scene that needed to be documented and that there were some people who'd done it before in an incredible way.

So, Nan because she used her peers and the contemporary society around her, and documented them as her own family from the inside, rather than going into a community and taking pictures of a different group as an outsider. Photographing from the inside; this idea became very important. Then Jeff Wall, because he not only documented, but he *re-imagined*. He constructed his images.

CM:

I can see very clearly how both those artists fit into what you do. Did you feel a responsibility to reflect what was going on in Hackney? It was so marginalised and attacked by the government and council.

TH:

That was very much part of it. I've always been quite political. I was very much involved in the punk scene, and now I would prefer society to be much more social but anti-establishment.

When I moved into a squat, we became part of a very big community living there. We became very attacked and marginalised by the council trying to evict us; and by the government with the Criminal Justice Bill, where they were attacking the travellers, the road protesters, the rave scene. It felt like all the groups I was affiliating myself with, was a part of, were being attacked. I thought it was very important to document that lifestyle and that was very much how I started.

But it felt like documentary wasn't really doing enough. I wanted to push the boundaries, so it could actually fight back against the negative representations that were falling down around me. I wanted to find new ways that I could really push back.

CM:

The peak of that was your image Woman Reading Possession Order. Did the image manage to change things with the local council?

TH:

Yeah, it did. It really did, actually. It was quite amazing what an image could do. That's why I believe in photography and I believe in images. The positive effect that image had was quite astounding.

> One of my students said to me a while ago, 'We've seen what you and the people like you have done and we couldn't make it better, so we have to reinvent it.'

It had so much publicity that people from the council were coming to me and asking me things. I was asked to become a member of school boards, *The Guardian* were interviewing me, the local paper were interviewing me… Suddenly, from having no voice within the wider community, our own community had a very strong voice, and it did open up negotiations with the council.

I'm not saying I did it singlehandedly, because we did form a co-operative. There were lots of people working together, so I'm not taking away from what all the other people did. But it definitely helped with that campaign. From that, we managed to form the co-operative. We negotiated with the council and we saved our houses. We saved our community.

The houses are still there, as part of a co-operative, rather than squats. My friends still live there. They've brought up their children there, and it feels very positive, the legacy of what happened to this squatting community in the heart of Hackney.

There's still social housing in that part of London Fields where ordinary people, teachers or whoever, can afford to live. As you know, most parts of central London have become so restrictive, people have to move out. Most of my friends had to move out of Hackney because it's so expensive. But this community… Again, it's about 80 people living in there. So that image was very important. It was a banner for us to rally around and it put us on the map. I had so many interviews and such publicity; it was incredible.

CM:

When I look at your work, I immediately see things like Christina's World *[Andrew Wyeth], the Pre-Raphaelites, Vermeer, the myriad of art influences throughout your work. Did* Woman Reading Possession Order *give you the confidence to continue working with classic scenes from high art, evolving it into something new, for a new audience?*

TH:

It did, because that body of work was an experiment. Before that, I was looking at other references, which were obvious but not as direct. I'd be talking about the golden age of Dutch painting by taking on colours or certain tropes within that visual language, but never directly referencing. Then from that, it went down so well that I really took it on board.

I think a lot of artists hide their references. Obviously, if someone says, 'Oh, you just copy someone else's work,' it's quite an insult, but you hope they realise it's not actually copying. It's reimagining.

And it can have a really powerful effect on a different audience – but a wider audience, which is very important. I didn't want to be stuck in a ghetto. I was living in the ghetto, as described by the local newspaper, but I didn't really want to just make work for me and my mates. When I got a wider audience, that made a big difference for me to change things, both for myself and my housing.

CM:

Was Life and Death in Hackney *at the White Cube your first big solo show?*

TH:

There were a few little things before that. *The Ghetto, Street Model* piece that went into display at the Museum of London was a big deal, to jump from a degree show to a museum. That went into a few little shows… Then the *Woman Reading Possession Order* was put in the Whitechapel open, and got bought by Saatchi. That was a big thing, but it was a massive jump from being an artist to then having a show in a very high-class, elite gallery.

Lots of photographers work away and have exhibitions in lots of places, but not many photographers show in a high-end art gallery. That was a jump in a different direction, which took me into a very different world. It was quite a big step to be represented by a big West End gallery who was a world player, especially at that time.

CM:

Was it hard to comprehend moving from, as you said, 'the ghetto', into that very elite world of money and galleries?

TH:

It was strange. It happened so quickly. I still lived in a squat when a limousine was sent round to take me to the Groucho Club, where I'd be given free drinks all night. Then at the end of the night, I'd catch the number 38 bus back to Hackney, back to the squat, and there'd be a party going on. At that time, it just felt normal.

Sometimes in your life things happen so quickly, you don't even notice. It wasn't till years later that we even thought it was strange. It was like, 'Oh yeah. Doing this, doing that.' It was just like, 'Oh, this is what you do. This is what happens. You make a piece of work. Gets taken by a gallery, gets taken there.' I think everything was just happening so quickly.

CM:

Is everything large format for you?

TH:

I try and do different stuff. I've been shooting this piece on the coast lately and I've been using an Olympus Trip 35mm. Lots of artists don't like to talk about their tools of the trade, but they are quite important. The way you use different tools really has implications on how you work as an artist.

When I use a large format, it slows me down because I used 35mm before that, which made me very quick and flexible. Then I went to large format, and it made me very slow, but also very thoughtful and very considered. I think it's very good to change tools every now and again.

I was using large format a while ago and that was so calming. You get so meditative when you work in that way, and you think about everything so carefully, which is really lovely, but I [...] like to change, do different projects with different tools, mix it up a bit and make it more exciting. I think if you stick with one way of working, you become a bit predictable and a bit too boring really, so it's important to try and change how you do things and do different styles.

CM:

You have about eight books. Do you find them to be a good vehicle for your work?

TH:

The books are really beautiful things. Most people are now on the internet, but there is a legacy about books that I really love. Now my kids are looking at my books and they look at things which are from 20 years ago, and that's really interesting. They found one with a photo of their mum last week, which was from 20 years ago, and they said, 'Oh my God, is this you, mama?' because that's when she had dreadlocks and piercings.

CM:

For several years you travelled through Europe and lived on a double-decker bus. How much did that travelling, punk lifestyle affect you and your work?

TH:

Massively. It's always made me, in some way, above a free thinker. As in, it was always about DIY culture. [...] I couldn't play an instrument, but that didn't stop me from forming a band. I've always had that attitude of, I might not know how to use a 5x4 camera or a 10x8 camera, but I'd just do it. If it doesn't work out, something will work out. It's just lack of inhibition, I suppose.

With the whole travelling in the buses, you make friends. You form your own communities. You take care of yourself; you don't rely on other people. I suppose it's about independence, about doing things for yourself. My dad making his own darkroom was a bit like that. It's really nice to just have that cottage industry, where you can make your own pictures. You can make your own art and you can use your friends around you as subjects. You're not reliant on other people. You're not reliant on anything. I'll always find that exciting. That's what I really like about photography. You can just start a project today, find a subject and get on with it yourself.

I was in a few punk bands, but I didn't really like it very much because there was always somebody who had a hangover who wouldn't turn up to rehearsals or know what you were doing. The community is great, but the great thing about photography for me is the do-it-yourself. If I've got an afternoon free, I can just go off to the marshes or I can get on with it myself, which I really like.

CM:

It must've been a really wonderful and circular thing to have a show at the National Gallery, having gone there as a kid.

TH:

I couldn't believe that I actually got offered a show. It was amazing to see pictures of my friends in Hackney actually at the National Gallery, and to be part of those pictures that I had grown up with. It was probably my artistic highlight to be shown in that space.

I had shows in a tower block on the holiday street just days before it was blown up and it was probably the most satisfying show I'd ever done. In some ways that made more sense, the location and the social context, and everything else was more interesting. As a prestige thing to do, the National Gallery was obviously huge.

But it was quite tricky. I had lots of negative reviews... For some reason, there was a bit of press saying, how can I compare myself to Velásquez or Picasso and so on, which I thought was quite a strange comment.

They thought I was putting myself on the same level as them, but I wasn't. I was trying to comment on art, historical art and contemporary art. It was quite a strange time. I really put myself out there. When you show something like that, you're open to a lot of criticism. It can feel like, 'Whoa, this is quite nasty,' which felt strange as well.

CM:

You were breaking the art world's mould, which unfortunately can be akin to making yourself into a punching bag.

TH:

I was really exposed by everything. It was a strange time. Afterwards, I got a residency in the Irish Museum of Modern Art and did a project about Dublin Bay with pinhole cameras.

CM:

Are there certain works of yours that you go back to and look at again and again?

TH:

The traveller pictures. [...] The choice people I was travelling with on my bus. It's very important for me, because that was such a mad time, having a double-decker bus and travelling around Europe for two years. It was such a fucking crazy thing to do.

The memories come back. We had such a close group of people; there's friendships and bonds we made, because it was so crazy. That brings those memories back. They're always there. The *Woman Reading Possession Order* was one of those moments. They're very important. In fact, the work that went to the National Gallery is probably the least interesting for me, because it felt in some way less connected to me.

The more personal the work, I suppose the more interesting it is when you look back. You always need a few years after you've done a project to let it settle and to think about it. Sometimes you think, 'Oh God, I was terrible with that work.' There's lots of work in the Persons Unknown series with the *Woman Reading Possession Order*, that I thought was really bad for years. Now I can actually say, 'Oh, that is quite interesting.'

CM:

Wolfgang Tillmans recently said it can take about a decade to actually see an image. Everything is so dependent on perspective.

TH:

Exactly. That's why I really like large format, actually. When I take pictures digitally, it's so easy to have in your mind what you want. You can take the picture, not get it and then delete it. Whereas when you shoot on 5x4, having not got what I want, a week later you get it back and you're like, 'Oh, what's this?' Then you leave for another couple weeks and you look at it again, and then at least you've got a bit of distance and can look at it as more of an image, rather than your original concept. Ten years later, you can *actually* look at it and see if it worked or not.

CM:

As a teacher at LCC, how do you feel about the ever-changing world of photography?

TH:

Every time you have a new student or a new cohort of students, their ideas of photography are always changing. I feel incredibly privileged that I'm a leader. I'm allowed to be in that environment where I can hear the new voices. You want to say, 'No, you don't do that. I know best.' But obviously, they know

best because they're living in the new environment and they have to want that new environment. I'm still living in my old environment, where I've tried and tested something and it still has a certain amount of poignance and recognition.

But it's really good when the new students tell me about this and about that. I have to remember not to be stuck in the past and to let them show me where it's going now. It's much more interactive now. It's much more digital now. It's much more disposable now. When I was making these five-foot-by-four-foot prints, it was all about making a permanent statement. One of my students said to me a while ago, 'We've seen what you and the people like you have done and we couldn't make it better, so we have to reinvent it.'

It was the same for me when I saw Martin Parr's stuff. It was very dynamic and in people's faces, very much the outside looking in. I really wanted to be the insider looking at my own environment. You really want to change the dynamic every time, so that's the tricky bit. You can't tell students what to do but you have to encourage them, and you have to trust in the new generation to find their way.

I read a lot – like, about the way that [photography] is not elitist. What [photographers] are doing now is so un-elitist, which is really great. In some ways, it's much more punk. I think it's much more about breaking down boundaries for yourself, and it's quite aggressive, which I think is interesting.

CM:

The elitism of photography has certainly gone now. Everyone can pick up a camera and go.

TH:

And there's so many more platforms to produce your stuff on. I find that really exciting. Again, that's a bit like the old punk thing: people do it for themselves, so they set up co-operatives, they set up their own galleries. They do it on Instagram. They do it on their websites, rather than waiting for the White Cubes to come along, the exclusive galleries.

CM:

You can be waiting your whole life for the White Cubes to come along. When you sit down to create a body of work, do you have a process that you go through?

TH:

[…] I have lots of ideas I'm working on. Lots of grand schemes and lots of things I'm shooting now and again. But actually, it's when someone like Purdy Hicks phones up and says, 'Let's do a show in January next year,' and I go, 'Fuck'. Then I've got a deadline. I find it a lot easier working for deadlines.

Otherwise, it's so easy to have a project that just gets bigger and wider and more convoluted. More interesting, maybe, but it can be never-ending. Deadlines really help me out a lot. I'm not very good at self-discipline in that respect, and I've been really lucky that I've had some great commissions and some great people to work with. We set some boundaries and set some discipline on the ideas I work with, and as soon as I've got that, the process becomes quite natural.

CM:

Are you working on anything at the moment? What deadline are you currently working towards?

TH:

Everything seemed to stop with the whole Covid thing. I have projects, but they're not running. I was doing some stuff on the coast; that's probably going to be a book project. I had a really beautiful project, working with the Royal Photographic Society and the Holocaust Memorial [Foundation], where I was doing portraits of Holocaust survivors. That's on hold, obviously.

I want to go back to Calais, to the refugee project I've been working on now for a few years. I'm still working on that and just trying to figure out how to get back to Jordan. I was working in Jordan, again with the refugees. There are a few projects I'm working on at the same time.

CM:

From what angle are you approaching the refugees in Jordan?

TH:

I took it from a perspective of Lawrence of Arabia. Lawrence of Arabia died in Dorset, in the next village to me where I grew up. I was looking at his legacy, actually: a young Englishman, the 'white saviour' going to the Arab Peninsula and trying to save the people, but who ended up destroying the whole place. Not him personally; the British and the French government pretty much did that themselves.

CM:

They had a wonderful way of doing that everywhere. Looking back on the British Empire is mind blowing.

TH:

Colonial powers tend to fuck up other people's lives. But I was looking at the personal side of one person trying to save something, and then the repercussions of that. I was looking at lots of different layers within that. One of my tools I like to use is to get people to relate to people, to see dignity and humanity in people. Photography can portray people in a quite beautiful way, and that's the language I really like using.

DOUGLAS KIRKLAND

On 9 April 2019, I sat with Douglas and Françoise Kirkland at their home in LA to discuss some of the more memorable moments of Douglas's career, which has spanned almost 70 years. Douglas is known for his work with many of Hollywood's major icons – Marilyn, Judy Garland, Jack Nicholson; the list is endless. As he says himself, photography has been good to the Canadian kid from Fort Erie.

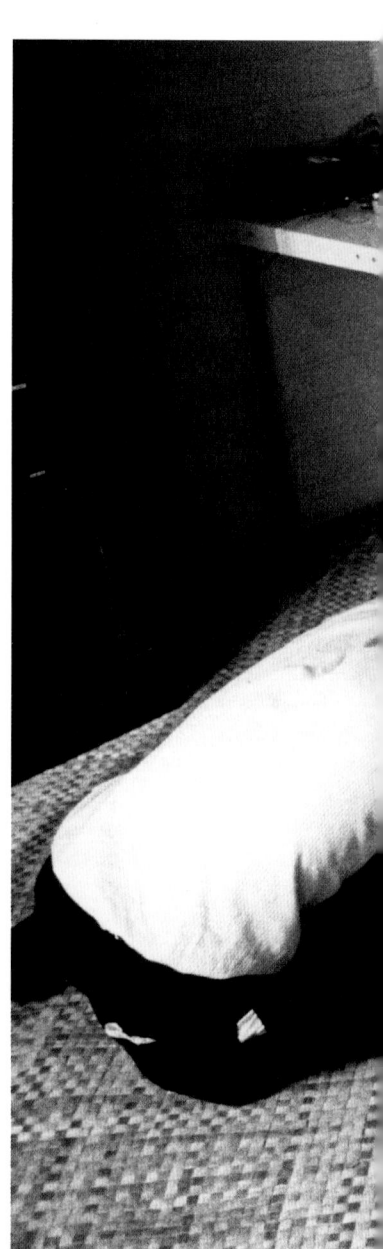

Douglas Kirkland, Photographing Marilyn Monroe on a White Bed, 1961
© Douglas Kirkland/Corbis via Getty Images

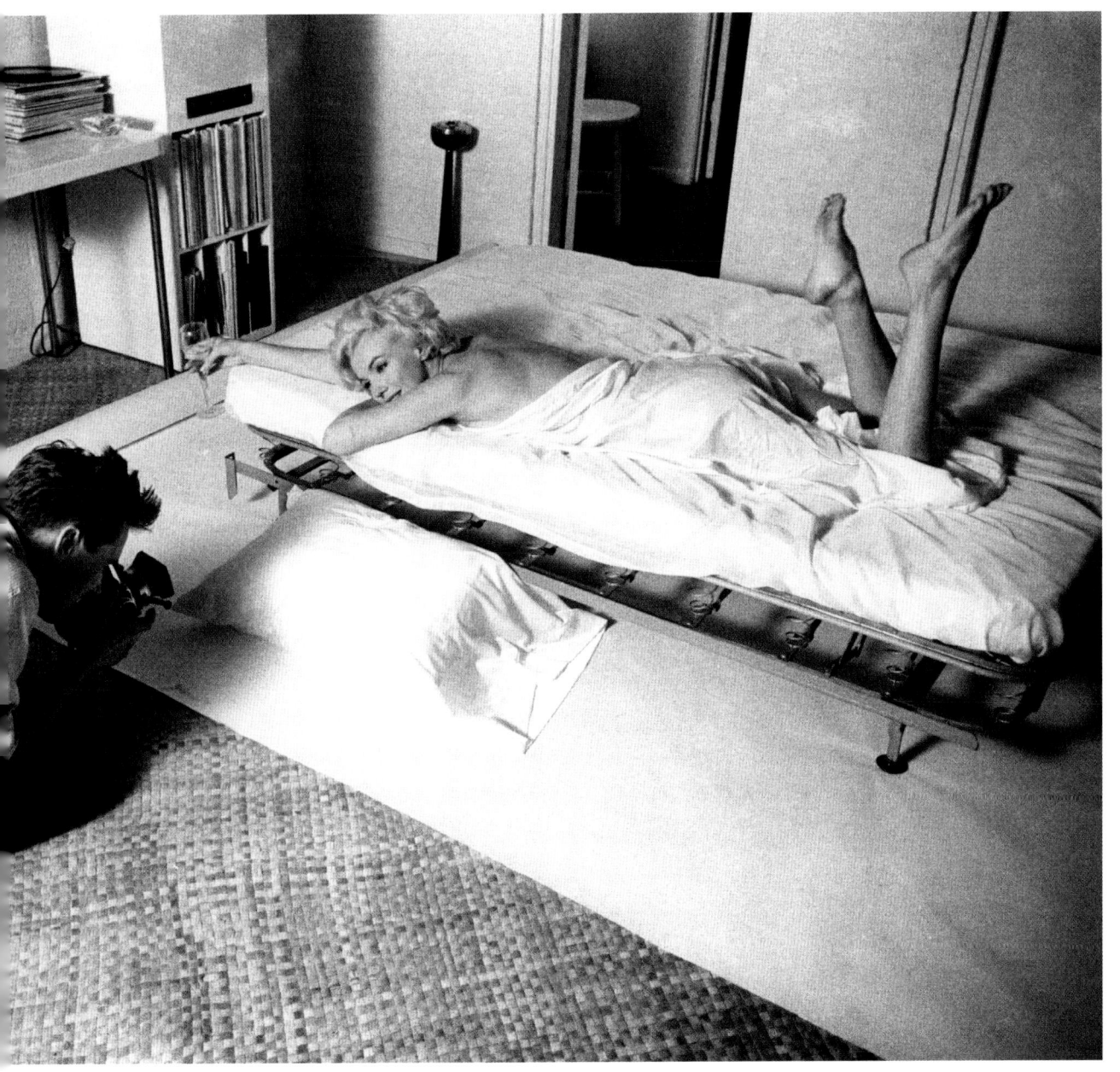

Charles Moriarty:

When did photography enter your life?

Douglas Kirkland:

The first time I took a picture was with our family box camera, and I was allowed to take one click. It was during the Second World War, and film was very rarely available in Canada. We had eight exposures on the roll. I still have the camera somewhere.

[The photo was of] my family – my father and brother in Fort Erie, our little, tiny town in Canada on the US border. It was Christmas Day. I was told I had to hold it very steady.

Françoise Kirkland:

And you never saw the film until later – probably six months later because they didn't process.

CM:

Did you know from then that photography was something that interested you?

DK:

It excited me. I had an uncle who was in the RCAF, Royal Canadian Air Force, who was sent to Europe during World War Two. He was a great inspiration because he would show slides at night of the pictures he had taken while there.

FK:

And your dad did home movies, too.

DK:

My dad did home movies, which we still have, and then my son Mark directed *The Simpsons* for 30 years, so it's in the blood.

FK:

Douglas was slightly dyslexic, so he was a dreamer. And I think the camera allowed him to express himself much better. Even now he still sees things in a different way. I know when we're adventuring somewhere, he'll start looking, and something happens to him – there's a glint in his eyes, and something takes over. It's almost like he gets possessed.

CM:

When did you start to take photos regularly?

DK:

It happened through going up to see my uncle in Wingham, Canada. He was into photography and had picked up a Contax camera in Germany. He brought it home and one day said, 'I think it should be in your hands'. This is after I had developed quite a bit of photography, and I'd gotten into the world.

CM:

What were your early years as a photographer like?

DK:

I started off in New York, where I initially spent a period working for Irving Penn. He didn't really have room for me, but I managed to talk my way in. I was with him for six months – I learned a lot, an enormous amount. He was very inspirational to me, but not the best teacher. You learnt by doing; Penn was interested in Penn. On the last day, he said he felt bad that I had to leave because he couldn't pay me enough money. He said, 'Is there anything I can do for you?' And I said, 'I'd like to take your picture.' He was rarely photographed, but sat for me.

I worked with anybody who would hire me in the beginning. I was this kid from Canada in my 20s, and I wasn't aware of the realities of New York. My first wife and I lived in New Jersey, my son with us. *Look* magazine would change all that.

Look used me with frequency because they needed covers; there were a large number of superstars. I could give you a list, and you would be astonished at the names. But I did everything: food and fashion. I love all photography. I love making pictures.

CM:

Can you tell me about your process of creation?

DK:

My process is simply to talk with someone, and care about capturing an image, no matter what it is. I look for something that excites me within the frame.

CM:

You are famed for photographing Marilyn, but is there a shoot that you recall or that you have some particular nostalgia for?

My ultimate message, if you are interested in photography: you should seize the opportunity.

DK:

Many years ago I managed to amazingly get a job at a magazine called *Look*, and they hadn't hired anybody in something like 12 years. They had two staff openings, and I got one of them. I came out here [Los Angeles] with the entertainment editor from New York. His name was Jack Hamilton. And we got a call on the phone...

We were staying at the Chateau Marmont, which is a legendary hangout, and we were told to go to Las Vegas because Elizabeth Taylor was there. So, I went with Jack to Las Vegas, even though we'd been told there would be no photographs. Jack was a very caring individual. I was the new boy around and he was the journalist, but he said, 'You've got to let me talk, and you can talk at the end.' So, when Jack had finished, I went over to her and I said, 'Elizabeth, I'm new at this magazine. Could you imagine what it would mean to me if you could give me an opportunity to photograph you?'

She had not been photographed in quite some time because of being sick. She thought for a moment and looked in my eyes. She said, 'Come tomorrow night at 7:30.' So I went there with my cameras, I shot and I scored. Those pictures went around the world because she hadn't been photographed in six or eight months. She was looking bright and sunny, and that was the beginning of my career at *Look* magazine. I had shot food and fashion for them, but this was for the cover.

CM:

I know you've always kept up with technology, cameras and everything. Are there particular cameras you've always been a fan of, that you prefer to use?

DK:

Originally I would use a Leica, and I used a Leica very briefly. And then it was Nikons and then it was Canons. I've used Canons ever since for my career, and the Canon company has been very good to me at all times.

FK:

He's an Explorer of Light. [...] Explorers of Light is the name of the Canon program for photographers that they sponsor.

CM:

Do you have bad days, Douglas?

DK:

No. A bad day would mean a cancelled shoot. Photography has been very good to me, Douglas Kirkland from Fort Erie. I was born in Toronto, but I grew up in Fort Erie.

FK:

I remember when Douglas would prepare for a shoot, I always wondered, 'Are you in a bad mood or something?' He said, 'No, I'm concentrating.' And then he would become completely obsessed and focused, which is admirable because it's been some 70 years of it.

DK:

My ultimate message, if you are interested in photography: you should seize the opportunity.

CM:

What do you think about the photography world today in comparison to when you started?

DK:

It's changed substantially, but frankly, I don't see a huge difference. You always want to be good. You want to do a good job, and I'm the same as I was when I began. Even though the reaches through technical possibilities, through digital, are unbelievable.

CM:

Do you have any favourite directors that you've worked with over the years?

DK:

I've worked with some incredible directors – like Stanley Kubrick, who had also been a photographer at *Look* magazine. [...] A long time ago, I worked on 2001: A Space Odyssey.

CM:

He was very famous for his obsession with composition. Is that something you think about a great deal?

DK:

Undeniably. That is your picture. I mean, how could you not think of composition?

Do you move the frame to the left, or right, is it long or wide? There are always these questions and that's what we all have to consider... These are our powers. You have to observe and you have to get along with people.

CM:

Are you still shooting?

DK:

Unquestionably. The amazing thing is, I'm turning 85 in August.

CM:

Congratulations.

DK:

Thank you. It gets better. And the world has been very kind to me, I think.

CM:

Do have a preference for studio or location?

DK:

No, I don't. It's the subject [that matters]. The studio is a location, and frankly -

FK:

You used to say a studio is a state of mind.

DK:

You can make one anywhere.

FK:

That famous photo of Sophia Loren that Douglas took – it's a very well-known picture. She was making *Man of La Mancha*, and it's a very sexy picture. But it was taken in the corner of an office during lunchtime.

CM:

One of my favourite images of yours is the Judy Garland photo where she's crying; it always stood out to me. Could you talk a little about that?

DK:

I spent a month with Judy Garland for Look and saw her highs and lows. We were in Toronto, the city I was born in.

FK:

Every night Judy would bring an audience to their knees – and when they brought her onto the plane the next morning, she'd be in a wheelchair. She performed her heart out.

DK:

We were getting to the end of the shoot, which had been a month long. I said [to Judy], 'I've done everything now. But I haven't seen you, as you feel lonely and without your kids around and without all the fanfare'. I was playing her music at the time, and then she started to cry. [That moment will] stay with me for the rest of my life.

CM:

Françoise – you've been working alongside Douglas a long time now. What are your thoughts on the medium?

FK:

I think photography is always going to be, and there are always going to be some great photographers, and some photographers who just document facts. But it doesn't matter if you use a mobile phone or you use a film camera, as long as you get what you're trying to capture. Those things are all just tools.

Douglas was one of the first people to use Photoshop. I mean, really – one of the very first. He embraced Photoshop and he loved it. He got so enthusiastic, he reinvented his pictures in Photoshop. We had an exhibition and he did a book. It created such uproar, we lost clients over it. This was around 1990–92 – a picture editor from *The New York Times* wrote, 'What is he doing?'

We were in Paris at our then photo agency, Sigma. The photographers surrounded Douglas and said, 'You are destroying photography,' as if Douglas somehow single-handedly was. They said, 'You have to stop that'.

Now all the photo editors want pictures that are retouched, that are perfect and that have no shadow – but back then, it was as if the world was ending. These programs are all just tools.

DK:

Just like the camera. An important tool, which should not be interfering with your shoot. You have to know your stuff. But apart from that, it's what you get out of your subject that matters. You have to seize every opportunity.

MARCUS LEATHERDALE

I first met Marcus in 2017, outside Café Orlin in East Village, a decades-old local haunt that was, sadly, about to close its doors. This is an all-too-familiar sight in a city like New York, where rents continue to skyrocket. We met to discuss publishing a book of Marcus's work, which would focus on his time in New York from the end of the '70s until the mid-'90s. Following this conversation, *Out of the Shadows* (2019) was published by ACC. A year after that, in autumn 2020, we sat down once more to discuss photography, during the pandemic, over Zoom.

Marcus Leatherdale, Larissa, New York, 1983
© Marcus Leatherdale

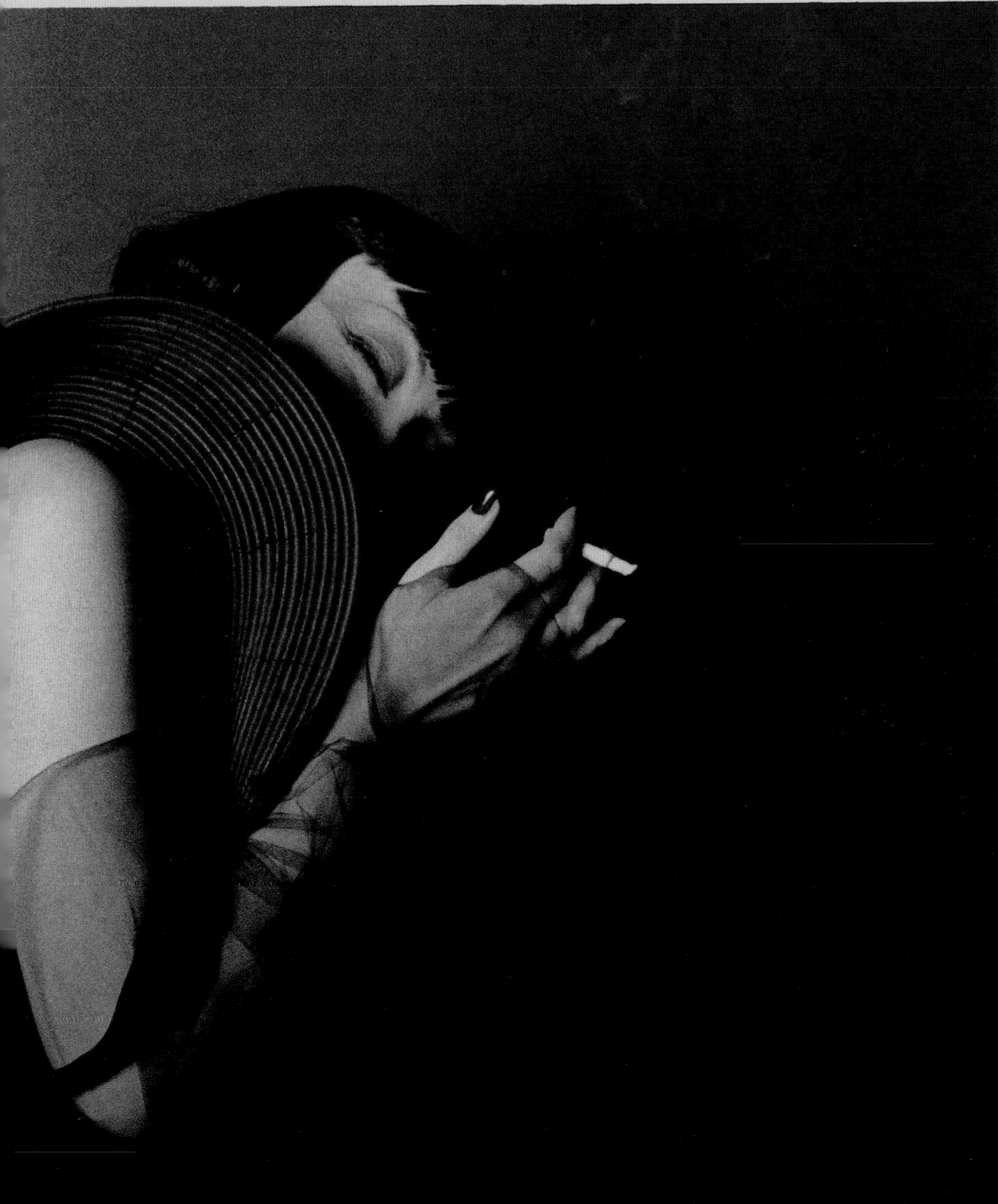

Charles Moriarty:

Canadian beginnings?

Marcus Leatherdale:

I was born in Montreal and I was there for 21 years. I went to École des Beaux-Arts de Montréal as a painting major, and it was the dean of the school who introduced a photography department and a film department. You have to understand, in the '70s that was rather progressive. Most art schools did not have photography and film as an option. He was rather revolutionary.

I had never picked up a camera. I just took it as an elective. I started with animation, because it was the closest thing to painting, and then from animation I went to film. I didn't really love film. I found it made me nervous. It was too much and it still makes me nervous. People always ask, 'Why don't you do any videos?' It's complicated enough to make a still photograph, without trying to do video. Plus, I like to work alone, and you can't really work alone when you do video. I'm not a good teammate.

After three years I transferred to LA ArtCenter, which I hated. You had to have a car. You had to own a car to even be accepted, and you had valet parking. It made me hate it. You were taught by teachers in technician coats and they called you by your last name. It made me absolutely hate photography. It was more about how to get a Kellogg's Corn Flakes box totally in focus with a view camera. It was products, and I hated it.

[It was] very commercial; I had no idea. When I went to leave, they said, 'You don't...' They were so funny, because they said, 'What? You're quitting? We refuse two-thirds of our applicants. What do you mean, you're quitting?' And I said, 'I'm quitting.' So I moved up north to San Francisco, and finished my degree at San Francisco Art Institute.

CM:

That's when you ran into people like Peter Berlin, right? Did he introduce you to the gay scene?

ML:

Actually no. My scene there was punk, which had nothing to do with Peter. The main people for the punk scene were actually students at the school. Penelope, who was my last girlfriend, more or less became the lead singer of the band Avengers, which was one of the main local punk bands, and I just got totally... My mania; it was my mania. I absolutely lived punk, and I was photographing them all the time. I was a black-and-white photographer and I was still shooting 35mm reportage, because I didn't have a studio. I didn't know much about studio work at all; I used white walls and backed people up against whatever, and I photographed that way.

I did meet Peter, but he was something very different. I mean, there was the whole punk scene, and then there was Peter. Peter was a scene of his own. He brought me to the baths for the first time. He brought me to a leather bar for the first time. He brought me to these places, like my guardian. I was 24. He would take me to the baths, and growl if anybody came near me. It was the same thing at the bars. He was like my bodyguard, because I was 24 and looked 18. When I lost my licence, I couldn't get into any bars for the longest time, even though I was over 21, because until I could prove that I was old enough, I really looked young.

It was through Peter that I met Robert Mapplethorpe. They were friends. All of a sudden Peter said, 'Oh, I'm meeting a friend of mine, he's

CM:

a photographer from New York who's coming in. I'll take you to his show.' So, I went with Peter to Robert's show.

CM:

Didn't he have two shows on at the same time?

ML:

Yes, he did. One I didn't understand at all; it was just flowers and art dealers sitting around, Park Avenue portraits, and I just didn't get it. Then he had *The X* [X Portfolio], which was all the really questionable ones, from *Double Fist Fuck* and this and that. All the ones that made him infamous at the time. I was confused with both of those shows, actually.

CM:

Did it feel like a different world?

ML:

Absolutely. I wasn't involved with the flowers and Park Avenue, nor was I involved with S&M in the gay world either. All of it was new to me. And Peter... People don't realise that Peter was like my mum. I mean, we spent a lot of time together. It was totally platonic. He would make me lunch.

CM:

It's good to have those kinds of people when you're growing up gay, right?

ML:

Yes. [...] Maybe you wouldn't realise, but actually he's a photographer in his own right, and he created himself. All the photographs of him are by him. He was the first person to really take self-portraits, selfies, to the extreme. He would do his pictures, and then they would be sent out by mail, mail order, and he created a whole business through self-portrait mail order soft porn.

CM:

When did you move away from punk and into the studio?

ML:

I had to move to New York. I transferred from San Francisco to the School of Visual Arts, so I could learn how to do studio. The San Francisco Art Institute was started by Ansel Adams and was very reportage. It was not about studio at all, so I was rather disappointed. I liked it as an art school. I really enjoyed it. It was my foundation and it gave me the freedom to create, but I really wanted to learn studio photography, and move to a larger format and all that, which is what I did. When I met Robert [...] the SX-70 Polaroid camera had just come out. So, I was going to go with a friend and do a conceptual tour of miniature golf courses in the desert of Arizona. That's what I was about to do, with my friend's baby blue Cutlass Supreme.

When I met Robert, I remember it was really odd, because he took a liking to me immediately. At his show he came over and talked to me, because I was leaving, and then he asked me out for dinner. The next night I had dinner with him, and I said, 'Well, I'm leaving now, because I'm going to Arizona at dawn.' He just thought I was out of my mind, that I would do such a thing, and that I wasn't more interested in his options.

He said, 'I understand you're graduating and you're going to be moving to New York; feel free to come and stay with me.' And I was like, 'Yeah, sure, sure, sure.' But when I came back from the desert there were at least two postcards reiterating that, with his address and his phone number and everything else, so he actually was serious. That was a good introduction and necessary, because you can't just go to New York and not know anybody.

It wasn't expensive like it is now, but it wasn't

87

cheap. This way I had a place to stay, and he was just about to go to Amsterdam, so he just left me his loft for a month or two. Just gave it to me. Trust. Very nice of him. Robert was not the shark that people make him out to be. He was very generous. To me, he was extremely generous and kind and funny, and personable.

CM:

When you were at SVA, was that a Master's degree?

ML:

I just took a few courses. I had my BA from San Francisco, and I just wanted to take a few courses in photo silkscreen and studio. I learned how to use a strobe. Robert was only doing tungsten, and Sam Wagstaff had bought him all the equipment, but he was afraid he would electrocute himself. So, we both learned how to do strobe, together in his studio, because I didn't have one.

[...] I wanted to do what I was doing, but in a studio format with one light. At that time, I was not doing daylight at all anymore. Once I moved to the Hasselblad from the 35mm, I was doing strobe for virtually everything. It wasn't until I went to India that I stopped the strobe and went back to using natural daylight. But I've always used just one source, one light. I didn't get tricky with bounce reflectors or anything else. I just kept it really simple, not much technology. I always felt that you shouldn't have to wade through the technology in an image to get to the soul of it.

CM:

It gives a wonderful continuity to your work.

ML:

My inspirations were never really... I appreciated photographers. I love Sanders. I liked Robert, at the

time. I liked... There's a lot... Penn, all these people. But my real inspiration was painters: Caravaggio and Rembrandt. That was the lighting I always went for.

CM:

What was the photographic scene in New York like through the '80s?

ML:

It was not like now. Financially, photographs were just starting to be worth something. Up till then, they were pretty much worth whatever you could get someone to pay for it. There were not a lot of photographic shows. I had to start showing in nightclubs, because I couldn't get shown in galleries. I created one-night events at Club 57 and at Danceteria, and places like that, just to get myself out there.

A lot of the people I photographed were going to those clubs, of course. In retrospect, they were all my friends. At the time they were all the 'it' kids, the reason New York was so cool. I was in those circles, but I've always been in more than one circle. I was a mudwumper; I could shift from going to the Mudd Club and being totally downtown, to going to Studio 54 and being totally uptown, with the likes of Iman and Tina Chow. Or I could be in Robert's circles, which were more the art world and galleries. So, I was pretty flexible.

CM:

What was Studio 54 like?

ML:

It was everything you think and more. There's never been a place like it. It made me like disco, and I hate disco. I was an ex-punk. It was in the age of new wave, and I would just wait for a song to play that wasn't Donna Summer. Duran Duran, please. But the energy – you'd walk through the doors and you would just be like... I've never experienced anything like that. I remember I went there; within a week I went over there and I went to the street and I was like, 'Oh my God.' The whole entire street, Studio 54's street, was just packed. I thought, 'I'll never get in. How do you do this?' So I went across the street and I stood up on a fire hydrant just to see, get a view. And luckily enough, Steve Rubell, who was the owner, walked out and was scanning this mob of people, and he just pointed to me. The seas parted and I walked in, and I never had a problem after that. He introduced me to the doorman and said, 'Always let this person in.' I was just very young, lucky and in the right place.

CM:

Did you bring your camera?

ML:

Oh no, never. I only owned a studio camera by then. I don't even know what happened to my 35mm; I never took a picture as a paparazzi, or something like that.

CM:

You mean, you only want to shoot when you're in the studio?

ML:

I want the control. I've always considered myself a studio art photographer. I would almost be offended if they would want me to bring a camera to somewhere, an event or something. I'm not a paparazzi. [...] I dabbled in fashion only when Issey Miyake asked me to do things. Ironically enough, they've become some of my most iconic images.

CM:

That's the stuff you shot with Andy Warhol, Tina Chow and everyone, right?

ML:

Larissa. That picture of Larissa, that picture

everyone thinks is Man Ray in the '30s. No; it's me in 1983. That is probably one of my most iconic images of all time, and that was fashion. It's like Penn. I love Penn fashion, and I love Avedon fashion too, almost more than their portraits – you can't compartmentalise, actually. You do when you're young, because you're idealistic, and everything is more black and white then. Pun not intended.

Nowadays, everyone can be a photographer or a DJ.

CM:

Was it hard to make a living at that point?

ML:

Fortunately, food and rent was a three-digit figure back then. When I did *Hidden Identities*, the page that I edited every month for 10 years, I started by making 50 bucks; that's all I got. But my rent was only 200. So, it was all relative. It was tough, but obviously I survived it; I somehow got through all that. I started selling my photographs at, I think, $100, and of course they're a lot more than $100 now. $100 doesn't get you anything except breakfast today.

CM:

You lived in New York during a time of great change. How does it feel to have been part of that?

ML:

[...] I didn't realise I was archiving an era that would be extinct in 20, 30 years. It was just, 'These are my friends, and this is what I was doing.' I didn't see it anthropologically as an archive. I'm so grateful to have been there, because my favourite time in New York was the late '70s, early '80s. I'm so glad I was there for that, even though that's when it was the most dangerous, and the dirtiest, and I was the poorest. It was my favourite time. It got gentrified, and then of course AIDS came into play, and that changed everything.

Nowadays, I remember sitting with a friend. [...] We were watching people walk by and he said, 'Do you see the people walking by? None of these are New Yorkers.' New Yorkers aren't really living in New York anymore.

The people that are in New York, the people you see go flip-flopping down the street in baseball caps, these are the people who wouldn't have come near New York, back then. It was too dirty, too dangerous. Too, 'Oh God, I'll never go' – you know what I mean? They would never do it. Now they're treating it like Disneyland.

As Debbie Harry said, 'You need shit; you need dirt for things to grow.' It got too cleaned up. You need fertiliser. I remember walking out of Robert's Bond Street loft and kicking the garbage, and rats would go in all directions. That didn't bother me at all. Not that I want rats everywhere, but you know what I mean? It's like it was just part of the course, and you never knew what was around the corner. Now you do: it's a Starbucks that's around the corner.

I feel very grateful that I was there at a time where it wasn't about branding. It wasn't about a credit card. It wasn't about any of that. It wasn't about money. I mean, you needed money, but you did not have to be... You could be fabulous and not have any money. You could be all those things.

CM:

Do you think we're a little doomed, now everything is based upon money and branding?

ML:

Branding, and how many likes you get on Instagram. Now, anyone can get their ego stroked and get notoriety just by having an Instagram page. Back then you had to be in it to win it; now you don't.

CM:

Do you have a process when you sit down to shoot a portrait at the studio?

ML:

My backdrop in those days and now is the same, and my light is constant. I don't get, 'Okay, we're going to shake it up... We're not going to do this kind of lighting today, and that lighting. We'll use a different background.' No. I always had a black canvas painted backdrop that I would keep till it fell apart. I had one strobe on a 45-degree angle, and it was one exposure. Everything was constant. What changed was what was put in front of all that: the subject. I usually had an idea when I wanted to photograph someone. There was a reason why I wanted to photograph them. I would somehow try to channel that. But I didn't have preconceived ideas. I never had artist sketches of how it was going to be. It was just a springboard for departure. I went with the flow. I really can't say that I knew... I didn't know what I had until I had it.

[...] For Joel-Peter Witkin it's not about spontaneity. Different people have a different approach, right? When I went to his studio and was looking at his work, it was like he had everything charted out down to drawings and sets. It was nothing spontaneous at all. For me, it was. In my picture of Larissa, she has this twinkle in her eye and she's smoking a butt. You can't plan that.

CM:

Was there a reason you left New York in the '90s?

ML:

India was my calling. All of a sudden, I got disinterested. Who needs another picture of Madonna or Jodie Foster? There are enough photographers out there doing that; I don't need to do that. I didn't see the worth in it. I went to India, and I just got the bug. I loved India: I loved the drama, the realness, and the human element. So, I got a studio in India, and I started spending half the year there, almost.

The first time I went, I was a guest of the Indian government. I drove around India for a year in a turquoise Matador van with an assistant and a manager, and I photographed virtually all over India, showing the diversity of India, which is what the *Bharat* series is. That was before I started getting involved with the tribal Adivasi. For a year I did that, and then I came back and I thought, 'Let me see what I can do with this,' and I went to the Paul Bridgewater Gallery. He [Paul Bridgewater] loved the work and gave me a show immediately. Then I had a show, and I realised that I could actually transcend to this subject matter. People didn't say, 'Oh, this is too ethnic,' or, 'I'm not interested in India.' It seemed to work, regardless. I was actually selling and being able to survive with this work.

Now I do both. Back then, I didn't have two bodies of work. I had really just focused in on India. [...] I went to Banaras, or Varanasi, on the river Ganges. I rented for several years, a haveli in the old city, and I would photograph on the roof. All the sadhus and the pilgrims came. Rather than before, where I was going all over India looking for people,

I thought, 'Why don't I just stay put in Banaras?' as it is a pilgrim spot for all Hindus, and also the Muslims are there for the silk and sari industries. I thought, 'If I could just stay put, I can get everyone in India coming to me.' So that's what I did for several years.

People always think, because I'm in India I must be going... Gurus, and swamis, and yoga, and pot and bong. I didn't do any of that. I had Indian friends and everything, but they didn't do it either. There's that whole part of 'spiritual India', which was relevant, but that's not why I was there. I've never been to an ashram. I was there for the people. Just the people at the moment, in the moment.

CM:

Do you think that's what's at the heart of your photography?

ML:

Maybe that's for you to decide. I mean, I've never decided. I've never thought, 'Why do I do this?' I let writers and critics decide. I'm always amused when I read reviews as to what I'm doing. They're not wrong, because the whole idea of making a photograph is creating a dialogue with the person who's looking at it. That's what they see; that's fine with me. They can be totally off. I'm never offended, like, 'Oh no, you didn't get it.' No – it just means you have a different frequency.

CM:

You don't go in with a concept?

ML:

As a springboard of departure, I may have a concept, but all hell can break loose. I just channel, and it goes where it goes. I can start off with a circle and end up with a square. I'm very laid back about all this. Technically, intellectually, spiritually. All these things are labels, I guess; I don't really know how I fit into any of those boxes.

CM:

Is there a particular reason why you always stuck to black and white?

ML:

There are certain people who do colour, like Annie Leibovitz. I prefer her colour to her black and white. But on the whole, I found that I could not make it my own. I did do a series of four Mapplethorpe portraits in colour. I like those, but if you notice, they were very 'black and white' colour. It was colour-ish. But it wasn't really colour. I just never felt I could make it my own, but I was happy to do that.

CM:

Any thoughts on digital photography?

ML:

Nowadays, everyone can be a photographer or a DJ. All you have to do is buy whatever it is, read the manual, and you can have a competent photograph. I mean, it took me a year or two before I could take a photograph that didn't look like shit. It took years before I had what I considered an exhibition-quality photograph that could be worth something in a gallery. Nowadays, all you have to do is buy an expensive digital, and have it spit out of your computer, and you've got it. At that level, I roll my eyes back as far as they can go. But at the same time, I have *Omen* magazine, and I feature digital photographers. They can be something. Every medium can be used, and I think that there are some phenomenal digital photographers.

But I do miss the fact that photography is no longer real. You can look at a photograph, and you don't know if it's a fake photograph or not. It's not even proof anymore, is it? Did you ever see the fashion photography book that Thierry Mugler put out? He photographed all his creations, but before Photoshop. Before digital. Before anything. It was all real. That was special.

CM:

Photoshop is not the same.

ML:

It's not the same thing as actually floating someone on an iceberg.

CM:

I guess it'll be something different when our generation, who were analogue to start with, disappear, and the people who come up only will ever have known digital.

ML:

It's totally true. I had to go to India, and I went with 100 rolls of film and my Hasselblad. You wouldn't believe the trouble I had going through customs, going through security. People were asking, 'What is this?' They didn't even know. 'This is film.' 'What's film?' I'm Dr Frankenstein now, with my laboratory.

They were used to digital. They didn't know what film was. They couldn't believe I had it. They were in lead bags and looked ominous. Obviously, they had to open them, because they couldn't see. It was a whole ordeal every time. They were looking at the film like it was kryptonite.

That's something interesting about India. All the years I was in India till recently, I would go for walks, and people would always want me to take a picture, because they couldn't afford a camera. And if they had the camera, they couldn't afford the film. And if they couldn't afford the film, they couldn't afford cleaning it. They didn't develop things; they called it 'cleaning the film'. But now, everybody has smartphones, so it's the other way around. When I go walking in the jungle, in the forest or whatnot, I get besieged by the villagers and their smartphones, wanting to take selfies with me.

The whole idea of making a photograph is creating a dialogue with the person who's looking at it.

The whole world is changed. I mean, I literally have tribal people coming up to me, wanting to take pictures of me, rather than the other way around.

CM:

Why is photography important?

ML:

The modern world has not existed without photography. Everywhere, we are connected via photographic images, be it commercially or personally. A photograph used to be a factual statement, evidence that for one instant, this was reality. No longer. Since the digital evolution of the medium, the photographic image can be just a pretty picture, enhanced and altered reality. Not real at all.

In certain ways, photography has lost its integrity and substance, reflecting an artificial and shallow reality. Everyone, anyone can be a photographer these days. It's like instant oatmeal: edible, but not the real thing.

CM:

What's next for you?

ML:

Currently, I am working on a charity book project for a girls' school in the deserts of Jaisalmer, India; photographing the women of the region. Most likely, this will be my swansong for my ongoing India series, started in 1992. It's the end of an era. In many ways I have lost interest in creating photographs. It has become way too pedestrian. Currently, I'm focused on sorting out and printing my archives, creating full portfolios and trying to make sense of my 30 years of work. Hopefully in Mexico. That said – never say never. Perhaps cultural and colourful Mexico will change my mind

GERD LUDWIG

It was 16 April 2019, and Gerd Ludwig and I sat at his dining table in east Los Angeles. Above him was a large photograph of a sculpture of Stalin, blindfolded with a red piece of fabric. The image came from the cover of his 2001 book, *Broken Empire*. We talked about Gerd's incredible journey, both in life and photos, his work with *National Geographic*, and his focus on Russia, particularly Chernobyl and what once was the USSR.

Gerd Ludwig, Ice Fishing, Magnitogorsk, 1998
© Gerd Ludwig

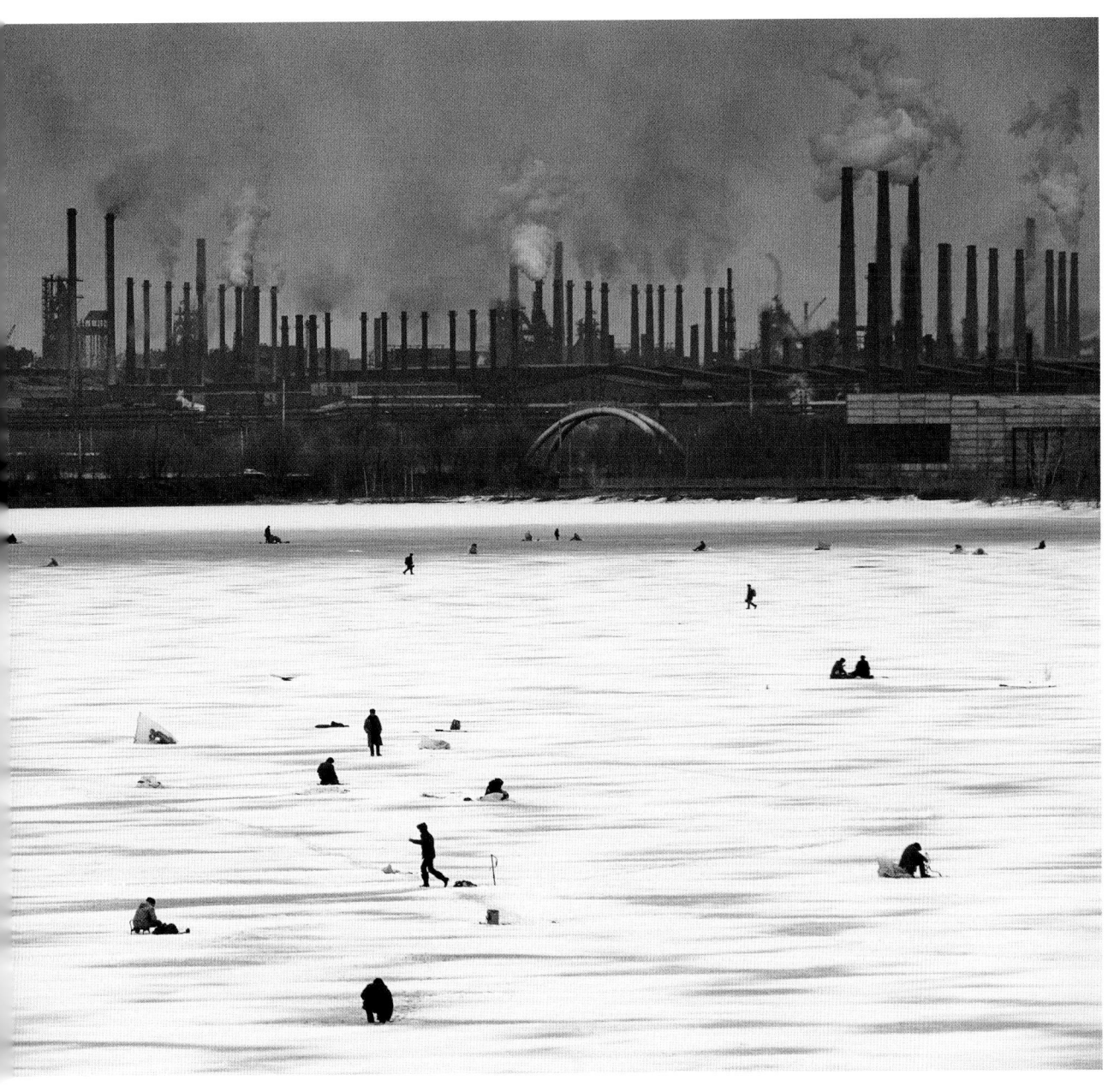

Charles Moriarty:

You've had quite an incredible career. Where and how did it begin?

Gerd Ludwig:

I studied German literature, political science and physical education at a university in Germany and I wasn't happy about it. I abruptly quit and started to travel with a friend of mine, through Scandinavia and then on to the US. During that time of travel, I started to read about sociology, philosophy, all the hip subjects of the '60s. I was searching for a new subject to study.

Normally, when people travel they bring back souvenirs, but I was on the road for a year, so I couldn't. Besides, I didn't have any money. So, I bought a camera and started to take photographs; they would become my souvenirs.

[...] I started to read magazines, trying to improve my technique, and came across an article that said 'Photography is highly educational, because you carry on your vision of the world and give it to other people.' I put down the magazine and I thought, 'Wow, I have so much fun taking photographs, but I haven't even thought about that aspect of photography.' I was in my early 20s – 20, 21. That night I discussed it with my girlfriend – we had hooked up on the road – and I decided I'd become a photographer.

CM:

Do you remember the camera you picked up?

GL:

It was a Voigtländer. [...] A 35 mm. I picked it up in New York, because I was a sailor on the road. I was on the Norwegian-American line. After having been a dishwasher in Norway for several months, I became a sailor and went across the North Atlantic a couple of times. I was a mess boy, and seasick all the time. Once I came back to Germany, I started an internship and applied to colleges.

CM:

Did you work with a particular studio as an intern?

GL:

I was totally exploited by a photographer who did portrait shoots. I did a lot of retouching at the time – pre-digital, of course. [...] The hard stuff, making people really beautiful by retouching negatives and positives and print. Except when somebody had some insurance issue, because of an accident. Then, we did the opposite.

CM:

Were you bleaching directly onto the negative?

GL:

No, just taking out the wrinkles with pens, pencils, very soft pencils on large-format negatives; stuff like that.

CM:

Painful work. How did the college applications go?

GL:

I applied at several art schools and colleges and was accepted at a college which had the best teacher in all of Europe at the time: Professor Otto Steinert, a legendary figure in educating people. The other students came from Africa, Scandinavia, Persia. [...] I was lucky to be accepted. Eighty people applied and 20 got in.

We tried to study as long as we could. It was 10 semesters, five years. When I started, it was a college, but by the time I finished, it was part of the university. So I ended up with a university degree as a photo designer, but specialising in photojournalism.

CM:

Did you go directly into that field after university?

GL:

It was a tradition at the college that you started to work for magazines while you were a student, because the education system was in touch with reality. So, we did real assignments for our studies. One assignment was photographing the work of the garbage collectors. It was the first bit of attention that was given to the huge amounts of garbage that we produce.

Everybody takes pictures, but that doesn't mean that everybody is a photographer.

The assignments were made up of black and white reportages telling a story in eight, 10, 12 images, which we would send in those days to local magazines, national magazines and weekly papers – the equivalent to *The Sunday Times*: *Der Spiegel*, *Stern*. Germany had a very thriving tradition of photojournalism.

These institutions had their own archives. So they kept the prints we'd sent and whenever they needed to publish a photograph about the amount of trash we produced, they would go and pick one of our images out of the archive and say, 'Here's a great picture that is very general in its approach, that we can use and print'.

So, we had our first publications in national magazines by the second term at college. After a while, the picture editors of magazines and weekly papers would say, 'Oh, we're getting images from this guy. He's in Essen; why don't we give him an assignment next time we have something in the area?' Many of us had already shot our first assignments for *Der Spiegel* or other publications, while we were still students.

Subsequently, we thought, 'What's going to happen after we graduate?' Now, we, my fellow students and I, had become close friends. We were a group of people working together, to the detriment of our professor, who said photographers are lonely wolves. Co-operation between photographers was a new thing.

Our idols were the people from Magnum, where people were working together. And we had already started to work together as students, so the last thing we wanted was to become fierce competitors. A decision was made, while we were students, to create an agency, and when we graduated, we could continue to work in this agency.

In our last semester at the university, three of us founded an agency, a co-operative agency, modelled after Magnum, where we three were the owners. We would distribute our material to those magazines that we had already worked with, since our second term at college.

The people at *Spiegel*, for example, thought it was a brilliant idea. They knew they could call one phone number and one of the guys would be able to do the assignment. So it was the three of us who founded the first serious German co-operative that was owned by the photographers, for the photographers. It still exists.

CM:

What's it called?

GL:

Visum, which is Latin for 'having seen' – and obviously, the reference to Magnum is there. Over the years, it has undergone a lot of changes. At some point there were more than 10 equal owners.

CM:

Do you still work with the agency?

GL:

I left after I realised that my future was out here in America. They didn't want to become an international agency. I wanted to open a New York office for them, because I lived in New York at the time. They didn't want to do that.

CM:

When did you start to step outside of Germany with your work?

GL:

Well, we were so incredibly successful with our agency that *Die Zeit*, the equivalent of *The New York Times* or *The Sunday Times* in London, did a huge story about us. We were the new idea and we paid ourselves equal salaries, no matter how much each of us made. Visum was so successful that we soon started to work for *Stern* and *GEO* magazine, which is the German equivalent to *National Geographic*.

[…] After the big article in *Die Zeit*, we started to do our first assignments for *Fortune* magazine in America. They assigned us across Europe. Then the *Day in the Life* books came around.

It was in the late '80s that Rick Smolan and David Cohen created the concept of sending 100 of the world's best documentary photographers and photojournalists to photograph one country. People would descend onto the country from all over the world, and there would be a good number of local photographers from that country too. We would be given assignments, receive a briefing and then spread out to our location, have a day of research or two and then shoot for 24 hours.

Then you flew back to the centre, wherever that was – usually one central location in the country. You'd turn in the film, and get debriefed. A book was then published, which was called *A Day in the Life of Australia*, *A Day in the Life of Israel*, *A Day in the Life of Russia*.

CM:

How many countries did they do?

GL:

Maybe 18 or 20. I worked on 13.

CM:

That must have been a mind-expanding experience.

GL:

Yes, of course, because at the time I still lived in Germany, and had no connections to the... It was a different world. Think of the '80s; you didn't have much information, or if you had information about what was happening in America, it got to Europe months later.

All of a sudden, I was meeting these people, these other photographers, in person, for my first assignment on the first project, *A Day in the Life of Australia*. Until I got to Australia, I didn't believe it was for real. I thought, 'Maybe it's just an Australian photo club that has invited us, because we are the antipodes, coming in from Germany further than anybody else'. Only three German photographers were invited, and two of them were from Visum.

When I arrived, there were people that I knew of, but who I never thought I would ever meet in my life. Mary Ellen Mark, Susan Meiselas, James Nachtwey, Alex Webb, Eddie Adams. The first day, I literally went and touched them to make sure they were real.

A Day in the Life pushed our names into the international market. Picture editors from international publications were selecting the images and editing the book.

CM:

Do you remember what your assignment was in Australia?

GL:

They had wanted me to cover a German Australian family circus, and even though I was one of the youngest people there and I was really overwhelmed by the whole situation, I refused. I said, 'I'm not coming to Australia to photograph Germans. Can't you give me something else'. I was very young and brash.

They gave me a small town of 5,000 people, Cowra, in the middle of nowhere. And then I said, 'I love that. That sounds really Australian'. I managed to get the second-most pictures in the book. Not the best ones, by far, but all of a sudden – wow, I

had 10 pictures in there. In subsequent books, I only had one.

CM:

Was this project what brought you to Russia?

GL:

Not yet. On one of the *Day in the Life* projects, I met my now ex-wife in Hawaii, and we got married at another project in front of 150 photographers.

CM:

Some good wedding photos?

GL:

You know how photographers are; they always promise and never deliver. Finally, a year later, we got a few wedding pictures. Everybody said they weren't good enough to show us, but we didn't care. So, I met my now ex-wife Dana Fineman, then a celebrity photographer in Hawaii. That resulted in me moving to New York. She lived in LA, I lived in Germany. We said we'd meet halfway and that was New York City.

CM:

Compromise: a good start. What year did you move to New York?

GL:

'84.

CM:

And that was when you wanted to set up the agency there, I presume. Losing that must have been a blow. How was the transition?

GL:

I started to work for American magazines. In the beginning illegally, because I had a journalist visa, but I soon worked for *Esquire*, which at that time did really interesting stories, journalistic stories. I did a special edition with other photographers.

There were five of us and we were sharing one issue. Lee Friedlander, William Klein, and I forget who the others were. But they were really top photographers, and I happened to sneak in there.

CM:

Was there a point when you felt like you weren't impersonating anymore, that you belonged?

GL:

No, I'm still impersonating.

CM:

Tell me about your time in New York.

GL:

Dana and I moved. I bought a loft in Manhattan and it was in the same building where Eddie Adams lived. Famous for the execution photo [*Saigon Execution*, 1968] from the Vietnam war, Eddie Adams was a legend, and he had created a tuition-free workshop, which is still around, even though he passed away more than 10 years ago. I became a teacher in that workshop as a young photographer and the director of photography from *National Geographic*, Tom Kennedy, was there as well.

Co-operation between photographers was a new thing.

During the workshop, each of the team leaders, the teachers, gave a short presentation. After my presentation, he came up to me and said, 'I not only liked your pictures, but I also enjoyed what you had

to say about them. Why don't you come and see us and present your work?' But I didn't go. [...] I thought it sounded great, but I also thought that I didn't want to go there and for them to say, 'Don't call us, we'll call you,' and never hear from them. I'd rather live with that feeling of being asked.

A year later, the same scenario: we're both teaching again and Tom says, 'Why didn't you call in? Come on, come over, we can discuss whether you fit in there.' So, I finally went and showed them my pictures. They said thank you, and then I didn't hear from them for three months. After those three months, I thought, 'Okay, that's exactly why I didn't want to go.' Not realising that in those three months, they had only assigned maybe 15 people, because at the time, *National Geographic* had only four to five stories per magazine, per issue. Finally, they gave me a call. They wanted me to shoot a subject in Germany, and I nearly turned them down because I didn't want to go back.

CM:

What was the subject?

GL:

It was the construction of a canal in the eastern part of Bavaria. I was really unsure about it, but then I started to think, nobody else can do this. The people in that area are so stubborn. If an American goes, they won't be able to do anything there. At least as a German, I can somewhat relate to the people. So, I shot the story and it became the lead story in the magazine a year later.

Then, German reunification happened while I was already living in the US, and they asked me whether I could see myself shooting a story about the changes in Germany. I did that, and they loved that story too; it became another lead story. And then they said to me, 'Do you think you can shoot a story in Russia, similar to what you've done in Germany, depicting the rapid economic and social changes?'

And just to describe the magazine at the time, they said to me, 'We would like you to fly out to Moscow and check for a week whether you think a story is possible. You might as well take your camera.' Can you imagine? Those were the good old times.

CM:

That certainly doesn't happen anymore. I take it that week went well?

GL:

It turned into a seven-month assignment.

CM:

There was a huge shift in the world at that point. What was it like being a fly on the wall?

GL:

It was total change. I didn't speak Russian; I still don't speak Russian, but I understand some. I started to work very fast with local interpreters, local assistance, which I always do when I'm in the field. I get my people working in the field, in the country of my destination, tapping into their own networks, into their friends' networks.

Russia was in so much turmoil. My driver was a military officer who just pretended to be sick for two weeks when I was there.

CM:

Did you ever run into danger?

GL:

I was arrested probably a dozen times in Russia [...] I was travelling with bulletproof vests.

CM:

Were they arresting you for being an outsider, or for having the camera?

GL:

For being there with a camera. It never really got scary for me, but what they often would say when they arrested me was, 'You can go home, but your Russian assistant needs to stay here.' I knew that he would be in deep, deep trouble. So I said, 'I'm not leaving without him. He works for me, I hired him, I'm not stepping out of this jail without him.' The arrests only really lasted for maybe five hours or so.

CM:

Long enough to incite fear!

GL:

Yeah. Scary enough.

CM:

So, seven months? Can you break that down for me?

GL:

Multiple trips, of course. The longest single trip was 11 weeks.

CM:

That's basically the backbone of Broken Empire, *your book?*

GL:

Yeah. But then, I returned to shoot a story on pollution in the former Soviet Union, a story on the Russian Cossacks, a story on Moscow, a story on the Trans-Siberian Railroad... I had started to focus mostly on the former Soviet Union. It has a deep, personal and historical connection for me. My parents had lived in this part of the world and my family, for generations had lived in Sudetenland.

You know where that is? It is the border

between [what was then] Czechoslovakia and Germany. Before World War One, it was part of the [Austro-Hungarian Empire] and then after World War One, when the borders were arbitrarily drawn, my grandparents, ethnic Germans, all of a sudden realised they were living in Czechoslovakia. Only a few kilometres away from the German border, but it was Czechoslovakia and so they became Czech citizens.

My father, who didn't speak a word of Czech, was drafted into the Czech army. And when Hitler annexed Czechoslovakia, he had to switch sides and was drafted into the German army the next day. Subsequently, he was part of the 6th Army that invaded the Soviet Union. He saw Stalingrad, which he survived. After the war, all the Germans were expelled in that area, and I grew up as a very, very poor refugee kid in West Germany.

I was born after the war, in a room of 80 square feet. That room served as living room, bedroom, kitchen, all in one. At night, I was tucked away between my parents' bodies to keep me warm, and I would listen at the age of two, three and four years old, to my father telling stories that I thought were bedtime stories. But it was my father telling stories about soldiers, about people hiding from soldiers during snowstorms in stables and barns. It was only later I realised it was my father's attempt to shed himself of the terrible memories of war.

He never said a bad word about Russians, nothing, not a single derogatory term about Russians. Later on, when I grew up as a teenager, I started to ask, 'What the fuck did you do? You had no reason to be in Russia.' And his explanation, 'It was war,' wasn't really good enough. So, I started to embrace everything out of my guilt for the deeds

of my parents' generation. I started to embrace everything that my parents' generation tried to destroy, like Russia. My Jewish ex-wife said to me, 'You only married me out of German guilt.'

[…] When I was first assigned to Russia, by *National Geographic*, it was not my first job there. I had already shot a couple of assignments in Russia for German *GO*. During those first assignments, I found images from my early childhood that had been implanted into my mind, images from those stories that my father had told about his time in Russia. It was like I knew this world.

During my work for German *GO* I didn't allow myself to be critical toward Russia, a nation that had suffered so much at the hands of my parents' generation. I did not shoot any critical pictures. It was only when Gorbachev himself pulled away the veil that I started to look beyond myself. Basically, my whole body of work in Russia and the former Soviet Union is based on guilt, on German guilt.

CM:

Is it something you've put to bed?

GL:

No.

CM:

How soon did you go to Chernobyl, after the reactor blew?

GL:

I was actually fairly late; it was seven years after the accident that I went for the first time, but I went deeper inside the reactor than any Western still photographer. I was in areas where I was literally only allowed to shoot for a few seconds.

On one of my journeys – I think it was 2011 – I photographed in a room… During my earlier explorations inside the reactor, my assistants had refused to go with me, which I understood. There was an engineer who accompanied us in 2011. He said, 'Hey, you need to get your cameras ready. This is going to be very short.' We had Geiger counters and dosimeters: he constantly checked how much exposure we had gotten during our trip. When we were getting close to the maximum, we needed to rush back. Outside the room he said, 'This is highly radiated; are you ready?' And then he started to prise open a heavy metal door. It took him a while, even to get it open.

I was arrested probably a dozen times in Russia [...] I was travelling with bulletproof vests.

I stumbled into a pitch-black room just lit with a headlamp. I fired a round of strobes. I wanted to wait for it to recharge, but he grabbed me by the shoulder and said, 'Well, that's it.'

Thank God, it was already the digital days. I looked at my display and I realised my auto focus had focused on some wires that were partially obstructing the view. I begged him to let me go in one more time. Thankfully, he did, because I had seen in the back of the room a clock that had been frozen at 1:23 a.m.: the moment when life stood still in Chernobyl forever.

CM:

How did it feel being there, in that space?

GL:

It gave me the chills. I managed to shoot one more round of pictures. Before, I had been with workers who were carrying oxygen and gas masks and were working one single shift of 15 minutes a day in that area. I mean, you needed to get to that area, so you stumbled more than you walked through dimly lit tunnels and walkways with obstructing debris and wires. They were drilling holes into the contaminated concrete floors to stabilise big pillars, which were to stabilise the roof, which was in danger of collapsing. [...] It would have triggered as much radiation again as the initial accident.

CM:

Do you suffer any kind of emotional trauma after shooting in places like that, or are you able to erect some kind of barrier?

GL:

I was shooting a story on pollution in the former Soviet Union, during which I photographed a dying child in Azerbaijan. The child was brought in, and they were really just skin and bones. They had this big belly of malnutrition, and because it was the early '90s, we were used to seeing these pictures from Africa but not from a child in Eastern Europe. It made me think about my own emotional prejudice. We accepted it in Africa, it was common, so it was much more shocking to see it in the Eastern European world.

After a while, I couldn't take it anymore. I asked the doctors if I could sit down and have a cup of coffee or tea. After a while, I thought, 'Maybe I didn't get the picture?' I couldn't check, as we were still shooting film. So, I wanted to go back.

I asked the doctors, 'Can I go back to this child one more time?' 'The body is in the morgue,' they said. A child, a human being, had died.

[…] The body had been discarded already. I kept myself together in that moment, but when I walked out and sat in the cab outside, I just started crying, and I thought about my own son, who was then four or five years old.

I started to embrace everything out of my guilt for the deeds of my parents' generation.

I'm normally pretty good in this situation, because I have to focus. However, people often mistakenly think that you can hide behind the camera. You cannot. You must never use the camera as a shield. You have to feel what is going on, and then you have to absorb that feeling and convert it into a picture. A camera must never be a shield from what you experience, because if you do that, you don't take a great picture.

CM:

You have to be emotionally present. Why do you think photography is important?

GL:

First of all, it's a universal language that transcends borders, which is understood not only on an intellectual level, but also on an emotional level. It needs to connect in both those ways.

And it's important because it stops time. It captures history, from the horrendous horrors of war to the gentlest acts of humanity. It shows us mankind's greatest achievements and mankind's deepest failures. One could say – okay, film does the same thing. But photography is the only medium that allows you to study something at your own pace. Film imposes a way of seeing. A single picture – you look at it, and you wander around it at your own pace; you look at it however long you want. And therefore, it's a very democratic medium. It allows you to turn away from that one moment whenever you want, whereas film carries you from moment to moment to moment.

At the same time, there is a dichotomy in photography. While photography is stopping time, freezing a moment, it is also accelerating it, through the digital applications that we have today. Without photography, without the knowledge of a situation, it took days and weeks for an event and for storytelling to reach another part of the planet. But with our technical advantages, photography contributes to accelerating time, so that somebody on the other side of the world can see momentarily the same thing. So: while photography stops time, it also accelerates it.

I would also like to say, it is important that you make emotional and intellectual pictures. A great photograph touches the soul and broadens the mind. But it can only happen if the photographer doesn't just show us what is out there in the world, but also how he or she felt at that moment when they pressed the button. How you see the world as a photographer is as important as the view outside.

The relationship between photography and reality is such that at any given situation, you can have one thousand, one million different perspectives and each of them are true. Wherever you stand and take a picture, it is true. It is your view of the world. And I'm interested in that point of view, where I think, 'Oh, I never thought about seeing it that way.'

But that doesn't mean there are no limits to what is true. You can look at a sheet of paper and you can say, 'I see a rectangle.' You can say, 'I see a square, a parallelogram, a trapezoid. I can also see just a line.' All of that is true. However, you cannot say, 'I see a circle.'

Then it's a lie. If you look at an unobstructed sheet of paper, everything else – the line, the trapezoid – all that is real and depends on your perspective. But there are limitations, and that's where photography is unique in comparison to language. You could say, 'Oh yeah, I see a circle and nobody can doubt it,' when you describe something with language itself.

It's a reflection on reality, but it is also connected to that reality. And what is so important in this visual age is that we have a language that transcends borders and that doesn't need a translation. We see everybody taking pictures today.

CM:

Everyone is a photographer?

GL:

Everybody takes pictures, but that doesn't mean that everybody is a photographer. The technical aspects of photography have become so easy. The early photographers needed chemicals; they had to put an emulsion on paper, etc. Even when I started out with photography, some photographers were still mixing the developer and the fixation liquids themselves. All these practices are gone.

Anybody can take a correctly exposed picture, but technique and composition in photography are the equivalent to grammar and syntax in prose. So many people call themselves serious photographers after they've taken a few iPhone pictures, but their compositions are off. You can compare it to doing a spell check, but even with a great spell check, you can create an absolutely nonsensical sentence that your spell check will not correct.

CM:

What would you say to younger photographers starting out?

GL:

Research is incredibly important. Know what you're photographing; know about the person, about the circumstances. And then, with that knowledge, try to make an intelligent picture. But don't forget about your emotions. Tell me how you felt in the moment when you pressed the shutter. That is really important.

SLAVA MOGUTIN

I first met Slava at a White Cube party in London, celebrating artists Gilbert & George. I was aware of Slava from the queer sphere of art, though I didn't know huge amounts about him or his work. Slava is an incredibly inspiring artist. Through his actions, his words and art practice, he rebels. He recounts his own lived experiences so that we might be bent to his vision. We sat down over Skype in October 2019 to talk.

Slava Mogutin, Lost Boys; Anton roof smoking, 2000
© Slava Mogutin

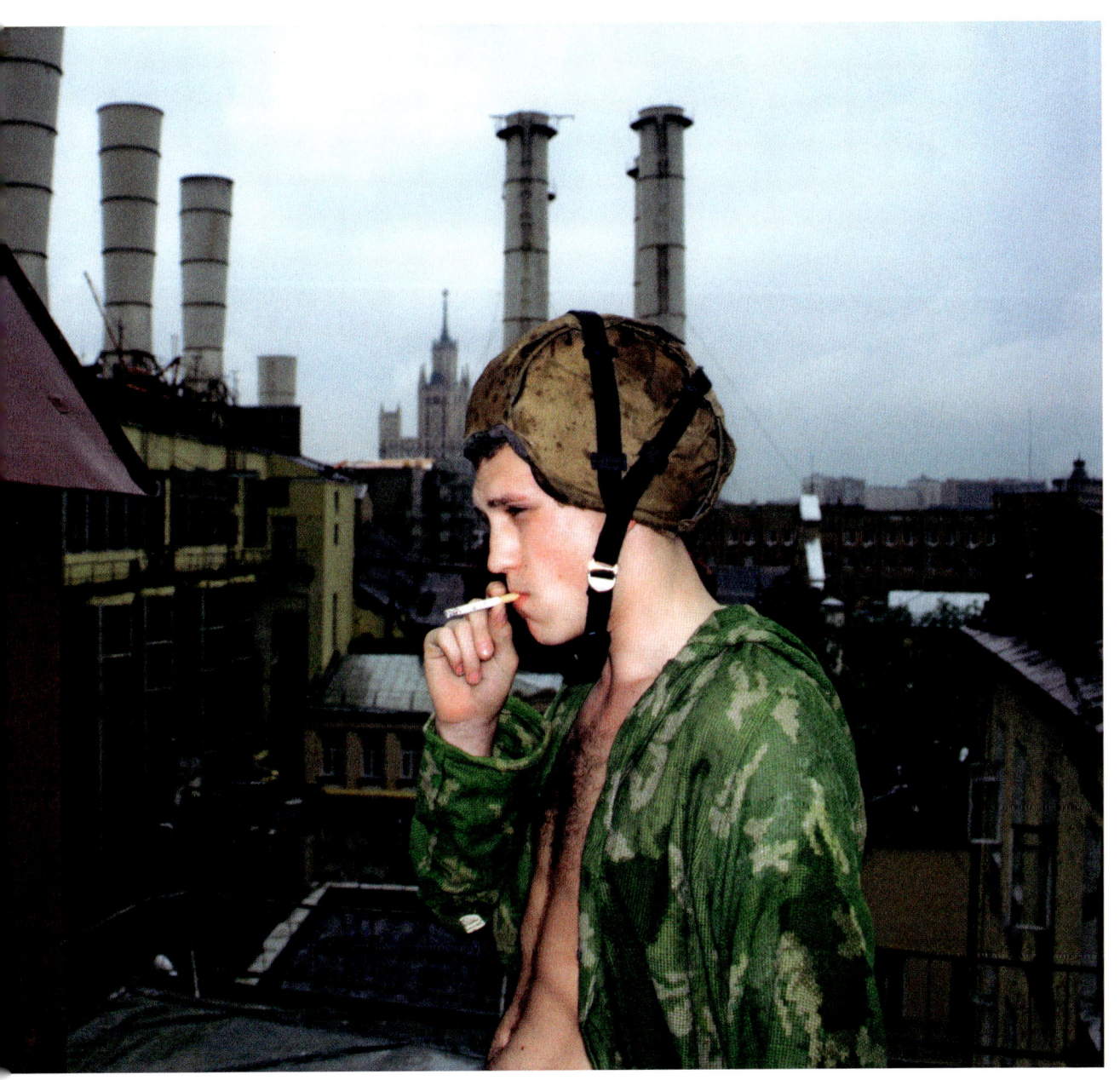

Charles Moriarty:

Could you please introduce yourself?

Slava Mogutin:

My name is Slava Mogutin. I'm from Kemerovo, Siberia, and I've lived in New York City for over 20 years now.

CM:

What was it like, growing up in Siberia?

SM:

I left with my family when I was very young. I was seven, and I don't have many recollections except that it was very cold and very uncultured. It's not really known for anything other than coal mines, chemical factories and pollution. That's what the place is famous for.

We moved from Siberia to this small town outside of Smolensk, in the middle of Russia, very close to the Chernobyl power plant, shortly after the Chernobyl disaster had happened. I always joke about how it must have affected me.

There was hardly any information about the accident. Rumours and stories had started spreading about gigantic mushrooms and deformed vegetables, but there was no official information until way after the fact. We were all affected by radiation, just like most of Europe; I just happened to be particularly close to the site.

My family moved several more times after that because my father [...] had a very nomadic personality. We couldn't stay more than three years in one given place, so we constantly moved around. It was very traumatic as a kid, because I didn't have a chance to make any friends before we had to move somewhere else. It was living on the go.

CM:

Your father is a writer?

SM:

He did a lot of travel journalism and made his living as a freelancer. He also wrote books for children. He wasn't a big name, but still, I remember when I was in my literature class and some of his work was part of our lesson. That was kind of weird and funny.

CM:

Did you learn from him, or did your writing practice find its own path?

SM:

I had a love/hate relationship with my dad, the antihero. He was quite abusive to my mother, my sister and I, and he had a big, big problem with alcohol. That made it difficult to respect him as a writer or as a creative human being, because there were so many other personality flaws that overshadowed his creativity.

CM:

Understandable then, that you left home at 14.

SM:

In retrospect, I do have a lot of respect for him. He was able to survive as a freelancer in a system that simply did not allow such a lifestyle or such freedom. Also, he was really strongly opposed to communism and its ideologies. It could get you in a lot of trouble with the authorities if you were openly discussing your anti-Soviet views.

When I was a teenager he did eventually join the Communist Party in order to get published and further his career. Then, when I was 13, he left my mother for another woman. It was traumatic, but we were all kind of relieved he was finally gone; he brought so much madness to the family. But even his absence added to my family's dysfunction.

After that I stayed with my mother in this small station settlement, three hours outside of Moscow. It was a place where they would send criminals. In the past, if you were arrested or jailed, you couldn't live in Moscow anymore. They would send you 300 kilometres outside of the city.

CM:

Right into your town. Perfect.

SM:

Exactly. That's where I spent some of my teenage years. When I was 14, I left my mother and went to Moscow to study. I went to two different schools and I was dismissed from both of them. I was kicked out for 'amoral behaviour' – that included the fact I was openly gay at the time. There was no place for such a thing in the communist system. I had also picked up my father's drinking habit, so I was drinking heavily and I was big trouble as far as the authorities were concerned.

I was an outsider; I identified as a punk. I had really long hair, and that was also completely out of line. I was going to underground concerts and getting into street fights, getting arrested for drunken brawls and stuff like that. I was totally antisocial.

Around that time, I started writing poetry and journalism, and I began taking my first pictures. The reason I picked up photography was actually because of my dad. He was an amateur photographer who brought his camera everywhere and took pictures of all his travels. Some of them were really, really beautiful, black-and-white pictures. I stole his camera and brought it to all the rock concerts I went to. My first photographs were a documentation of the underground rock scene in Moscow and St Petersburg.

CM:

What camera did you nick from your dad?

SM:

It was this old Soviet camera called FED. It was a manual, really beautiful, well-designed 35mm camera. I mostly shot black and white, so I had a primitive darkroom in my bathroom where I was printing my first pictures. I think my mother's got this whole archive of my very early photography somewhere.

I was experimenting with photography, but I didn't think of it as my language or form of expression until much later. Not until I moved to New York, when I was in exile from Russia. I did publish my pictures with some articles I'd written about my first trip to Paris and my first trip to San Francisco. I took lots of pictures on both trips. But I was thinking of photography in a more utilitarian way. I thought of it as something that was as a part of my journalism.

My main form of expression was my language, my poetry, my journalism – and photography was a part of the larger picture. It wasn't until I moved to New York that I realised it was going to be really difficult for me to get over the language barrier and start writing in English.

CM:

At one point in the early '90s, you were facing jail time in Russia. Was that quite distressing?

SM:

In all honesty, I'm the kind of person who doesn't hold grudges. I don't want to remember all the bad things. But there was plenty of hatred and death threats, anonymous threats I was facing on a daily basis.

In '94 I tried to stage the first same-sex marriage in Russia with my boyfriend, who was a conceptual American artist called Robert Filippini. He was also a member of ACT UP [AIDS Coalition to Unleash Power] and Queer Nation. We tried to do this Western-style happening slash political performance in an environment where homosexuality had just recently been decriminalised. The cultural climate was still very hostile and homophobic, and most of the press covering any kind of issues relating to gay rights or lifestyle was tabloid-style journalism.

I was the first journalist who started writing about my own personal experiences, without that stigma of being morally fraudulent or morally corrupt. The way they tried to present homosexuality in the Russian mainstream press was always very, very negative and dismissive, and it was all deemed to be the corrupt influence of the West.

CM:

You moved to New York after receiving asylum. That must have been daunting.

SM:

Language was an immediate barrier. Instead of writing I was working as a model and assistant. I wasn't doing professional modelling, but I would seek out people who I thought were important and interesting to work with. I also interviewed a lot of artists who ended up taking my portraits. For example, Wolfgang Tillmans was one of the first people I met in New York. I interviewed and photographed Wolfgang in his old studio, which later on became my studio.

Then I met a lot of great artists who ended up helping me with my own visual work. That gave me enough confidence to actually start publishing and showing it as art, as opposed to just an addition to my journalistic work.

CM:

You've worked a lot with Bruce LaBruce.

SM:

Bruce was one of the people I sought out when I was specifically looking for queer figures who were inspiring to me. A lot of them I introduced to Russia, because I was still writing as a correspondent for several Russian magazines and newspapers while I was living in New York. I introduced people like Wolfgang and Bruce LaBruce and Gus Van Sant and Larry Clark to the Russian audience for the very first time. It was very cool to meet and become friends with those people.

That was 1995 and I continued to write in Russian up until the late '90s. One of the first people I was fortunate to meet in New York was Allen Ginsberg, and I worked with him closely on his Russian translations. He was very helpful with my political asylum. He organised a letter of support for me and introduced me to other important writers and artists.

CM:

Is your photography a direct revolt against Russian attitudes towards homosexuality?

SM:

Absolutely. When I first started thinking about photography as a new language and as my main creative outlet, I felt I was continuing my work as a journalist, just through a different medium. I started focusing more on portraiture, and I wanted to preserve the snapshot quality of my pictures. In some cases, they were actual snapshots that just happened, on the street or in some random situation.

But in most cases, I was already thinking about composition, lighting and the camera I was using.

I then started experimenting with different types of cameras and film processes. I was very interested in developing my own aesthetic and style. After I got my political asylum, I went back to Russia for the first time in 2000, and that's when I shot my first coherent series [*Lost Boys*].

What I did in that book was an experiment, not just in terms of the language I was using, but also in terms of the narrative; not just from the technical perspective, but also with the narrative that I tried to present. There's this whole art of storytelling, and normally it's directly related to my poetry and journalism. *Lost Boys* was something that I felt was strong enough to stand on its own.

For the first time in my life, I started thinking of picture taking as something that could be my main form of expression. Also, I tried to subvert a lot of narratives that were fatwas in Soviet and post-Soviet propaganda. Russia is a heavily militarised society. Everyone was drafted from the age of 18 for two years. It was a mandatory military draft and I was able to avoid it, because I told them I was a homosexual and they simply didn't know how to deal with me. So I was dismissed right there and then.

CM:

I feel, looking at your work, that you are often at war with the overbearing, heteronormative communist society, but also heteronormative society in general?

SM:

That's where my fascination comes from, because I was part of that system. I was the last generation that grew up under communism and I remember

the Soviet Union disintegrating in front of my eyes. I was there at the barricades when Yeltsin was using tanks and shooting at Parliament. I was an eyewitness to all those events.

I was experimenting with photography, but I didn't think of it as my language or form of expression until much later. Not until I moved to New York, when I was in exile from Russia.

Russia is a society where you see more uniformed men than any other country I've been to. I was always fascinated with the saturation of paramilitary uniforms that you see. You can join the army in Russia from the age of 10.

The naval and military academies target disenfranchised kids and orphans. If they join the army they are set, before they're sent to some random war and killed. It's the system that forces you into conformity and that conformity is represented by various uniforms. In *Lost Boys*, you can see a lot of young men and boys wearing uniforms, yet they seem completely lost, and on the fringes of society, outcasts. I was trying to show how conformity leads you to this emptiness and isolation and bankruptcy: essentially that intellectual, moral, creative bankruptcy. That's what uniforms signify.

But at the same time, I was always fetishising uniforms. It was common when I was growing up for young guys in the army who didn't have any money to prostitute themselves. You could pay 30 rubles, which is like $1, to a soldier and suck his cock or something. It was a common thing to do.

CM:

Lost Boys *is clearly intertwined with your own sexual desires, but the people wearing the uniforms in the book are not who you would ever expect to find in the military.*

SM:

It was interesting for me to see the contrast between people who were representing order and also other groups that drew from the alternative marginal subcultures, who were representing chaos. I always wanted to show this dichotomy of uniforms that represent rebellion and uniforms that represent oppression and system.

In *Lost Boys*, you see this whole area, this whole range of different types of uniforms, and they all represent different segments of society. The people in the book are punks, ravers, skinheads and people from the fetish community. They're all in one book. I'm showing this whole spectrum of different lifestyles. To signify their affiliation, uniform is what makes them belong to a particular group or movement or system.

CM:

Did you have any training in photography? Who influenced you?

SM:

I never went to photography school, but I did study. I would say my main influences were documentary photographers and my favourite photographer of all time is Alexander Rodchenko, who basically [...] in my view, he invented the language of photography as an art genre. He was the first to experiment with photomontage and incorporating graphics with his own photography. The kind of angles and compositions he used were very influential.

Experiencing all this amazing sexual, creative and personal freedom, I really wanted to go as close to my subjects – their lifestyles and their personalities – as possible.

He was considered one of the classic artists of the socialist realism movement, which was the official propaganda vehicle during Soviet times. I found that style, socialist realism, very homoerotic, because it was all about the celebration of masculinity. Powerful male figures were always presented in a very victorious and empowering way. Also, if you look at Rodchenko's documentation of the Soviet parades, you see all these topless athletes in large numbers. If you look at my pictures of more recent parades in Moscow, they were definitely inspired.

I always try to imagine what Rodchenko's photography would look like if he was shooting in colour. A lot of my pictures borrow his ideas and his inventions and translate them into a more modern visual language.

Other influential artists are Brassaï and Henri Cartier-Bresson, Diane Arbus and Leni Riefenstahl; there are so many great artists I'm influenced by.

CM:

They were your teachers?

SM:

Yes. When I moved to Moscow, there was a lot of previously unseen artwork. It was before the internet, so the only way to experience someone's work was through books or cinema or going to galleries and museums. At that time, there were hardly any independent galleries in Moscow, but there was a really great Museum of Photography that brought a lot of amazing exhibitions from Europe and other countries.

My main visual influences were the Russian avant-garde, Russian constructivism and Rodchenko. There were also many other artists who worked with him who I found very inspiring and several socialist realist painters, most importantly Aleksandr Deyneka. There are several paintings of his that I recreated in *Lost Boys*. I remember looking at his work as a teenager and that was the first time

I realised I was gay. I found his work incredibly sexy. He was mostly depicting, again, really powerful male figures, and a lot of them involved full-on nudity.

CM:

What's your photographic process like?

SM:

When I started, I was picking up things from people I met and worked with. Bruce LaBruce was one of my main influences and I really appreciate his punk aesthetic, or homo-punk, queer-punk, whatever you want to call it. I did a gay skinhead movie with Bruce LaBruce, so I was very much interested in that scene. I would stay with my skinhead friends in Berlin and photograph them having sex. They brought me to these crazy, raunchy sex parties in Berlin that I also documented. Looking back, I realise how fortunate I was to be at that place during that time, because as you probably know, if you go out nowadays and try to take pictures –

CM:

No camera.

SM:

No cameras. Later on, I did a book in New York that was called *NYC Go-Go*; it was my second book, and I remember a lot of people at that time thought of it as a piece of pornography. I think only later, with the emergence of social media and iPhone photography, could people look back at that series and realise it was actually a really brave attempt to make a completely raw, documentary-style documentation of that underground gay scene, at the time when [Rudy] Giuliani was trying to clean up the city.

Also, I felt like, being an immigrant in America and experiencing all this…

CM:

Lifestyle?

SM:

Exactly. Experiencing all this amazing sexual, creative and personal freedom, I really wanted to go as close to my subjects – their lifestyles and their personalities – as possible. So that's when I realised I could actually go way further with my portraits than just doing staged snapshots. Because up until that point I was basically doing snapshot photography.

With *NYC Go-Go* I was specifically interested in close-up documentary. I think it's probably my most personal and most honest book because it wasn't something I conceived as a concept. It was something that was actually a documentation of my life at that time.

CM:

A moment of self-discovery for others to experience through your work. That was 2005?

SM:

It's around that time. Yeah, 2005, 2006.

CM:

A lot of your work looks at ideas of gender.

SM:

It's actually a very personal exploration, because there was a point in my life when I identified as a bisexual; I was dating girls and I was always interested in questioning the existing stereotypes and canons of what it means to be a man, to be an attractive man. What it means to be a sexual being in general.

How does masculinity translate from the gay perspective into the mainstream perspective and vice versa? How are male figures being portrayed in mainstream culture versus gay culture?

For me, it was always interesting to push the boundaries and question existing stereotypes. I always thought of traditional studio photography as something that was very, very rigid and almost outdated. It wasn't until I got my first photo studio that I realised you can achieve so much with proper lighting and a blank wall, that you actually don't need scenery to tell the story.

That's when I started thinking of gender as performance. During that time, I started shooting for magazines. I was toying with the idea of becoming a commercial fashion photographer, and every magazine shoot I did, with no exception, would be subversive; I was trying to play with those gender roles and stereotypes and turn them upside down, subvert them.

When you look at my new book, *Bros & Brosephines*, there are several trans models. They were my friends and I was really fascinated by trans people for a long time; it's still very intriguing.

I'm not really interested in traditional masculinity, as such. I'm way more interested in the spectrum of sexuality and how our sexuality and my own sexuality is evolving with time and age through exposure to many different and new ideas.

But going back to your question, I do think that gender politics are important and I feel like it's so politicised right now. Maybe I'm more interested in the formal aspect of it than the ideological or the political aspect of it. I do believe that the power of photography lies in documentation, but you can also create your own reality, your own world, and that's what makes photography an art form.

CM:

I know you have a very intimate relationship with a lot of your subjects. Is that something that allows you to go further, push boundaries with people and expand on ideas?

SM:

I'm interested in personal connections. For the most part, I work with people who are my friends and fellow artists or performance artists. I'm very interested in performance as a genre, and that's part of my photographic practice and artistic practice. I do like to work with certain subjects over and over again.

There are several people, like Brian [Kenny] and a few others, who I've been working with on a regular basis for nearly 20 years. I think of photography as a form of collaboration. I look for people who can challenge me and who can bring something to the table other than 'the look'. It's about getting to the core of the person and the core of any particular situation or movement or emotion, or the relationship between me and this particular person.

A lot of people assume I was intimately involved with all the hot guys I've photographed, but it's actually quite the opposite. I never push anything on anyone and I'm not a particularly promiscuous person, so I'm not really interested in fucking my models. But I feel like nudity is such a natural thing. I don't necessarily want to sexualise naked human bodies.

CM:

Is the body now hypersexualised?

SM:

For me, nudity doesn't equal sex or porn. It's quite the opposite. It's the most natural thing. The body is like a blank canvas; you can portray so much with the naked human body, and I tend to think of my body as an instrument. Back in the day, when I was a total exhibitionist, I loved to be photographed in the nude by a lot of great artists. Nowadays, I hate being

photographed, I hate being in front of the camera, but when I was in my early 20s, I was living for it.

Now, when I meet these young kids who are so eager to be photographed, I just feel it's something that goes both ways. It's not that I'm looking for exhibitionists. A lot of people who approach me, they kind of expect to be photographed in the nude, but honestly, it's not at all a focus of my work anymore. I'm way more interested in their personality.

I was trying to show how conformity leads you to this emptiness and isolation and bankruptcy: essentially that intellectual, moral, creative bankruptcy. That's what uniforms signify.

Exhibitionism is so common now, and on social media everyone is constantly posting selfies. It's the most boring and pointless thing. But if you have a point, and nudity is a part of it, then I think it makes sense.

It's such a hypocritical time, because on one hand, if you post slutty selfies, you get the most likes. But on the other hand, anything to do with the naked human form is so heavily censored, regulated and marginalised. It's almost like a war on human nature by the corporations who run these high-tech giants.

CM:

I actually really wanted to talk to you about censorship. As artists we are coming up against a lot of it, particularly online, where large corporations such as Facebook are shaping people's visual journey on a daily basis. You've said you have to fight back doubly strong, but how do you see that fight manifesting?

SM:

I think it's a very troubling trend, and I've been speaking out. I always fight censorship in any shape or form, but the traction that has been created by these huge multinational corporations creates a homophobic and sexphobic climate worldwide.

It's basically destroying the fabric of our society and our culture for the sake of consumerism. The only reasonable explanation that I can find is because it's just so tied in with the revenue they generate. It's all to do with consumerism and advertisement. It is in the interest of profits, corporate profits over human nature. Now more than ever, when photography is being devalued by the gazillions of selfies that are being uploaded every second.

Online, I feel photography as an art form has a responsibility and function in society. It doesn't just have an aesthetic function but also an educational one. As I said, I think of a photograph as a document before anything – but it's a document that can be transformative, a document that can be enlightening and challenging. Look at Mapplethorpe's work and imagine someone like him emerging in contemporary culture. He would be considered a marginal character and he would never get a fraction of the exposure he was given during his lifetime. We live in a very, very rigid sexphobic and homophobic time.

CM:

I think back to Larry Clark when he brought out Tulsa, *which he had to self-publish in order to get the work released and seen. Are we going full circle? Do we now have to return to demanding basic equality, and is the best way to be heard in print?*

SM:

I feel like we're being squeezed between different corporations that control our minds, every aspect of our lives; between Google, Apple, Facebook, Twitter, God knows what else. Let's face it. Grindr destroyed the fabric of queer communities and is being used as a data-harvesting tool and as a tool of entrapment in countries like Turkey, Egypt, China and Russia. So, it's a scary, scary thing when we're giving so much control to corporations. I feel now is the time for artists to speak out. We have to fight back and continue with our work. We cannot let these corporations alter our sexuality and our creativity. This is what's happening every day, every moment and every second.

I'm being censored continually, almost daily in fact. Most of the people I know, most of my friends who are real creatives, the ones who make original content – they're the ones who are being censored the most. It is a completely distorted and unfair situation, but I also feel, 'What doesn't kill you makes you stronger'.

I'm not the kind of person who would give up my rights easily. I come from a background where being censored was in some ways empowering. I think it's also a sign that my work is still relevant and still radical enough, that I'm being constantly censored by these fuck heads.

Going back to your question about censorship and the internet, the project I did after *Bros & Brosephines* was very interesting, because it's a collection of pieces called *Stock Boyz*, and they were printed on financial newspapers. The images were appropriated from obscure gay websites, porn websites that are now defunct. The main source of those pin-up pictures was Tumblr. The series was a documentation of the market crash in 2008. I was collecting financial charts from business dailies, like *The New York Times* and *The Wall Street Journal* and *Financial Times*. Last year, when Tumblr wiped the entirety of its adult content, I realised that the main source of images I used in *Stock Boyz* is now completely gone.

CM:

A little scary what you can do with the press of a button.

SM:

It's crazy. It felt surreal and I had this sudden realisation that our history and our database can be wiped out with the click of a button. That's what reaffirmed my belief in the importance of print media and hard copy and the importance of physical work, versus what's posted online. That's when I did this limited edition portfolio of *Stock Boyz*, that were reproduced as risographs.

It's physical image, to image-uploaded-online, becoming a virtual reality and digitised image – then it's manipulated and reproduced again. It's a full circle from reality to virtual reality back to print media. This was the first time I started thinking of my work as a concept. It's interesting because it was an experiment, not a book. It was a portfolio of 50 prints, like a show in a box. It was very labour intensive, because everything was hand-printed and bound in Berlin. I spent weeks working on it. I had to sign 6,000 prints by hand and that alone took me two weeks.

I would never do it again, but I did it. It was a project I'm actually very proud of, because it's very different from my personal work. It's a concept, but I feel like it directly relates to my ideas and the different subjects I was trying to convey over the last 20, 25 years. This is probably the most conceptual and the most elaborate thing I've done to this point.

CM:

What next?

SM:

I'm working on several projects and one of them is a book, a survey of my Polaroid photography. I'm working on a couple of artists' books – one is with Brian [Kenny]; that's a limited edition artist book. Then I'm also working on the collection of my English language journalism, which will cover nearly 25 years of my journalistic work in English. Lastly, I have a new collection of poetry written in English and Russian, which will be a very experimental book, because it's bilingual.

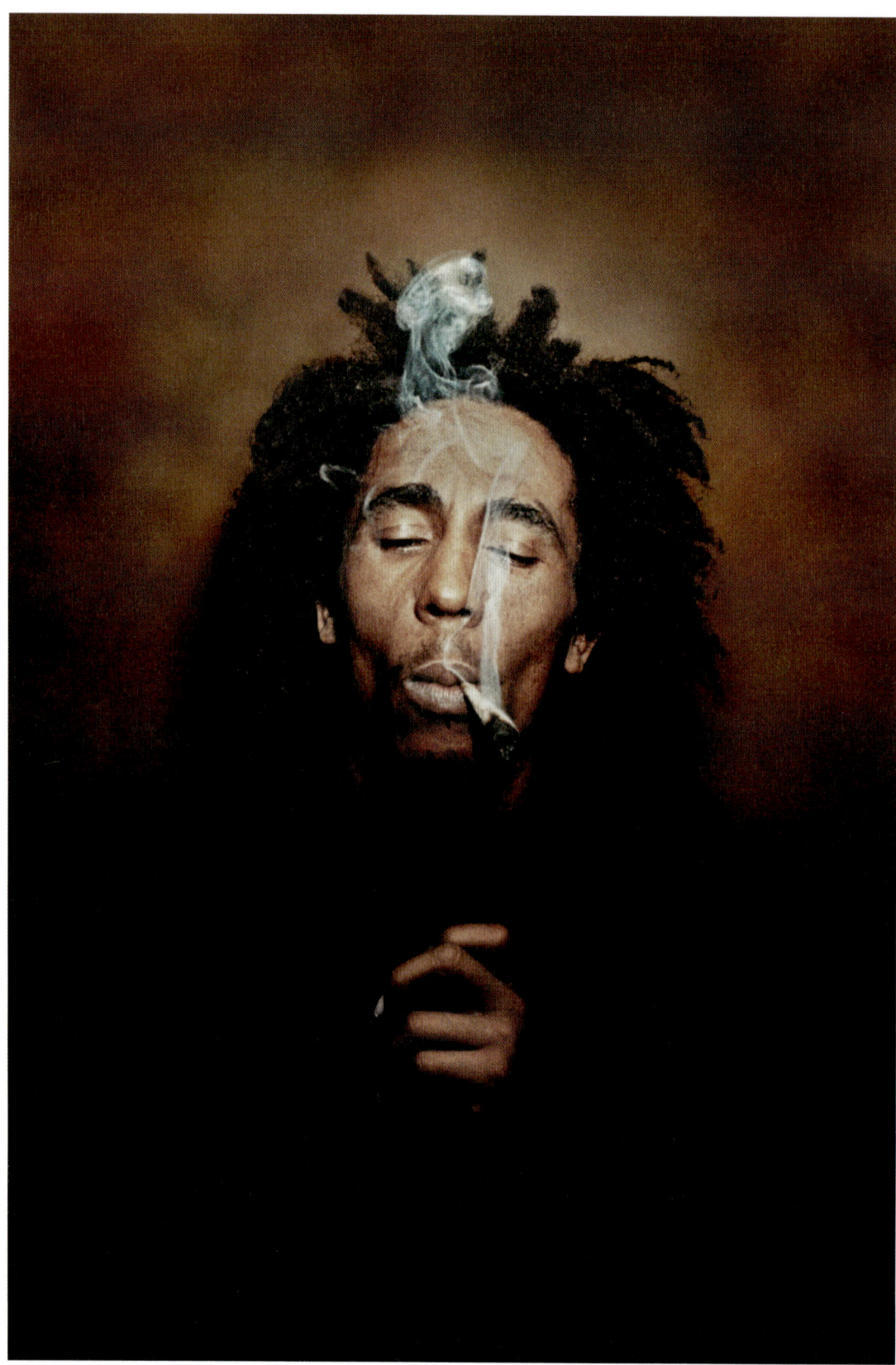

DENNIS MORRIS

On 4 August 2020 I spoke with acclaimed music and reportage photographer Dennis Morris over Zoom, from his home in Los Angeles. Originally from Hackney in London, Dennis exploded onto the music scene in the 1970s with his intimate photographs of Bob Marley and went on to create a body of work that almost seems impossible now. His close-quarters work with the Sex Pistols and Marianne Faithfull, along with his documentation of London and England's Black and white communities, stand as testament to his years behind the lens.

Dennis Morris, Bob Marley Spliff, 1974
© Dennis Morris

Charles Moriarty:

How's lockdown been for you?

Dennis Morris:

Yeah, good. I'm in LA, [though] Dalston still has a space in my heart.

CM:

You got into photography through the local parish. Was it with Father Pateman?

DM:

No, it was the Reverend Donald Paterson. He [Pateman] was the vicar of the church, while Donald Paterson was the inventor of the self-loading spiral, which was a big breakthrough in darkroom photography. He had a company called Paterson Products that made photographic chemicals, developing tanks, enlargers – anything for the darkroom. He made a huge fortune. Being from a Christian background he wanted to, I suppose, at some point in his life do something for society. At the same time, Mr Pateman wanted to create a choir. But he wanted the choirboys to wear Eton suits like they wear in Eton College. You know the big, white...

> As you progress, you realise that [the camera] is just a tool, and the tool is only as good as you are.

CM:

The frills.

DM:

Yeah. But he couldn't afford it, so he put an ad in *The Times* looking for somebody to help. Mr Paterson saw it and got in contact, and they became great friends. So he more or less bought the clothing for the choir and created a photographic club for the choirboys. That's where I discovered photography, when I was nine.

CM:

Were you given a camera?

DM:

Mr Paterson had built a darkroom in one of the rooms in the vicarage. And every Thursday any choirboy who was interested would meet, about 10 of us. And we were all given little cameras and a roll of film to go about and take pictures. Nothing expensive in the beginning – just a Kodak camera; that kind of thing. We'd all go off and take pictures, then come back and develop the film. [...] Paterson, I think, saw potential in me, and took me under his wings and taught me everything I knew. As I progressed, he would loan me his cameras. I was using Leicas from a very early age.

CM:

The M3, right? Are you still using a Leica?

DM:

Unfortunately, I don't really use Leicas anymore. They're the celebrity camera now. [...] Not so long ago, it was my birthday. My wife decided she'd get me a Leica. So, she bought me one: the equivalent of a Canon Sure Shot. It was very expensive. I went home and the thing blew up in my hand. [...] When I was growing up, I always felt the need to try out that camera, or this camera, or that lens, or whatever. As you progress, you realise that [the camera] is just a tool, and the tool is only as good as you are. So, I've had various cameras over the years.

CM:

Do you still shoot?

DM:

Yeah, I do still shoot. Before, my name was always coming up in magazines or whatever, but now it crops up in museums and galleries. […] That's where I always wanted to be.

CM:

When you fell into that great relationship with Bob Marley, did you see that as the beginning of a career, or were you just caught up in the moment?

DM:

A little bit of both, but I must say that on my first meeting with Bob I knew straight away he was someone special, somebody unique who would play a part in my life. My ambition had never been to become a rock photographer. My ambition was to be a war photographer, reportage. I got that influence from Mr Paterson and some of the great photographers such as Capa, Maltighe, Cartier-Bresson, Tim Page... They were my inspiration.

Rock photography was never really on the cards for me. But through that first meeting with Bob, and because of how I was influenced, the images I produced of him were taken in the same vein as reportage, which gave them a closeness and uniqueness. Because […] I was the only one who had images of Bob prior to that show – that gig at the Speakeasy Club, London – I suddenly got on the front page of *Time Out* magazine. I was thrust into the rock world – but I continued with my own technique and style, within the music business.

CM:

Do you regret not going into war photography?

DM:

No, because I don't think I would have been around years later, when I met one of my heroes – Tim Page, a great war photographer. He was very close to Jim Morrison and did a lot of work with The Doors. […] I actually met him at The Doors' reunion, years ago at the ICA. There was this lonely figure out and about, smoking a joint, so I went out and said, 'Hey, can I have a puff?' And he said, 'Yeah, join me'. So we started talking, and I realised it was Tim Page.

I knew the story that he had a bullet in his head, which is still there to this day. He turned to me and I said, 'Why did you go to Vietnam?' He said, 'Well, after Jim Morrison died, I had to find another war'. So he went to Vietnam, said he needed more action. But he's hated by all the war photographers.

CM:

Why is that?

DM:

He took too many risks. There was a code amongst all the war photographers, such as... What's his name?

CM:

Don McCullin?

DM:

McCullin, yeah. McCullin hated him. No one liked [Tim Page] because he just didn't play by the rules. There was a certain rule among those photographers, but he came from the outside and did what he did. I suppose, in some ways, it was the same for me within the music business. I wouldn't say they hated me, but I was completely left field compared to everybody else.

CM:

In some ways, punk was your war.

DM:

Punk was my war. Yeah, and Bob Marley was my war. I was quite happy in that way, because with Marley at the time, all the troubles were going on in Jamaica. There was a lot of physical violence, so it was very dangerous. And then with punk, the genre was more or less hated. The whole movement was hated, so it was very tricky for us on the streets. [...] I found my wars. I was very happy.

CM:

When you started out, you must have been one of the only Black photographers in London. How did that affect you when you were starting out?

DM:

Well, I was very aware that some of the work I went for at magazines or whatever, when they turned me down, it was because of [me] being Black. But at the same time, Bob always instilled in me... He said, 'Look, they're always going to tell you that you can't do this or you can't do that.' He said, 'If you've got self-belief, if you believe in yourself, you'll do it.' So I always walked away from those meetings just feeling, 'Okay, next one.'

It didn't faze me – and in some ways, it helped me. I think some of the work I got, [my employers] felt sorry for me. One of the key things for me as a photographer is that I actually own the rights to all my work. Many photographers don't – and that is your pension. Because people felt sorry for me, they

were like, 'Oh well, what does he know?' What I'm trying to say is: you've got to take something good out of everything bad, if you see what I'm saying.

CM:

I do, completely. Do you still think of yourself as a reportage photographer?

DM:

Yeah. I worked in the studio when I did the session with Marianne Faithfull. My approach to it was exactly the same [...] I just used two lights. When I speak to a lot of young photographers, I say to them, 'What you have to remember is, there's only one sun.'

That one sun can give you any amount of light you need. All you have to do is understand light. When I see people in studios with literally 50 lights, I think it's madness. So, that's how I work. With the Marianne Faithfull shoot it was two lights. That's all I had. One chair. A leather sofa, an armchair, and then we took it from there.

CM:

Outside of Tim Page, who influenced you as you were growing up and finding photography for yourself?

DM:

Gordon Parks. As a Black photographer, I realise the word 'photographer' is a word used to describe someone with a camera, but I see myself as an artist. My tool is the camera. With painters it's the brush, the paint. Gordon Parks... I've read about him, and he also saw himself as an artist. As an artist there are no boundaries. Like Picasso – he could do sculpture, poetry, paint and even design houses. Gordon Parks made films and all kinds of stuff. That's how I am. That's how I approach it.

CM:

When you started working as art director with Island Records, did that take away from being a photographer? Or did you find an easy middle ground?

DM:

Well, Island for me could have been a great experience – except they were trying to turn me into a corporate designer. The way I worked when I first joined really upset a lot of people. [...] It was Chris Black who brought me to the company personally. Although I was art director, I also had A&R capacity, so I signed Linton Kwesi Johnson to the label. I signed The Slits to the label. I oversaw Marianne Faithfull.

You've got to take something good out of everything bad.

But I never had a design table in my office. What I did have was three TVs. I had the biggest stereo there was, because I'm a very visually driven person. Even when I'm at home I always have a TV on and I always have music playing. I need to hear music. I need to have vision. I would be watching Sky One, BBC One, BBC Two... All at the same time. Music too...

That's how I function – which really upset a lot of people because they were very regular, straight down the line. Chris was okay with it, but in the end I just thought, 'This ain't for me.' It really upset Chris. He was very upset. I just could not stay there.

CM:

The music industry has changed a lot.

DM:

Well, it used to be the music business. [...] In the early days, when I was at Island Records, you went to record companies. From the minute you opened the door, all you heard was music. Music played in every single room. You go into a record company today; you don't hear any music. Everybody's in front of a laptop or computer.

CM:

You photographed Bob Marley before anyone really knew him. What was your relationship like years later?

DM:

Bob was always the same; he never changed. Despite his success and increased wealth, he was always the same. He never wore anything more than denim. He was never really caught up in the 'I've got to have a mansion; I've got to have this; I've got to have that.' For him it was more about spreading the message, spreading the word, spreading the gospel, spreading the music, spreading the love. [...] And so to me, having known him from the early days and through to his success, he was always the same. He always used to greet me with 'What up Dennis? Where's my photographer at?' [...] He never treated me differently. He was always very cool.

CM:

I'm a huge fan of the three spliff shot. It's a beautiful triptych and such a great moment of friendship.

DM:

That was my lesson: there was no fourth frame.

CM:

How long were you with the Sex Pistols for?

DM:

When I work with a band, I normally go and see them live first, without a camera. That's the only time I'm ever going to really see them live. I go without the camera and watch and see what it was all about, how the fans react, how they perform. So, when it comes to actually photographing them onstage, I know what it's all about.

I saw the Pistols at the 100 Club. I didn't have my camera. So, I knew they were going to 'happen'. [...] We all grew up in the same area. John grew up in Finsbury Park, but he went to Dorsen Technical College. That was on my route, so we all used to hang around the same places without really knowing each other. By the time the Virgin deal happened, John actually wanted me to work with them. [He more or less turned to Ian Richards and] said he wanted me to photograph them.

So that's how that came about. I went down to Vernon Yonge, where the Virgin office was at the time, there in the courtyard. We just clicked instantly and it went on from there.

CM:

How long were you with them?

DM:

One year. Then they went to America for a couple of months, and that was it. It was all over.

CM:

Would you take breaks or were you with them all the time?

DM:

I filmed them more or less all the time. 24/7. [...] As a reportage photographer, as a war photographer, I was down with the troops.

CM:

How do you feel about photography today?

DM:

I still love photography today. I think the problem for photography today is that with the development of all the technology, it gets to a point where everybody thinks they're a photographer. Truth and reality is, everybody could take a photograph before these advancements. But not everybody is an artist. Not everybody can take a great photograph. Because of the digital age everyone thinks that they are geniuses – but it doesn't bother me in any shape or form.

CM:

I really enjoyed your shots of London during the '70s – especially the pictures of Hackney. Can you talk about photographing during that period and what London was like for you growing up?

DM:

Those images are from my book, *Growing Up Black*. My parents' generation were called 'coloured people'. Then my generation, because of the Black Power movement in America, we called ourselves Black. So that's why it's called *Growing Up Black*.

In the very early stages of my development as a photographer, from the photographic club at the church, I developed a reputation in the neighbourhood for being very good and very cheap. I'd make extra pocket money to get film, etc. I would take pictures of people in the local community and stuff like that. But I would also walk around, looking for images that represented what the community was about and what I saw.

So over a period of years I created all these images. I knew what I was doing and I knew the importance of it because, again, it stemmed from what I'd learned and read from Gordon Parks and his body of work. So, I just kept doing it.

CM:

Was there a certain point when you stopped photographing like that?

DM:

No. At the height of my career, when I was supposedly earning a lot of money, I would take that supposed 'lot of money' to finance all these other projects I was doing. So apart from *Growing Up Black*, there's *Southall: A Home from Home*. Or *This Happy Breed*, which is a look at more of the English, white side of the community. So that's what I did. I took the money I earned from the commercial work, then used it to finance my other side of things.

The problem for photography today is that [...] it gets to a point where everybody thinks they're a photographer.

CM:

What are you working on now?

DM:

I'm working on several things. When the Olympic Games was in China, I got a commission from the Chinese government to produce a body of work. So, I spent a year going around China and produced a series to portray my vision of the country, which was part of the Olympic programme. On the opening day of the Olympic Games there was a museum exhibition of this work in Beijing.

Then when the Olympic Games came to England, the British government asked the Photographers' Gallery to commission a set of photographers to produce a body of work – same sort of thing, but more specific. Each of the photographers was given a country. I was given Haiti. We had to find someone who was originally born in Haiti but was now residing in England and was part of the community in England. So, I found this young woman – a young girl who was a foundling in Haiti. A Canadian couple found her on the streets, adopted her, took her to Toronto, and then as she grew up and turned 20, she moved to England. When the earthquake happened in Haiti, she created an earthquake fund for the people. So, I did a portrait of her and then there were billboards all around London.

CM:

It sounds similar to the A Day In The Life *project.*

DM:

I do a lot of work like that. As I said, you don't really see them in magazines. They're big projects.

CM:

Do you get more gratification from doing that kind of work rather than the magazine stuff, or does it matter?

DM:

Well, the problem for me is… I won't mention names, but not so long ago I worked with a very prominent musician. This person was in LA at the time, but one day they went into a management office and the management had my book, *Growing Up Black*. They saw it and said, 'Oh wow, I really want to work with this guy'. So I met them, we spoke, we chatted. Over about a month we spent time together, went out into the deserts, etc., etc. I was thinking 'Great. Great shoot.' Then they went back to England and presented the images to the record company […] who just said, 'Oh well, we're not paying you.'

I said, 'What are you talking about?' They said, 'We never commissioned you.' I said, 'The artist commissioned me.' They said, 'Yeah, well, he's not paying.' I said, 'What's wrong with the images?' They said, 'There's nothing wrong with the images. It's just that you've gone off in a completely different direction.' I said, 'This is the direction decided after discussing it with the artist.' They said, 'We don't care.' So I got into an ego scenario, and then I showed them my clout, and they said, 'Oh God.'

I ended up getting paid. And I also own the rights to the images. But what I'm getting at is that the artists today, they have no say. They have absolutely no say.

When I worked with the Pistols, when I worked with Bob Marley, when I did the Public Image [Ltd] work – all those things, Marianne Faithfull… […] In those days I would print all my images and stuff.

Then I'd bring the work in and show it to them. They'd be like, 'Oh wow. Let's go.' These days…

CM:

I suspect you're in trouble if you're the artist and you bring in pictures unapproved.

DM:

Exactly. So I try and stay clear of it unless on paper I've got complete carte blanche. Otherwise I just don't want the aggravation.

CM:

Have you been involved in any of the current political movements in Los Angeles, or are you keeping away during the pandemic?

DM:

America, LA, is a very strange place. I'm in West Hollywood. I can see the marches going by, but it looks to me almost like it's some kind of fashion show. A few days after the first wave of demonstrations, there was a lot of violence; shops were smashed. What was weird was, my wife and I would always go out for walks in the morning. Then, all of a sudden, because of this whole thing, we'd be walking down the street and then a complete stranger would come and say, 'Hello, good morning.' But now we walk down that same street – no one says, 'Hello, good morning,' anymore. Because Black lives only mattered for the first two, three weeks.

CM:

Everyone's fallen back into their standard ways of operating?

DM:

Yeah. I remember the days in London in the '70s in Lewisham, Broadwater Farm. You know? […] We wanted change and we brought around change. It wasn't about being photographed in front of a shop as it was being smashed and saying, 'Look, here I am.' [...] I find the American approach to these things a little bit too *media*. You know what I mean?

The artists today, they have no say. They have absolutely no say.

All the TV channels, they milk it dry because, basically, it's advertising. News in America is a commercial entity. I was in Tokyo the same day when the Fukushima reactor blew because I had a big show there. The same day I arrived, it blew and Tokyo was hit quite bad, but it was nothing compared to Fukushima. What I'm trying to get at was, we were there for a few days – weeks, in fact. And we'd watch the news and CNN would say, 'The radiation cloud is sweeping across Tokyo. Everyone is wearing masks.' And I was like, 'Everybody wears masks anyway.' Then they said, 'We're at the airport, everybody's rushing away at the airport.' And it wasn't even the goddam airport – it was the main train station.

CM:

Media has become a very powerful tool for manipulation – but maybe it always has been. Opinion distorts truth.

DM:

If there's a war zone, photographers aren't even allowed into it because they don't really want the truth. [...] Proof of that is through the Second World War, when Capa was one of the first true troops landing on the beach. He sent back a batch of something like 20 rolls to be developed. Nineteen rolls disappeared, or returned developed wrongly. One survived. When they saw what was there... no way.

CM:

Didn't tell the right story?

DM:

Yeah. When they had the first Gulf War, none of the photographers were allowed in until after.

CM:

What's your advice to young photographers or people who are trying to get into the world of photography?

DM:

You have to follow your own vision. Follow your art. As much as I was aware of the works of Gordon Parks, I would say I never actually copied that mould.

As a photographer I've never been bothered by what anybody else was doing around me. I just did my thing. A lot of photographers are influenced by what another photographer is doing. I never did that. I always kept moving down my own route. I developed my own style: it worked or it didn't. Like I said, it's no different from being a painter or a sculptor. You're an artist. Either you're instantly recognised or you're recognised 20, 30, 40 years down the road, whatever it may be [...] You just have to keep doing it. Keep believing in what you're doing.

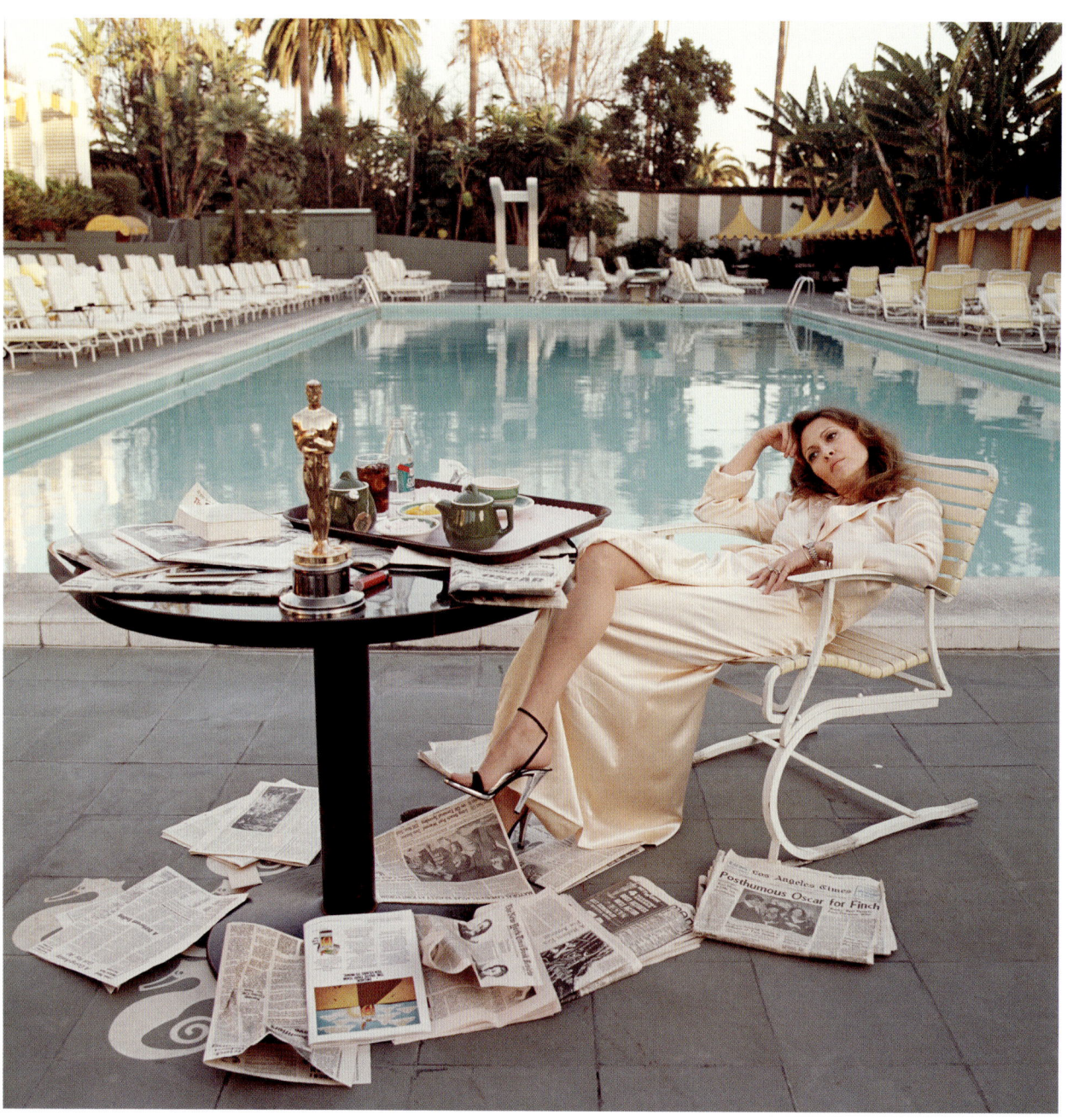

TERRY O'NEILL

Charles spoke to Terry mid-2019. Unfortunately, Terry was too ill when it came to the follow-up questions and sadly passed away in November 2019. To help the reader gain a better understanding, I have taken the liberty of adding some additional context to Terry's interview. It was an absolute honour to work with Terry O'Neill for four years, primarily helping him publish a series of books that highlighted his vast archive, including his work with David Bowie, Elton John, The Rolling Stones, the James Bond films, The Beatles and Michael Caine. He was always very humble, kind and willing to help me understand his photographs and tell me the stories behind the pictures. He loved publishing his books and was a real trooper when it came time to do publicity and events – even in his last year, when I knew he wasn't always feeling on top form. Meeting people who loved his work really made him happy. He is very, very missed.

Carrie Kania, Creative Director at Iconic Images, a leading company that specialises in owning, managing and representing photographers and their archives.

Terry O'Neill, Faye Dunaway, 1977
© Iconic images

Charles Moriarty:

Thank you, Terry, for taking the time to speak to me. You've taken some of the most iconic photographs of the 20th century.

Terry O'Neill:

That's nice of you, but it was all luck. I didn't know what I was doing!

CM:

How did you start off?

TO'N:

When I worked at BOAC [British Overseas Airways Corporation], there was this man, Peter Campion, who helped me understand photography. I wanted to be a jazz drummer and I thought the best way to get to New York would be to work at the airline. I'd fly over for a few days, then fly back and work. The life of a travelling drummer. There weren't any jobs going for stewards, so I joined the photographic unit. Anyway, Peter took a liking to me and would bring in all these photo annuals for me to study. Cartier-Bresson, W. Eugene Smith – I'd take the books home to study. One day, at Heathrow, I happened upon this old bloke taking a kip in the departures lounge. He was surrounded by African chieftains – head-to-toe in their regalia – and I grabbed a few snaps. A man tapped me on my shoulder and said 'If you got a picture, have it on my desk in the morning and my paper will publish it.' Turns out the man was Rab Butler! The picture ran. Soon after, Peter turned down an offer to join a paper on Fleet Street and thought it was more suited for me.

CM:

You worked with The Beatles and The Rolling Stones quite early on in their careers.

TO'N:

The papers wanted stars. Stars sold the papers. And the stars – the new ones – really needed the photographers back then.

CM.

How things have changed.

TO'N:

I wouldn't want to be working today. You can't get that close anymore. When I started, we didn't know what you couldn't do.

CM:

When you started, what was different? You didn't work in a studio.

TO'N:

I hated the studio. I wanted to be on the streets. That's where the editors put me. I used to have six or seven jobs a day – going to see this person wave, running to catch so-and-so leaving the hospital, then over to an event at the Palladium. It was non-stop. But I was young and I could run around back then.

CM:

When did you realise this was going to be the job for you?

TO'N:

I don't know. Taking those shots of The Beatles did lead to other jobs. I was one of the youngest on the papers, and most of the other photographers didn't really care for The Beatles or what was happening. The editors knew – the editors knew that the youth were going to change the decade. They were right.

CM:

How did you get from those early photos of The Beatles to where you are now?

TO'N:

I worked. When I was on the papers, I was given

assignments. Go here, go there. But there was this terrible plane crash and the papers needed someone to cover the funerals. I just couldn't do it. I couldn't go there and take pictures of people crying, mothers, sons – I couldn't. So, I quit. The editor told me 'Without the papers, you are finished.' The next day, I called everyone I knew and told them I was looking for work. I've never worked so hard to find jobs – anything.

CM:

Is that when you started to work on film sets?

TO'N:

Yes. I was brought in as a special photographer. I'd go for a few days and then feed the papers and magazines early looks of the big upcoming movies.

CM:

Was it competitive?

TO'N:

I wasn't the only photographer on-set. I'd cross over days with some of them. We were all selling to different papers, though. The papers couldn't get enough of it. The new James Bond, the new Audrey Hepburn; those were big stars. We could all sell pics of Audrey – she didn't take a bad photo – so it wasn't competitive. I think the fashion shoots were harder.

CM:

David Bailey and those people?

TO'N:

I wasn't going to be Bailey. He was his own person. Life imitates art [laughs]. I didn't want to be famous. You know, only a few days before he died, I was walking down Mayfair and Terry [Donovan] drove by and shouted 'Tel, how much money did you make today?'

CM:

What gave you the edge, then?

TO'N:

Maybe it was that I liked talking to people. I was also fast. The cameras I used were portable, easy to focus, and I'd just fire off some photos. After a while, I started to learn what was going to work for the papers, so I'd come back with shots I could sell. Sometimes I would hold my breath for weeks until I got the rolls back to see if I had got anything. I wasn't setting up the shots.

CM:

You'd make suggestions, though. Like with The Rolling Stones?

TO'N:

I wanted to make them look like a travelling band. Those blues bands that would come into town from America. They already looked great. Style. Each one was different from the other. I think The Beatles were individuals acting as a band, The Stones were a band acting as individuals. Anyway, I got the idea to put them in Soho, around Tin Pan Alley, carrying suitcases like they just got into town.

CM:

I read that Keith Richards admitted he didn't own a suitcase, so had to buy one before meeting-up with you. The suitcase was still filled with the tissue paper from the shop.

TO'N:

[Laughs] That's probably right.

CM:

When was the moment when you thought, 'This is me, this is what I want'?

TO'N:

A decade or so in, I thought I was starting to get good at this. During those times, we weren't looking back – it was always about what's next.

CM:

Which brings me to the 'Bardot with cigar' photo. Are you asked about it often?

TO'N:

It's a great shot, I have to admit. It was a photo I saw before I took it. And it was the first time I remember thinking 'That's the shot I need to get.' We were on the set of the film, *Frenchie King* [*The Legend of Frenchie King*, 1971]. I had already worked with Bardot before and I knew she had several, well, assets going for her. She took a great picture and the press always wanted them. They were getting ready to film a scene and the wind kept blowing her hair in front of her face. I thought if I waited for that exact moment, I'd get it. I took at least two rolls — hoping.

CM:

Did you know right away when you shot it?

TO'N:

No! No idea. You had to wait until the end of the day, get the film off, and you waited. And waited. Sometimes it would be days before you'd see the sheets. And there it was.

CM:

Your 'Faye Dunaway at the pool' shot, The Morning After, *is pretty iconic. Can you tell me about that? You set that up, right?*

TO'N:

You're not suppose to take pictures by the Beverly Hills Hotel. A few years ago, we were in LA opening an exhibition and we went over there and there's a big sign saying 'no pictures' [laughs]. I knew the pool boy. I asked if he'd let us in. I told Faye, 'If you win tonight, meet me downstairs at the pool at 6 and bring the Oscar'. To her credit, she did. She probably had only slept an hour, if that, but she looked beautiful.

I was asked to take a picture of the winner that year for Best Actress. I didn't want the obvious shot – the minutes after, when you're waving it above your head and you don't know what's just happened. I wanted the morning after, when you've realised that your entire life has just changed. You went from a $600,000 pay check to a few million. So, I asked Faye if she'd do it. I had it all set up: the breakfast tray, tea and all the papers with the headlines. It's become one of the most famous pictures of Hollywood. It was just us, and I don't think we took more than an hour to do it.

CM:

There's a lesson in that.

TO'N:

If you have time to think about it, do.

CM:

Who out of your subjects has had the most effect upon your own life and why?

TO'N:

I suppose it was Frank Sinatra.

CM:

And that's not a picture you saw coming!

TO'N:

It really wasn't. I was going down to Miami to do some on-set work for *Lady in Cement* [1968], starring Raquel Welch – someone I've known now, five decades? – and Frank Sinatra. I was nervous about Sinatra – who wouldn't be? I knew Ava – Frank's real love – and told her. She said, 'Don't worry.' Days later, she gives me this letter. 'Hand this to Frank.'

I got down there and I'm at the boardwalk, waiting for him to arrive, when I looked up and saw them coming at me. I fired off a few snaps and he walked right up to me. I stood up and said 'Ava told me to give this to you,' and handed him the letter. He read it and smiled and said to his boys, 'He's OK, he's with us.' That was the start of a near 30-year relationship working with him. He taught me not to get in the way.

CM:

You've worked with such a variety of icons – actors, musicians, politicians, sports stars – even royalty.

TO'N:

I have. I was so nervous when I got the invitation to take photos of The Queen. You know months in advance, so I would just sit there and think of every possible thing that could go wrong. I shouldn't have worried one bit. She's the most photographed person in the world.

CM:

Where do you see photography going in the future?

TO'N:

It's not the same. We've lost that trust between the photographer and subject, when the subject is famous – or wants to be famous. There are too many people involved now; everyone has to have their say. And they're photo touched. Sometimes the pictures are so retouched, they don't even look like the person. There's no one I'd want to work with like that.

I was onstage with Elton John when he played at the Dodger Stadium. Maybe the managers and PRs will see that – they are losing out on a lot of pictures.

CM:

Do you often find that your work has been about being in the right place at the right time?

TO'N:

Not really. I didn't take my camera to the clubs or to restaurants, I wasn't there to snap a picture of someone eating their lunch. They trusted me. The

I wouldn't want to be working today. You can't get that close anymore. When I started, we didn't know what you couldn't do.

people I took photos of knew I wasn't there to make them look bad. I wasn't the one taking a camera on holiday, if you can believe that.

CM:

Why does photography matter in society, and to you personally?

TO'N:

I think photography documents moments in time. Its great to see so many people taking photos. At openings, I'll have these young people ask me questions about equipment and what lens to use, tips. I keep telling them, just keep shooting.

CM:

Thank you, Terry.

TO'N:

That's it?

CM:

Unless you have anything else to say?

TO'N:

I've been really lucky, I really have. I've had a great life.

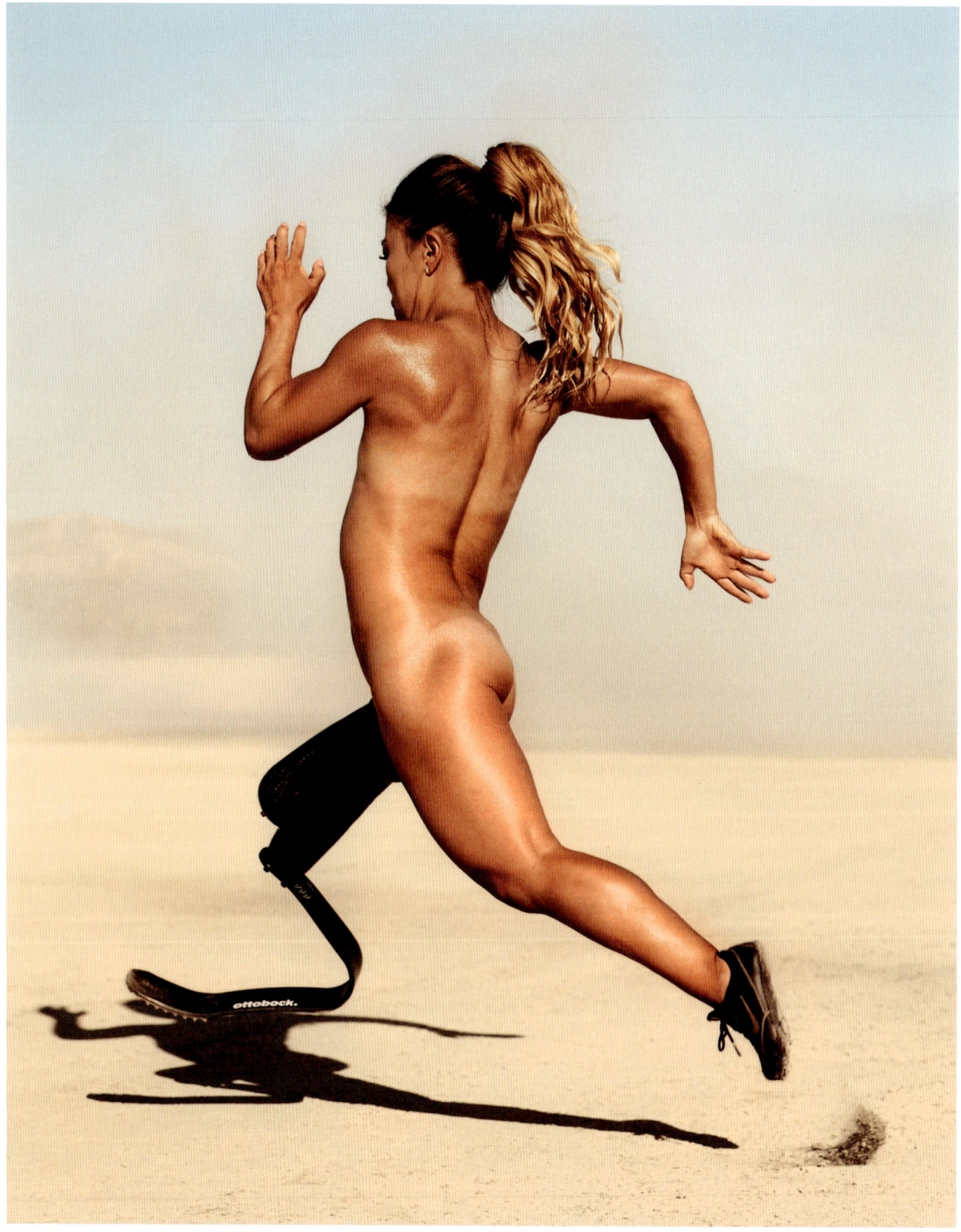

RICHARD PHIBBS

I first met Richard through Instagram, the day a mutual friend of ours – Isauro, also a photographer – tragically died. It was a true shock. Several months after, we met in London and became friends. Although Richard often jumps between cities, he lives in New York and London. I managed to meet him in London for some lunch and a chat about photography and his career.

Richard Phibbs, Scout Basset, 2019
© Richard Phibbs

Charles Moriarty:

Where in Canada are you from?

Richard Phibbs:

I grew up in Calgary, Alberta, the west.

CM:

Were you out in the pastures, or in the city?

RP:

I lived in the city. It was in a neighbourhood with a downtown, but the country was very close by. It's a beautiful part of Canada, where the prairies turn into the beautiful Rockies.

CM:

Were you a bit of a cowboy?

RP:

It's not really an option when you are part of that world, so yes, I do have cowboy boots, and did have cowboy hats. Actually, my first job as a child was sweeping floors at the Calgary Stampede, which was the biggest rodeo in the world.

CM:

How often was that on?

RP:

Every July. It's the biggest moment of the city. It's this huge rodeo, this international rodeo. I went back as an adult and photographed it many times, so it was interesting to revisit it.

I went running out of [Calgary] when I was 17, about to turn 18. I wanted to go to the big urban centres. I went to Toronto, which is a four-hour flight, but it's one of the cultural centres of Canada. That and Montreal.

CM:

What were your early years like in Toronto?

RP:

At 17 to 18 I just wanted to get away, and university was required by the parents. They didn't care what marks you got, you just had to go. So, I went to a great university. It was super challenging and super academic. I was so young. I thought I wanted to be an architect, because that was a creative job that dad could maybe handle. My very conservative father. Then I thought, let's just see how it goes. I actually did a Bachelor of Arts degree in art history and English.

I'm fascinated by the power of pictures and the power of photography, and what a wonderful thing if I can take a picture that lessens some suffering on the planet?

CM:

That's what I did. [...] It was a wonderfully broad spectrum for understanding and learning. That was three or four years in Toronto?

RP:

That was four years in Toronto, and then I thought

to myself, 'I need to be creative.' I took some fine arts studio classes at the University of Toronto. I did some figure drawing, and some basic stuff.

I enjoyed it immensely and I had great teachers, but I was all right, so I dabbled in that. I knew that being creative was important for my happiness. I was thinking of creative jobs where money was a possibility: advertising was one and architecture was another. Something about advertising really appealed to me, so I did a year at what they call the Ontario College of Art and Design. It was a foundation year, and after that, I got accepted to Parsons School of Design in New York, for the communication design program. I'd never been to New York, so I went down for my interview and got accepted. It was a life-changing moment for me.

CM:

How did you find New York?

RP:

I was terrified. I got into my room, which was part of the YMCA. Parsons didn't have residences, so they would take floors from YMCAs. They were horrible; each room was six feet by 10, and I'm 6'2". It was just a window, a cot and a small wardrobe, and then a little space that you could work at.

When I got dropped off at my room, I remember the wardrobe had been positioned to cover half the window, so when I walked in, I had half a window and a nasty cot. I closed the door, and I remember sitting down and just crying, and going, 'What the fuck?'

I was in my early 20s. I did a two-year degree, an additional Bachelor of Fine Arts in two years. But I had inspiring instructors who were great people in the industry.

CM:

Which makes all the difference.

RP:

A big difference, because your teachers are working people in the industry. I was exposed to a lot, and I worked my ass off, so I did well.

CM:

You were an art director before you became a photographer, right? Did you have large visual influences in your life by then?

RP:

I did have some. I was fortunate enough to have a mother who loved art, so there were always art books around me, big coffee-table art books.

I remember seeing *The Death of Marat.* It was on the back cover of one of those books. It would haunt me, but it's a beautiful image. I remember that being frightening to me, but beautiful and compelling at the same time. So painting, probably, was the first visual influence, then photography started to slowly creep in. My first job in New York – after a struggle, because it wasn't easy, finding

One day, the therapist and I talked about creativity, and he said, 'Creativity can be a healing thing, you know.'

my first job – was working at a big ad agency. I had two creative directors and they were working on a fashion account, which was great for me. It was there that I started to get exposed to photography and fashion photography.

CM:

Who were your first photographic influencers?

RP:

A girlfriend gave me Bruce Weber's *O Rio De Janeiro*. That had a powerful impact on me. At the same time, I happened to be reading *GQ*. Donald Sterzin was the art director, and Bruce Weber was his colleague/friend, and mostly their photographer, as well as this guy named Barry McKinley. Donald ended up being my first boss at this ad agency.

So, here he was, this guy that I had admired. In the early '80s, Bruce and Donald were the first guys to do women without makeup, and they were the first guys to put the man as the hero, and the woman as part of the image, but not necessarily the focus, which for fashion was an unusual thing.

CM:

Do you think they were changing things up, like Avedon did after the '50s, when he brought in a lot of movement to fashion photography?

RP:

For sure – and there was a group of them that did it. They really changed the path of men's fashion.

CM:

How did it work at the agency?

RP:

I worked on a couple of fashion accounts throughout those years, and then I left one year to go to another agency that focused more on TV and TV commercials, because I thought I was more interested in film and wanted to give that a try. I did that for a year, then a load of personal shit happened, and I ended up back at the first agency. I also had immigration issues and Sandy, my old boss, had said she would sponsor me, so that all happened at the same time. It was the mid '90s, and that's when AIDS was…

I like imagery that doesn't age, that's timeless. I also think it's an interesting challenge when shooting fashion, to create an image that's timeless, something that lasts through the decades. That's always the goal.

I mean, the city was exciting, and it was New York, but I was terrified. I was terrified of AIDS. Nobody really knew how it was contracted. I knew some people who had become ill. By 1994, '95, I had found a group of friends who I really connected with – but they slowly became ill and died. That was a really horrific time for me. In those same years, in '95 – I think it was in one year – my boss, the beloved boss who had worked in *GQ*, he died; my dentist died and my doctor died.

I hit a freaking low. I mean, they were hideous deaths, too. It was really awful. When your best pal suddenly gets a Kaposi's sarcoma spot, which is a cancer, and then it leads to more and more, and then wasting syndrome, and then just a horrific death…

On top of this, there was the bigotry, and people not being kind. That was a very difficult time. I hit rock bottom and got myself to a therapist, and went on antidepressants because I was in the darkest of places. Then, one day, the therapist and I talked about creativity, and he said, 'Creativity can be a healing thing, you know'. Even though I was going to group therapy, and I was on antidepressants, and I was going to individual therapy. I needed that much help.

I had never experienced loss like that. You become scared of your own existence. I didn't even want anyone to touch me. So then, it was that one line that [my therapist] said: 'Creativity can be a healing thing'. I perked up, and the following day, I picked up my camera.

I had taken a basic photo class at Parsons, which was required. Then I took some pictures out at the beach, of my friends. The contact sheets ended up on the desk at the ad agency, and the creative director walked over and she said, 'Whose are these?' And I was like, 'They're mine'. She said, 'Those are your pictures?' I'm like, 'Yeah'. She said, 'Come here'. And she hugged me, and she said, 'They're beautiful'. And I was like, 'Really?' And she said, 'Why don't you try shooting something for us?' That's the way the whole thing started. I began to do tests for ad campaigns, so we would use them to show an idea. I was in my late 20s, early 30s.

CM:

Did you find yourself going in at the deep end? Or were the tests a really great way for you to play and figure things out?

RP:

It happened quickly, because the tests were liked so much, they ended up using them. They didn't use the other photographers they had spent a huge amount of money on, down in Santa Fe. I happened to be in the room when the owner of the brand Ralph Lauren, looked through the pile of C-prints and pulled out a print and was like, 'It's this one'. He turned it around, and it was mine.

I remember leaving that meeting and it was winter in New York. The [UNICEF crystal] Snowflake was there at 57th and 5th, and I remember going late at night, walking home and thinking 10 days earlier I'd had this conversation with the therapist, now this was happening. Suddenly, I had a picture that was running in *American Folk*, *The New York Times*, all these different—

CM:

There must've been someone watching over you.

RP:

You're right, Charles. I walked out of there going, 'What the fuck just happened?'

CM:

Did that push into creativity lift you out of that hole?

RP:

Yeah, completely. 100%. It forced me to see beauty again.

CM:

Did you continue to work with Ralph Lauren?

RP:

I did, but then it got political, and of course I didn't have the right visa for that kind of job. It's funny when we all have these personal shifts that happen. Sometimes, other people around you aren't so encouraging of the shift. I ran into some disappointments and challenges; friends suddenly were not so supportive. But I got my visa within the next year, and off I went on my own.

CM:

Was there a point with photography when you felt like you knew it, and had confidence?

RP:

It was more like, 'Wow, there's healing power to this,' or, 'This is what I'm meant to do,' or, 'It never bores me.'

CM:

How do you approach a photo shoot?

RP:

I don't sketch or anything like that, but I do think of the elements I'm going to put in there. I'm trying to think of what elements can I put in there to make it a more interesting picture, or to bring more humanity to the picture. I do think about that, but I don't plan, I don't draw it out.

I always see picture taking as having a beginning, a middle and an end. Where you're searching, you're on this internal path towards finding that moment where everything collides and combines to become this magical thing in imagery. When it happens, I physically feel it in my body. I *feel* it. When you're shooting, and you can feel it, and it's happening, it's such a moment of joy.

CM:

Do you have a favourite subject?

RP:

My favourite is portraiture and fashion. I like imagery that doesn't age, that's timeless. I also think it's an interesting challenge when shooting fashion, to create an image that's timeless, something that lasts through the decades. That's always the goal. How to make fashion not really look like fashion, in a sense.

CM:

Do you prefer working in women's fashion?

RP:

I do more women's fashion at the moment, but that's just the way the business goes. In the beginning I only did men. Then portraiture – whether it's of an animal or a human, it brings me a lot of joy.

CM:

Does your kit matter to you?

RP:

As long as it works. I'm not a techie; I don't get off on looking at cameras. I do love my film cameras, and I do love my Mamiya RZ. But I had to switch to digital, you know? It was just required, so I had someone help me through that transitional period. You put that image from the film beside an image shot in digital, and it's not a heck of a difference. You know?

CM:

What do you think about the current state of the industry?

RP:

There's so much to be said, but I'm just grateful that

I'm still taking pictures. I'm still wanted, and needed, and desired to take pictures. So, because I've been doing this a couple decades now, I feel grateful. But I also believe our business has changed dramatically in that people need...

We hear it all the time. 'We need our assets.' They need stuff. They need their shit. And they just need imagery. [...] In the past, we really tried to focus on creating something special for an ad campaign, something iconic. With digital, the path shifted, and I think there's... I don't think there's as much care that's taken in taking pictures now.

Everything is so fast. I think about Avedon, who used to do three pictures a day. On a good editorial job with a great fashion magazine, you can do 15 to 17 looks in a day. And you're not just documenting looks; you're trying to create an image.

CM:

Do you have any major photographic influencers now, who you admire?

RP:

I like the greats: Horst, Cecil Beaton, Edward Steichen, Penn and other ones like Herbert List. I love all of those.

Anyone alive? [...] Annie Leibovitz. I respond to her images. Nick Knight does great imagery. Tim Walker has got a great point of view. There are many I admire. I tend to be more inspired by the guys from the past, or from paintings. I look at Caravaggio, I look at any of the Dutch guys.

CM:

Would you say your lighting in your photographs is very similar to painting?

RP:

Yeah – the one light source. I like to get inspired by the light. If I take a picture of you and I put you near the window, I can shape the light and see it, do interesting things and get inspired by it. But when you're doing strobe, it's a free-for-all. You set it out so maybe you can get inspired a little bit, and then you just go for it. Who knows what you're going to get? But I really get inspired by the way the light rolls across a face, or doesn't roll across a face. I'm into that.

You can't unsee things.

CM:

At what point did you find the dogs?

RP:

It came out of a need to take a picture that did more than sell clothes. It came out of a need for a picture that did more than promote someone's career, which is basically what I, we, do. And I'm grateful I can make a living doing that, selling product. But I think I'm fascinated by the power of pictures and the power of photography, and what a wonderful thing if I can take a picture that lessens some suffering on the planet?

So, I thought, 'How can I do that?' I did a project in Romania from 2001 to 2009. We photographed HIV-infected kids, mostly orphans. We helped a group of kids down there, and helped raise a lot of money. They were all infected through needless blood transfusions because of this guy named [Nicolae] Ceaușescu. They called it a medical accident. Other people call it a horror show. I photographed all these kids, and that was an incredibly moving time. But the problem was, if the child was alive... I thought we could use these photographs as a way to promote the cause.

CM:

You couldn't use the photos?

RP:

No, because they're alive and the state has the rights to them, because they're an orphan. But if any of them had died, which most of them did, I could use those photographs. Those pictures started it, and then that crisis ended, and we closed down that NGO, but we did raise hundreds of thousands of dollars for them, me and my friends.

CM:

When you're dealing with a subject like that, does it follow you around for a long time?

RP:

Being a sensitive human is a blessing and a curse, you know? It sticks with you, that shit. Us artists are the creatives, the sensitive ones, and you really... you can't unsee things.

I remember we drove up into this village where nothing had changed in, it seemed like, hundreds of years. We were dropping off medication and rice and a chicken to the family, and some toys, because they didn't have access to the city. We walked out to this cardboard shanty building, and there was a child covered in acne holding what appeared to be her brother. The child with the acne was the one who was HIV infected. We walked into their home, which smelled really funny, and there was just... it was the weirdest vibe in there. We found out that the baby she was holding was actually hers. She had been raped by her step-father.

It was her second child through the step-father. He was in jail, but she was there with her mother. And I thought, 'How did the step-father rape her...' [...] Twice. Who knows how many other times? Then, there's two dogs in the back that are tethered, and have no shelter, that are terrified of humans. A big pot of this stuff is boiling on the stove, bubbling away, and the ceiling is cardboard. It was pretty haunting stuff.

But the point is... I thought, I have this love of animals, and when I travel around the world with work, I saw the volume of suffering in the world of animals, and it was heart-breaking. Not only dogs and cats, but camels, donkeys, the whole thing. You try to do your bit when you're there by helping out or getting a vet. But I came back to New York, and thought, 'I wonder if there's a way I could do something here.' Long story short, I ended up contacting my local shelter, which I was friendly with, and then I started to do portraits of dogs in a little makeshift studio that we would create out of an examination room in the animal shelter.

We started to do that, and then it was pretty spontaneous. Suddenly, the shelter was getting way more traffic and more interest, and then Instagram came around and Facebook, and there's this amazing vehicle to spread all these beautiful portraits of these animals in need. So that's how it started. It's already been about eight years now.

CM:

Where do you see your work going forward?

RP:

It's interesting, because as long as I've been shooting, I don't even think I've taken my best pictures yet. I really don't. I still feel I have a lot to say and a lot to do.

CM:

You'll go until the eyesight starts to crumble?

RP:

Oh, for sure. I think us photographers don't ever stop or retire. To be a great photographer, you really need the passion. You need to love it, because it's not an easy business.

CM:

Does photography become a money game? Does that differ between Europe and New York?

RP:

There are more money-jobs in New York. But it's interesting. If you shoot for a magazine in the US, you could produce 18 amazing pages for them, and they'll say, 'Sorry, we can only do our eight, as we had originally thought.' Whereas, in Europe, if you give them 18 pages and they're only expecting 12, if they are of value they will make space for them.

[…] There are amazing times in Europe where often, I'll do a fashion story and then I'll lay it out in a pdf. I'll do actual layouts because I envision a story in a certain way when I'm shooting it. I'll then present the pdf and very often, the editor in chief will run it exactly as.

CM:

What stages do you go through when you get a job?

RP:

You're normally briefed by the client. You're given your restrictions and your limitations and also the objective. What is the objective of the job? If it's an advertising job or an editorial, what are we doing? Of course, in editorial, there's much more freedom and creativity, and there's more opportunity for new things to be discovered. But you follow a brief and then probably do a little bit of research on that. Then you go through meetings with all your colleagues, you present your ideas and you collaborate, trying to sort it out.

CM:

Do you work with a strong team?

RP:

You work with a group of people that you like, and you're always open to introducing new people. But it's about finding people who have a similar aesthetic to you, or who understand that we're creating a photograph together. It's not about the hair person's hair, or the makeup person's makeup; it's about the photograph. You have to find those people who are really into the photograph.

CM:

Would you like to add anything?

RP:

I think an important part of my story, which is helpful for people to know, is that had I not gone through all that suffering and loss I don't think I would be where I am. […] The point is, good things can come out of great suffering.

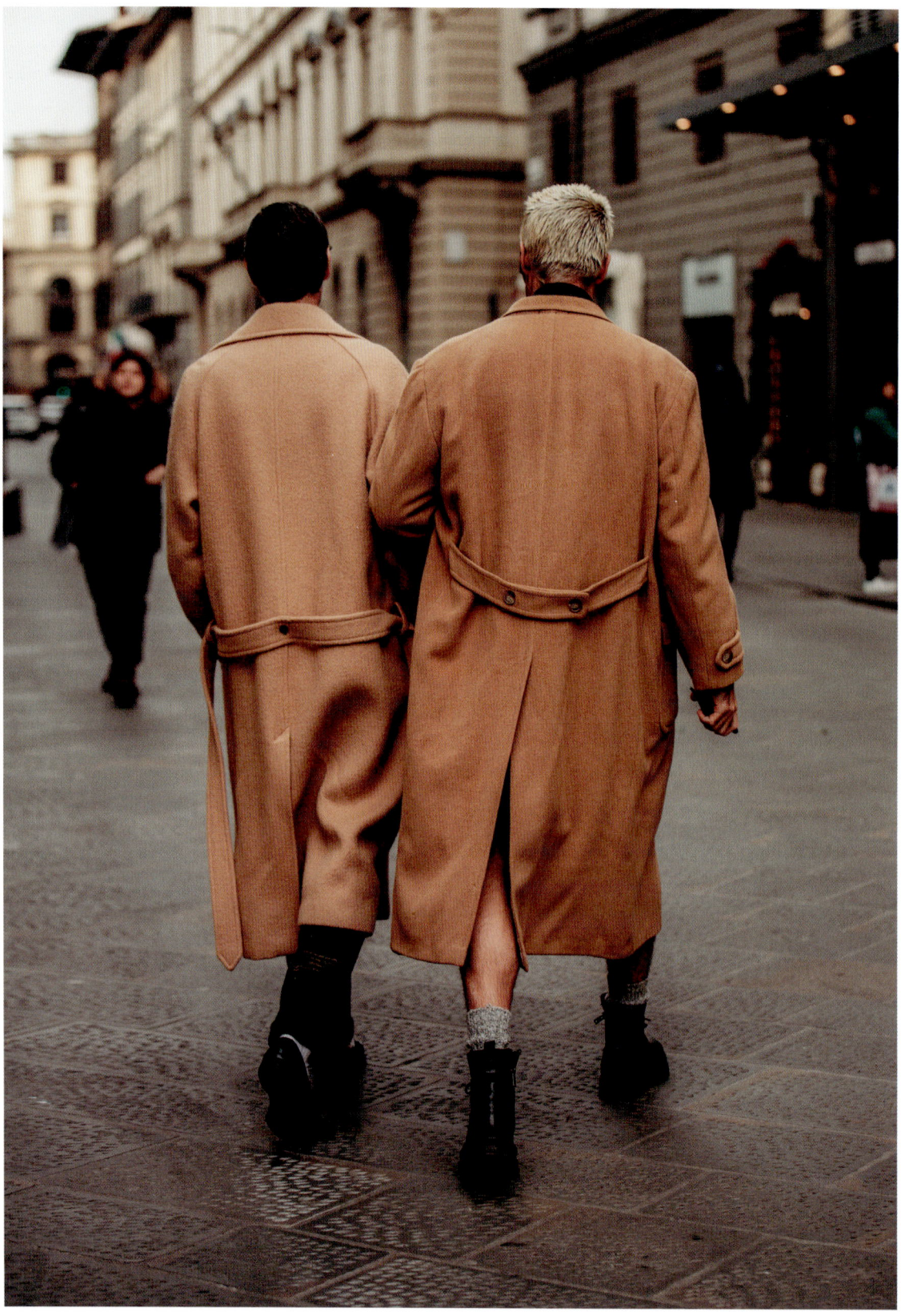

JONATHAN DANIEL PRYCE

On August 7, 2019, I had lunch in Canary Wharf with Scotsman Jonathan Daniel Pryce, aka '@GarconJon', the famous street photographer. More recently known for his continued work with *Vogue*, Pryce was thrown into the global limelight with his first book, *100 Beards*. We talked about fashion, art, Instagram and the ever-changing world of photography.

Jonathan Daniel Pryce, Camel Coat Florence, February 2020
© Jonathan Daniel Pryce

Charles Moriarty:

Please introduce yourself.

Jonathan Daniel Pryce:

I'm 31 years old. I am originally from a village called Kilmacolm in Scotland, but I guess it's more easily remembered as Glasgow.

CM:

What are your photography roots?

JDP:

I remember my first camera. I was about seven or eight when I found it in a charity shop on a family holiday. It was a little red 35mm point-and-shoot. It was actually a panoramic camera, which I didn't realise. We'd take it to the pharmacy to develop the film and all the pictures would come back with a black band across the top and the bottom. It would be a 6x4 print, so there were these cropped-in images, which I always found quite annoying. It's funny to look back on that time with the knowledge I have now.

I also remember my early interest in imagery and pictures. My mum did a college course in photography when she was about the same age, and she also, somehow, blagged herself a part-time job as a photographer for the new-born babies at the local hospital. She had camera equipment in the house, and I remember her going to learn about darkrooms, and she had paper in the house. She told me that you couldn't take it out of the box in case it got exposed. So, I have memories of photography as a process and a thing that people did. I don't think I ever grasped that it was a job people did seriously, other than my mum doing the baby pictures, which I don't think I even perceived as a proper job.

CM:

Outside of baby pictures and misunderstood panorama, what were you first exposed to from outside the home?

JDP:

Imagery from music. Mum and dad had a record collection that we would go through, and I would just look at the photographs. I really strongly remember The Beatles' *Help!*, with the white background and them doing this sign language, body language thing, with the airplane symbols spelling out 'help'. I asked my parents about what they were wearing and what they were doing. And it just... It is really strong in my head, the idea of the images telling a story. Same with the Paul Weller CD we had. We only really had two or three CDs in that time. It was like, the mid-'90s, and we didn't have much money, so we didn't have a CD player till, you know, way after everyone else had CD players. I just remember looking at the artwork and spending an unusual amount of time looking at the photographs.

My mum had also been given a couple of photo books. She had two about Marilyn Monroe, one of them being the Bert Stern last shoot — *The Last Sitting*, I think it was called – and another one, which was more like an overall view of Marilyn's career. I loved looking at those. I remember finding it amazing that this woman had all these outfits and looked different in each of the pictures. I wanted to know who she was, and why she was doing what she was doing.

CM:

When did you move from being interested in images to realising you could be taking them?

JDP:

When I was about 10, I entered a photography competition for my local village. I took photos in my garden of the river and stuff. It was in the middle of the country, so there wasn't much to photograph other than nature. Surprisingly, I don't remember being particularly inspired by it. I was always more interested in drawing than using my camera, but I guess it had some impact on me.

Then in high school, it was the same thing. I was really into art and I'd spend a lot of lunchtimes in the art department, drawing and stuff. It wasn't until I was maybe 17 when I started to see photography as an interesting medium. That came from being a teenager and getting into magazines, when you begin to experience the world through pop culture. I remember seeing *i-D* for the first time. I was captivated by certain photographs, but also the fashion and the world outside of my own existence.

CM:

At what point did this fascination turn into your own experience?

JDP:

I remember the first shoot I ever did was with a girl I'd met while studying abroad for my degree in NY. As soon as I saw her, I thought she looked like she'd stepped out of *Dynasty*. I had recently bought this book by Guy Bourdin, and I'd never seen his work before. It had this really '70s American feel... or I guess, not all that American, but there were some New York shots in the book. And then I saw this girl and I thought, 'Oh, I want to try and recreate this.'

Of course, nowhere near did I recreate the shot.

But I went to a thrift store and bought a fur coat. It was the first shoot where I'd used studio lights, shot it and developed it myself in the darkroom. It was a full circle moment of realising that you can create something from nothing.

There's also something really magical about being that age, a teenager. There's an excitement around what is possible. Nowadays, I know the limitations of doing certain things. The anticipation of *doing something* gets caught up with the finer details and the annoyance of logistics, whereas at that point, I was just like, 'Let's try it.'

CM:

Talk to me about being an outsider for the first time in a new city, in a new place.

JDP:

There was a real benefit to choosing America as my year abroad, because they love British people and they're quite positive from the offset. Sometimes in the UK there's a suspicion around you if you approach someone on the street to ask him or her for a photograph. They would be thinking, 'Why are you asking me? And what do you actually want?' Whereas in America I always felt like they were just down for it. 'Let's try it. Cool. Okay.'

Even if you're busy and you're in a rush, the rejection wouldn't feel as cutting because I wasn't from there. And so, coming from the city of Glasgow, which also was a very friendly city – despite what I said about British culture, there are positive cities like Glasgow... I'd gone to university at 17 and had all of these really great experiences, going clubbing and making friends very quickly and people just being open to you and the situation. So I came with this idea that, 'No' was not going to be an answer. That people were going to be open to me asking for a photo, asking for help on a project or whatever it was. And that, I think, is really conducive to creativity and ideas and just experimenting.

CM:

What happened when you got back to Scotland?

JDP:

I was studying marketing in Glasgow. I had always been creative, but my dad had said a good business school is a lot more stable, and he was right. I have since thought it would have been nice to actually go to art school, to have the space to just think creatively. But now, as a business owner – which you are when you do any kind of art – it has helped me. So, going back to Scotland, I was very focused on doing well in my degree and I really wanted to get a first.

In order to do that and keep my mind stimulated – marketing is not the most interesting topic – I wove in photography, or fashion, or art; just some sort of interest into my dissertation or coursework. I think that helped a lot, because there was no one else on the course doing that. I was handing in these quite interesting-to-read pieces of work. I was taking more unusual examples of marketing and branding in a different world, so I did get a first degree, and I was very happy.

[…] Twelve years have gone by. Right after I finished, I realised I didn't want to go and do what all my friends were doing, which was either going for graduate positions in big firms or working in an agency. So I started a blog, which was called Le Garçons de Glasgow, because of the famous artist group, The Glasgow Boys. When I was in America, if anyone had ever heard of Glasgow, a response I got frequently was, 'Oh my God, isn't Glasgow dangerous?' So I really wanted to show Glasgow off as the creative and musical place I knew it to be.

I started the blog with my best friend. We covered clubbing and nightlife, and shot people in the club and did street style. This was in 2008, 2009. Blogging was this exciting new thing, which felt very grassroots. You had a lot of community.

CM:

Was that when you first started creatively placing photography alongside your writing?

JDP:

Yeah, I guess so, but I didn't think about it so strategically. I just knew there was this new thing that was starting to explode. I had been to this tutorial with Scott Schuman, who had done an exhibition, his first exhibition, with dozens of galleries in Chelsea and New York in – I think – 2008. I had just started following his blog and thought, 'Oh, this is a cool thing.' With street style, I didn't really know much about it in terms of a blogging format. I thought I'd go to this gallery and speak to him and see what he said, see what his opinion of it was. I went and there was a queue around the block, and I was like, 'Whoa.'

I got in the door but you couldn't get anywhere near him. I thought, 'This is huge.' That was a real moment of realisation about how blogging and the Internet can touch people. There were blogs where people were becoming names or going to these cool clubs in Paris and London and taking nightclub photography, and people would go on the next week and see if their photos had been uploaded.

It was all a part of this 'culture of online'. So that was me at 20-21, just caught up in the wave of the

Internet. About three months into Le Garçons de Glasgow, we started a Facebook fan page, which was the only real format to [offer that]. I think Twitter had maybe just started or was just about to start. [...] We had a Facebook fan page and we gained five or six thousand followers in a few months. That was huge to me then, and even now I think that's a pretty big deal. It became a thing.

I remember a friend who I used to photograph quite a lot. Glasgow is slim pickings, as there's a small population and not a lot of fresh blood like in bigger cities. So the same people would crop up time and again on this blog and become a face. This friend called Stevie – who was about 17 at the time – was quite extreme in his style. He would change up a lot and he would dye his hair so he looked quite different every week. He went to T in the Park, which is the Scottish equivalent of Glastonbury, and came back saying that a bunch of chaps shouted at him, 'Oh Garçon de Glasgow, what's going on?' You know, sort of making fun of him – but also the fact that they were aware of it [meant it] felt like this was real.

CM:

You were being heard by the average Glaswegian.

JDP:

Totally.

CM:

Do you remember the first time you took a photograph and thought, 'Yes'?

JDP:

I do. And it was for the blog actually. And it's funny because now I look at these early photos and think, 'I can't believe I loved that photo so much.'

I'd stopped these two guys who looked so fucking cool. The coolest guys I had ever seen in

my life because I was green, really green. They did look cool but at that time it was monumental for me. They were in a band called Local Natives – I think they might actually still be together and touring – but they were in Glasgow for a gig.

It's a photo of two people standing very straight. They were about the same height and they were dressed vintage style, which was cool, but looked really relatable. Something about it felt controversial, but it's just two guys standing side by side, looking to the camera. It's an okay photo. It was a time when I was starting to do digital photography; I was learning how to use the camera and how to get a certain effect.

I really wanted to show Glasgow off as the creative and musical place I knew it to be.

CM:

Do you have a preference now between digital and film?

JDP:

If I was to do personal work, it would always be film because, as you know, you shoot in such a different way depending on the camera, the lens. I feel much more connected and present doing film. With digital, I know when I've got the shot, but with one set up I'm taking 20 frames, whereas with film I'll do two. […] So I enjoy film more, definitely.

CM:

At that point in Glasgow, were you looking at other photographers' work? Who inspired you? Who were your teachers?

JDP:

It has been quite a journey. I started it 13 years ago and I take things really seriously. In the early days, I was absorbing as much about photography as I could. I would be looking at all sorts of photographers. Then, when I started the blog, I really did get into street photography a lot. I would be looking at what the other 'street style' – quote, unquote – photographers were doing. They were Tommy Ton, doing Jak&Jil, Scott Schuman, who was doing The Sartorialist… Even Yvan Rodic, who was doing FaceHunter. And then a bit later on it was Adam Katz Sinding, who did Le 21ème.

Those were the big boys in my mind and that was maybe the first year I was doing it. I was super into them; I would read their blogs and try to emulate their work, try and get the lighting that they got. After that first year, I decided to start shooting fashion weeks. I think when you do it yourself, the magic goes because you realise the reality of what is entailed. So, for example, when I was looking at Scott's work… I used to think he was doing what Steve McCurry was doing: walking around Florence and seeing all these amazing people in cafés and having these experiences.

Now I realise it's so concentrated, and these are old-fashioned people. That's why they dress well. There's a bit of jadedness that comes with it, where you know half of them are specially dressed. So, it's not that amazing that they look so impeccable, because they just got given [the clothes] that morning. The magic of finding a moment is gone, because it's complicit. They are complicit in the scenario of wanting to have the publicity of being photographed. So, the magic left a me a little bit after certain fashion weeks. I still love street photography, but it would be more like Garry Winogrand, or something more classical that looks at a historical time or culture, rather than anything to do with fashion.

CM:

When and how did 100 Beards come along?

JDP:

That was in 2012. I had just moved to London and I was starting to feel that the fashion street stuff was not nurturing my soul creatively. But there was a lot of work in that; everyone was talking about street style. Every magazine wanted a street style section on their website and every clothing brand wanted a street style look to their images. So I was getting a lot of jobs, but it was boring.

I wanted to do something that people would still know me for. I wanted it to have the immediacy of doing street style, but not be about clothes. I was thinking it has to be some kind of character trait … I also felt like female street style and female fashion was so dominant. You'd see a million photographs of a woman in nice clothes. But there were far fewer of men. It was around that time when I started to think, I'd like to pursue looking at either men's fashion or creatively try and do something around men.

It was February 2012 and I thought, 'I should do something about facial hair. It's becoming really popular.' And then by May I still hadn't done anything, and I thought, 'Fucking hell. Why have you not started it? It's easy. You just go out and fucking start shooting; just do it, do it, do it.' So, it was the 31 of May and I set up a Tumblr and I thought, 'I need to put a finite date on this or I could just keep shooting forever. So make it a hundred, do it for a hundred days, do a Tumblr blog, do it every day for a hundred days and it will be easy. Even if nobody sees it, it's fine. It doesn't matter.'

On the first of June, I went out and took my first picture. By 20 days in, I stopped someone in Soho, London, and I said, 'Oh hi, you look great. I'd love to photograph you. I'm doing this project, 100 Beards.' And he said, 'Oh yeah, cool man. I love 100 Beards.' And I was thinking, 'I've only been doing it for 20 days. How do you love 100 Beards? It's so new. How do you know about this thing?' But I also thought maybe he was bullshitting me.

Ten more days passed and a few more people would say it. And I was like, 'Oh, people are really seeing this.' In Tumblr you have stats and you can see how many subscribers you have. But you know, I never thought I could replicate that feeling of what I had with Le Garçons de Glasgow. London felt so huge and I didn't think I could tackle it, but actually it was great timing. It was the right time and the right place. I happened to hit the cycle when beards were highly searched for online. Everyone loved it, but no one was creating content around it. So I was posting all these beard photographs and there were both girls looking for hot guys, pictures of hot guys with beards, and guys looking for beard inspiration.

CM:

It was also that time when Tumblr was still this enormous publicity machine. The access to imagery was phenomenal and with Tumblr you had the power to send a photo you uploaded everywhere. We now have Instagram, but it works very differently. I'd go so far as to say it doesn't work as well for the individual.

JDP:

You're right, 100%. With Instagram, yes, you can share other people's work and sometimes that happens. But because of the reblog functionality of Tumblr, within 10 or 15 days of starting, I would be looking at it and one of the photographs would have 10,000 reblogs because someone who had a lot of followers on their Tumblr would have reblogged it and it would be exposed to this whole new audience. It was a spiral effect.

By maybe 60 or 70 days in, Jeremy Paxman wore a beard on *Newsnight*. BBC Radio One were talking about beards and did this tongue-in-cheek piece about beards being really popular, even on Jeremy Paxman. They mentioned 100 Beards on it. I was getting all these tweets saying, 'Oh my God, Radio One just talked about you.' Then *Metro* wrote about it, followed by the *Evening Standard*, and *The New York Times*. I thought, 'It was just this Zeitgeist thing, it was out of your control.'

CM:

At the same time, it must have been a great moment personally. Was it validation for moving to London?

JDP:

Totally, you're so right. In London, there were a lot of challenges, and at that point a lot of money was being put into digital media without knowing what it would really do... [without knowing] why or who was connecting, or what it meant for brands. So, it would lead to unsuspecting things — like, Urban Outfitters would want to see how they could make their website more social. They would approach me, because they had seen 100 Beards, and say, 'You know, we want to put a blog on our website, would you create content for that?' It was very exciting, and I was walking a line between street and corporate work for brands.

CM:

Was that photography giving you creative joy? Or was there something else that you were shooting that connected to you on a more personal level?

JDP:

100 Beards, even though it was seemingly quite commercial looking and very mass market, mass appeal – that doesn't detract from the fact that I love people. That's the number one thing about doing this job for me, and I loved meeting a different person every day and having even a five-minute conversation. And then the validation beyond that, you know.

One of my favourite photo moments ever is when I stopped a man who was maybe in his '60s at the naval college in Greenwich. He had a long white beard, so I photographed him and emailed him the photo. And then a few months later he told me that his mum was terminally ill at that point, and that she hadn't smiled for months until he showed her the photo. It was the last time she smiled with him before she passed away. That's so heavy, and that's the power of photography.

Is it my best photo? No. Does that matter? No. The point for me was that I had created work that meant something to someone. Even if it's just those two people in that room, you know?

That's the really lovely side of doing that kind of project. I loved that. Artistically speaking, was I being fulfilled? Not necessarily. I spent the next three or four years after that doing all these jobs and being a workaholic. I just took on any job that came, obviously not publicising everything I was doing, but running on the treadmill. In 2018, I started to think, 'I'm just churning out all these images and contributing to this world of too many images, which has devalued what a photograph is.' I thought, 'do I really want to contribute to that?' I decided I didn't, so I took a little step back.

I was a bit more selective with the work I was doing. Then within that period, I was approached to do my new book, *Garçon Style*, which would in a way act as a retrospective. They'd asked me to do a men's stylebook of street photography I'd shot for *Vogue* over the past few years, so it was a nice time to start reflecting.

CM:

Are you coming to an end with the fashion and street style stuff? What do you think will motivate you over the next five to 10 years in photography?

JDP:

A very good question. There is a shift happening, culturally, not just in my world. Street style is now a totally different beast and I have just had to accept the beast for what it is. It is now a very corporate venture, especially in women's wear. [...] I mean, 99% of the people are paid to be there, or are wearing something which will have some monetary value attached to it. It's not like in 2007, where it was someone who just had this really unusual, interesting style and you were documenting it.

But I am lucky: four times out of the year, four months out of the year, I'm going to these interesting cities and I have pretty much free reign. The client just says 'go out and shoot', and I just send them a batch of images every day and then they're posted. So it's a good job to have. It's a nice job to have. Most of my energy and focus though, is on the work outside that experience.

I'm trying to focus on personal work. There are two things I'm working on. One project is about body image, specifically about male body image. I don't think it's a new conversation, but with men it's a broader spectrum of something that's still not really spoken about. I was also thinking, 'What would make me learn something about myself in the process?' I think for someone else looking at me, they would think I'm just an average looking person who is slim, and yet I quite frequently feel fat and ugly. It's something that crosses my mind at least once a week.

Street style is now a totally different beast and I have just had to accept the beast for what it is.

I don't want to be vain enough for that to be a thought in my head, number one. I also don't want to have those thoughts anymore. I think it's silly, so I want to do something that might help other people and also help myself in the process.

CM:

When you started doing street style in 2008,

everything was a lot more spontaneous in fashion. Do you think the evolution of the image through sites like Instagram, etcetera, has changed how people behave within society, how they dress, and how they interact with you, with cameras?

JDP:

That reminds me of this conversation that was being had, maybe up to about 2015, when in an interview someone would ask about how street style has changed people's way of dressing and street style blogs. Now that's almost exclusively been taken over by the Instagram outfit of the day, or an Instagram account where it's all photos of one person that you follow because you like their style and you're inspired by them. The content is aggregated into one feed.

Maybe this is actually just nostalgia and we all think [the past] was a simpler time, no matter how far back. Because 2007 was hardly like it was in 1950, but [...] people are a lot more self-aware now.

I wonder sometimes how 15 year olds get their money, because if I look at a 15 year old that I would've seen on the streets when I was maybe 20, I could see they were borrowing their big brother's jumper and wearing a charity shop item of clothing. Now they're wearing Supreme and a Louis Vuitton collaboration and trainers that are so expensive, and I think, 'How, how?'

CM:

We live in the world of Instagram and the influencer. How do you feel about all of that?

JDP:

It's to be expected. If someone had asked, I would have predicted that this was how it was going to go down. The sad side is, before it I remember you would comment on other people's blogs and you would find them because they had this really interesting point of view. There would be some girl living in Ohio who couldn't fit in any clothes that Forever 21 sold, so she'd make her own clothes at home and post an outfit of the day because she was plus size – or Tavi [Gevinson], that girl who was 12 and had a style blog. She ended up being accepted in the fashion world by being invited to shows and stuff. There was a real grassroots feeling to it.

Now, you're 13 and you know who Margiela is, and you know a reference because you're so overfed with stimuli, you don't have to go to a book to find it. So, the jaded side of me says it's a shame because the learning curve is not the same and also, you are aware that you can make money doing this thing. Especially if you're good looking, which is the downside in the conversation. There's not much of a look in for the girl in Ohio. The real winners of this scenario are the…

CM:

Good-looking people?

JDP:

Yeah. If you're a guy with a six pack and broad shoulders who looks great getting out of the water on a beach, you're a success. You don't need to have great style.

CM:

What's your relationship to your work and photography like now?

JDP:

The more I learn about myself and about photography… Because I'm learning constantly, I'm still not happy with things I did last month. I try to push myself forward, and then on the art level – and the 'creative saboteur' level that we all have, as crazy

people – it is, 'How can I get over my own insecurity in order to start doing stuff I really want to do?'

CM:

I think anyone who would consider themselves in any way a creative is their own worst enemy, most of the time. Is there anyone who's on your mind these days, inspiring you to create?

JDP:

I photographed Nadav Kander recently, which was a mad experience. The most nerve-wracking thing I've ever done. And you know, obviously, my photography style is not anywhere near the calibre of his. But it is amazing seeing his studio and getting to humanise a process. Having seen his work, and then seeing that he's just a human being… It was such a great experience.

I saw the Stephen Shore exhibition in New York. It must've been a year ago, in summer or something. I love what he does. And there's a guy my age in New York called Ryan Pfluger. […] I love his narrative and his transparency [regarding] the queer world; it feels so human. It's just very personal, and that's something I feel I struggle with.

CM:

Connecting to yourself?

JDP:

Yeah, and making sure that I'm making work that actually says something about me, because I think for a long time I've hidden behind brand work or just done some job, and it's not necessarily me. I don't know, I guess I'm figuring out what that is.

CM:

Why is photography important?

JDP:

I actually think it matters now more than ever,

because it's the way most people communicate. Even if you think about a text, an emoji isn't a photo, but it's an image, and people think in images now a lot more than they ever have. We also need to make [photography] physically real, by printing the good stuff and sharing it.

I think [photography is] how we understand the world, and I'm not actually a photo snob. I think you can take a brilliant photo on an iPhone or whatever; it doesn't have to be a Hasselblad. Photographs can be important when at the scene of an event. [...] If you think about things like police brutality, photos and video are proof of reality in America at the moment, so you know people with badges aren't necessarily following the law. We wouldn't have that without the use of photo equipment.

How can I get over my own insecurity in order to start doing stuff I really want to do?

CM:

What are you shooting on these days?

JDP:

I use mainly Pentax 645, which is the meter for my film camera. I still use my Canon 5D Mark III a lot. For fashion week that's the main thing I use, and I often carry around a point-and-shoot camera. I've got two. I use a Contax T3 and a Yashica G3.

About a year ago, I got a Polaroid 600SE. That's the one that comes with ZEISS lenses. You need to change lenses, and that's just so much fun to use. But I'm so, so strict with myself in using the film, because I have expired film in my fridge. It's so expensive to get.

CM:

If you could have any photograph on your wall, no matter the price, is there one that's always spoken to you or that you connect to?

JDP:

The ones that stick in my mind most are of my mum. She was trying to make it as a singer in the '70s and she had these photos taken of her. She was probably about 18 or 19, and I don't even know where those photos are. Mum tends to just get rid of things, doesn't even think. So, she's probably gotten rid of them. I think I'd like one of those photos. She was in Hyde Park. She's from London, so it was like this tie-in before I moved here, to this city I've never been to. A picture of my Mum in Hyde Park at 18, fresh and starting out life. If I could find that photo, I would want that.

CM:

If you could say anything to someone who's looking to get into photography, what would it be?

JDP:

Don't add to the noise. Try and figure out what makes your voice special. Buy a camera from eBay; I probably spent $10 on this little film camera. It's the best thing to do. The gap between taking a film picture and then having it developed, especially if you don't develop your own, gives your brain the space to breathe. And I think it's a really great way of learning. So, yeah; get a film camera and try and figure out what it is you have to say.

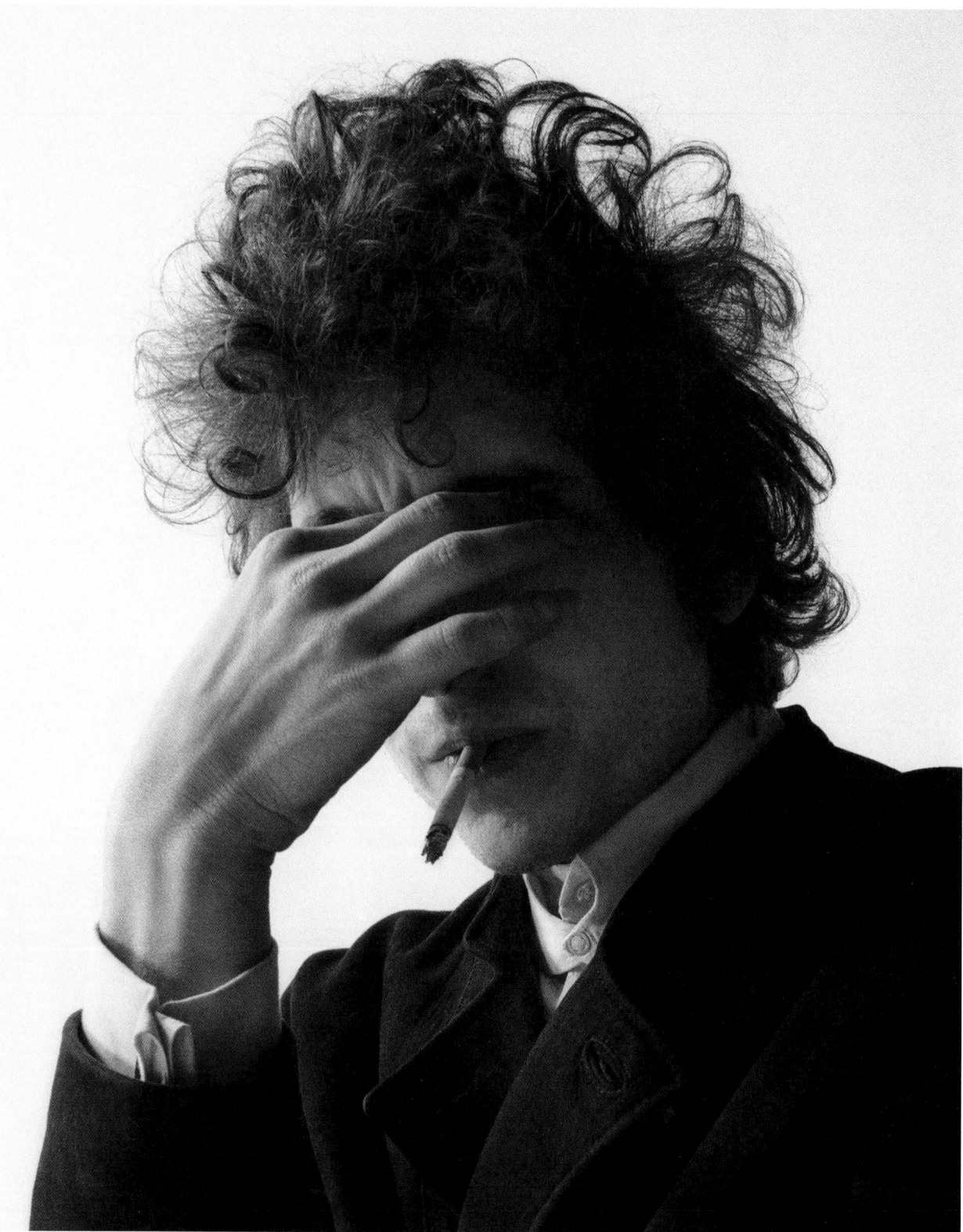

JERRY SCHATZBERG

I met Jerry Schatzberg at his apartment, close to Central Park in New York City, in the winter of 2019. We sat for an hour and delved into his long, illustrious photography career. I didn't even get to his films. Jerry is still full of energy and continues to take pictures into his 90s. He is famed for his work with Bob Dylan, but I find myself more often caught up in his fashion photographs, with their sweeping New York street scenes and the intimate moments he captured in the back of big American cars.

Jerry Schatzberg, Bob Dylan Covers His Eyes, New York, December 1965
© Jerry Schatzberg/Getty Images

Charles Moriarty:

Your family were furriers in the Bronx – how did you discover photography?

Jerry Shatzberg:

I really found it after I was an assistant to somebody, between 1954, or '55. I took a good job with Bill Hepburn and I was lucky to get that job because I really knew nothing about photography. I just answered an ad I saw. It was a way of getting away from the family business, which I hated. I didn't really know what photography entailed. I explained my situation to a head-hunter, and he laughed and said, 'Well, come in, I'll see what I can do for you.' I was about 24.

I was working with Bill and he was fantastic. I liked his personality. I liked his attitude. It was great, and we'd work sometimes late into the night, but as long as we'd do his work, he'd let us work in the studio at night. That's how I started doing tests. It was through that process that I became a photographer, because I worked for him for two and a half years, photographing almost every girl who came into New York to work. It was good for them and it was good for me. [Bill] was a commercial photographer, a fashion photographer. He did very interesting commercial work.

CM:

How soon did you move from assisting to picking up the camera yourself?

JS:

I started to experiment because I had nothing to lose. It wasn't good. You throw it away, you know? It was a good way to start and a good way to work with the camera at that time. All Bill's commercial work was done on an 8x10 Deardorff or a 4x5. He almost fired me in the first three weeks, because I wasn't very adept at using the cameras and changing the negatives. But his stylist talked him into giving me another shot at it, and after two and a half years, he offered me a piece of the business. Only when I told him I was leaving, of course.

CM:

Did you stay?

JS:

Yeah. Maybe six months after I left Bill, I took my portfolio up to [Alexander] Liberman at *Vogue*, and he gave me an assignment.

CM:

Good timing and portfolio I guess.

JS:

All from just experimenting and working with the girls.

CM:

Was the 8x10 where your own work started?

JS:

I started with a Rolleiflex and then I got into Nikons. But when I started working, I bought an 8x10. The commercial people, they wanted 8x10.

CM:

They're beautiful pieces of machinery. Did you stick with Nikon throughout your career?

JS:

No. A friend of mine, an English photographer, came over and said, 'I've got this brand-new camera, it's so fantastic.' He went on and on, so I said, 'Well yeah, what is it?' 'It's called a Hasselblad. [...] It's really great. It's fast.' I said, 'What do you mean, it's fast?' 'It works so fast because when you finish a roll, you just take the roll off and put another one on.' I said, 'I do the same thing, but I take the camera off. I put another camera on.' He must've convinced me of something though, because when he went back to England I went and bought three

Hasselblads.

Then I worked mostly on Hasselblad, for my work. For my own personal photography it was Nikon, until just about a year ago, when I got into the Sony AR.

CM:

With the progression of digital, have you left film behind?

JS:

I'm not nostalgic. I'm not a technical person. I used to talk to somebody like Mary Ellen Mark who wouldn't change. She stayed there, and I'm sure she sees what she says she sees, but I don't. What I'm interested in is my subject. My subject is what I like; that's good enough for me. I don't care if the blacks come out like this or that, you know?

CM:

You're looking to make sure you have the moment, rather than anything else?

JS:

Yeah. Exactly.

CM:

When you worked with your subjects, was there a process you stuck to?

JS:

If I was doing a job for somebody and we had a purpose, a brief, then I'd stick to that as much as possible. Otherwise, I think the subject was always the most important thing to me.

CM:

You recently released a Bob Dylan book. How did working with him come about?

JS:

One of the models I was doing tests with kept talking to me about Dylan. I had heard of him, but I'd never listened to him. She was a Dylan nut. Then Nico from the Velvet Underground also started to

> In those days, you'd have six photographers working on an issue and every one of them was different. But you could tell who it was just by looking at the photographs, because everybody had their own style.

say, 'Dylan, listen to Dylan.' She kept bugging me. I said, 'Nico, next time you see me, I will be fully aware.' So, I started to listen to him, and I really got hooked. I was in my studio one day with a rock and roll journalist who was a good friend of Dylan's, I said, 'Hey, next time you see him, tell him I'd like to photograph him.' The next day, I get a call from his wife and she says, 'Bobby hears you want to photograph him.' I said, 'I'd love to.' So she said, 'Okay, he's recording at…' It was a Columbia studio.

His wife was the first model who was telling me about Dylan. She kept pursuing Dylan till she married him. I hadn't talked to her in about four or five years. She told me where he was recording, I went there, and I was greeted and welcomed. I had good references.

CM:

That would have been, what? Early '60s?

JS:

It was '65. I left Bill's in the late '50s.

CM:

Was there a specific focus with the subjects you photographed in the '60s?

JS:

No. I think, through the magazine and through my Dylan pictures, I started to get more musicians. When you work for a magazine like *Vogue* or *Glamour* or *Harper's Bazaar*, they always want to photograph the person who is happening. So, I started to get assignments in that area. I was doing a lot of fashion for *Vogue*, too.

Eventually I quit *Vogue* because *McCall's* was coming in with a whole new plan. I had a new art director, and they were coming out with some good photographs. I went to Liberman and I asked him, 'Would it be all right if I did some work for *McCall's*?' He said, 'No, it wouldn't be.' He wanted exclusivity. He didn't want anybody, any of his photographers working for anywhere else. I said, 'Oh.' And through the conversation, he said 'If you want space, I got space. But I'm not your psychiatrist.'

I thought about it, and then decided I wanted to try *McCall's*. I left *Vogue* and I went back to Condé Nast and worked for *Glamour* for a couple of years. But my days at *Vogue* were over.

CM:

Who inspired you?

JS:

The obvious New York photographer is Penn, but also Avedon. Louise Dahl-Wolfe – I liked her a lot. I didn't photograph like her. Well, you know, everybody has a different style. In those days, you'd have six photographers working on an issue and every one of them was different. But you could tell who it was just by looking at the photographs, because everybody had their own style.

CM:

What sort of style would you associate with your own work?

JS:

A lot of people say my photographs are very cinematic. I take that as a compliment because I like cinema and I like movement. I like what happens.

We copy all of [the people who influence us]. We study all of them and something comes out of it. It used to bother me that I copied. I talked to Liberman about that. He said that there's nothing wrong about copying people, so long as you copy good people and you copy them well, because eventually your own personality will take over.

CM:

Are there any particular shoots that stand out for you in your career?

JS:

Dylan, of course. You could just point the camera at him and you knew something was going to happen.

CM:

Was he a big performer?

JS:

He was for me. I think he probably was. When I look back at some of his sittings with other people, he liked to put it on.

CM:

Can you talk a little bit about how you approach your subject?

JS:

I liked controlling the situation. I didn't necessarily let them know what I was doing. I liked to surprise them – I might pick up a prop and throw it to them, just see what they did with it. I don't know how to describe what I do. I know I do a lot of research in my head for myself, and what I feel I want to get or try to get. I copy what I see in the streets. I like real people and what they do.

What I'm interested in is my subject. My subject is what I like; that's good enough for me. I don't care if the blacks come out like this or that, you know?

I've got a photograph that I love. It's of a woman, about 65. She was sitting on a park bench with a snake, a huge snake. She was holding it by the head, and next to her on the bench was a shopping bag. It said 'main course'. That was the shopping bag from Bloomingdale's, when you bought

something in the culinary shop. I loved finding that.

I did a lot of photographs of Peggy Moffitt. She used to photograph in all of [Rudi Gernreich's] clothes and he had really extreme clothes. She was a great model and I just loved photographing her because she was bizarre and the things she'd do were so unusual.

I've got a picture of her walking a chicken on a leash. That's the way I like to think. When I think of Off-Broadway I don't think of plays I'll see on Broadway, because it'd be a little different, a little more challenging, a little more bizarre. And I like to think I do that with my photographs.

CM:

When you started working in moving image, did photography take a back seat? Or did you continue to work in both mediums?

JS:

Once you're a photographer, you're always a photographer. You pretty much always have a camera, and now we're lucky enough to always have an iPhone that allows you to get images that you would never have gotten previously. I started off shooting colour on 8x10, and now I'm shooting with an iPhone. I walk down the street and I have no qualms about shooting something on an iPhone.

CM:

They're getting pretty good, now. Are there lessons you've learned that you would impart?

JS:

All I can say is, if you want to be a photographer, photograph. Get out there and photograph. The only way to find something new – or to find out what you don't like – is to do it and see it and not like it, and just go and try it again.

You don't always get the shot. I mean, if you walk the streets, I see no reason for a photographer not to be able to get a photograph. But it depends. If you say that you won't photograph rubbish in the streets – okay, so you miss out on that. But some people do photograph rubbish in the streets, and they get wonderful photos.

CM:

Similar to Penn and his cigarette butt?

JS:

It's funny you mentioned that, because I've been doing a series for myself, I guess, since the '90s. I photograph everything I see on the streets; I'll get down on my hands and knees. I don't move anything. I never move anything. I move me. I change the light by doing that. I was looking through Penn's official Instagram. I turned a couple of pages and I see him down on his hands and knees doing the same thing. Doing the same thing that I'm doing all the time.

So, there's nothing new. I've copied him or – not copied, but I've studied him through the years, and I look back. I've either learned from him or I've done things that are because of him.

CM:

Are there any images that have spoken to you?

JS:

[...] I'm sure there are thousands of them, but I don't...

CM:

You don't hold onto them in memory?

JS:

No. You ask me what I had for breakfast. I can't tell you. [...] I take it one at a time and I don't plan it. But, as I say, if I go out the on street, I'm just looking. Looking down or looking up, because most people when they're out, they don't look down, they don't

All I can say is, if you want to be a photographer, photograph. Get out there and photograph. The only way to find something new – or to find out what you don't like – is to do it and see it and not like it, and just go and try it again.

look up. They just look straight ahead or on the sides.

You see lots of things. They're still lifes, for the most part. What Penn did with the cigarettes, he took them out of the street and put them in the studio, which gave the butt a whole new dimension. The picture that I'm talking about, when he's in the street, I'd like to see what he did. He's got an assistant with him and his assistant is a reflecting light or whatever. And he's doing it with a Hasselblad. I do it with anything, whatever camera

I have.

CM:

Is there a defining moment in your career that helped shape you?

JS:

I think Dylan and working for *Vogue*. Have you heard of [Alexey] Brodovitch? Brodovitch was a teacher that we all studied from and it was a great, great learning course. He didn't teach you how to work the camera but he taught you how to think. Almost every photographer in New York took his course, at one time. Then he went to the new school with his course and he adjusted it there, and lots of kids who came along later on went there and studied with him.

CM:

Personally and in general, why is photography important?

JS:

It's given me so many beautiful moments. I've seen so many beautiful women, I've seen so many odd situations. It's captured life for me in so many ways.

CM:

You've worked with Faye Dunaway, Jimi Hendrix, Bob Dylan and Steve McQueen, among many others. Is celebrity work challenging?

JS:

It's a difficult question to answer. It's like saying, 'How do you get a good picture?' Or 'Which of your photographs do you like the best?' Every occasion is different.

CM:

You've watched New York change through the decades. Is there a particular period you loved the most, photographically?

JS:

No, because there's always something new each year, and if there isn't, I make it happen. I keep on walking and looking until I find something that pleases me. It's funny because with Brodovitch, before I took the course, he had many students and he used to teach in a studio – I think it was John Rawlings's studio – once a week. There was a 10-week course, and he was usually half drunk when he was teaching. First, we'd all introduce ourselves to each other. Then he'd say, 'Okay, the assignment for next week is the Brooklyn Bridge.' Everybody said, 'He's going to give you the assignment for the Brooklyn Bridge.' He never gave us the assignment for the Brooklyn Bridge.

Maybe 30 years after I took the course, I said, 'Damn it, I'm going to do the Brooklyn Bridge.' I had a lot of fun going there and I think I got maybe a few photographs that hadn't been done before. If you keep looking, you'll always find something.

CM:

A new aspect.

JS:

Yeah. And as Liberman said, you just photograph it. If you copy, copy somebody well, but your own personality will take over. You'll see something or you'll be doing a still life in the street, and you'll see that if you pull back a little bit, there's a match lying there that'll help make the whole picture complete in some way. We all think differently about what we see.

NORMAN SEEFF

It was a real pleasure to sit down with Norman Seeff in his Los Angeles office in the spring of 2019. Surrounding me were large-scale prints showing just a few of the incredible artists he has worked with through the years. We connected over his work, the power art has to heal and his incredible journey.

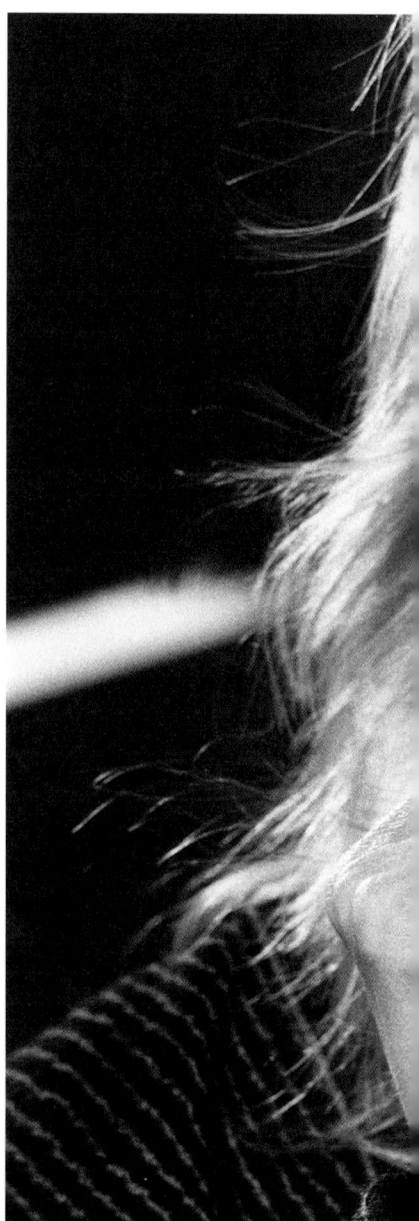

Norman Seeff, Joni Mitchell, Los Angeles, 1975-1976. © Norman Seeff

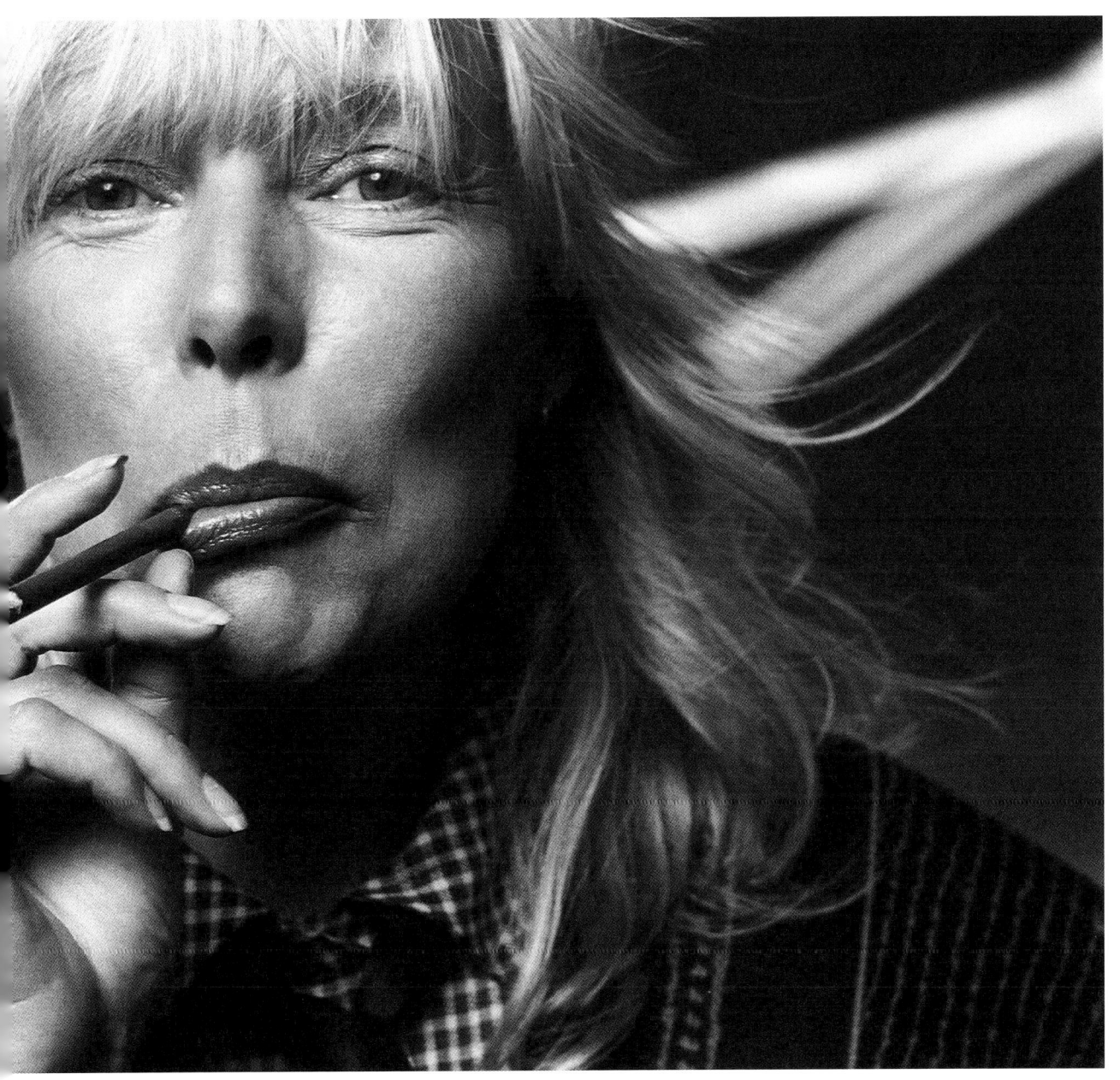

165

Charles Moriarty:

Photography came later in life.

Norman Seeff:

Well, it's an interesting vocation, and the way that I look at photography is that it's part of a multidisciplinary flow of creativity and it's just one face of what I do. There are some people, I've been told, like Avedon or Annie [Leibovitz], who opened their eyes in the crib and knew they wanted to be a photographer. I never even conceived of the idea until much later in life.

In my early days, my father was this amazing doctor who went to sick people, to their houses, and gave them his medical expertise and love. I saw him as a healer and wanted to do that too. But I also had this creative side, which was being able to draw and paint and sculpt.

CM:

What was it like to grow up in Johannesburg?

NS:

As a boy you had to figure out your manoeuvres, two, three steps in advance. The intellect of thinking one step ahead became a kind of survival mechanism. As I got older and understood how fucked up the Apartheid system was, I was trying to find a way to bring about change. My friends, about 50 of them, were into bringing about change through violence. On weekends they'd want me to go into the countryside with them and blow up the electrical grid.

CM:

What age were you?

NS:

Early 20s – 20, 21. The big debate was, 'Are we going to sit aside and let it be?' There were no means for freedom of speech. The only way was violence. I don't believe in violence as a substitute for violence;

it's just a recycling of the same kind of mental consciousness, and it doesn't bring about change.

So, what would bring about change? This was the question that came up for me. The truth is, I didn't know, but there was something in me that got sparked at that point. How do you bring about change?

Straight out of med school I elected to go and work in Soweto, in the Black hospital, because Johannesburg and Soweto were completely separate. One was Black and one was white.

When I was young, I came across a book about the Left Bank in Paris in the early days. There were these gorgeous girls everywhere hanging out, bare breasted, and I would often ask myself, 'Why be in the emergency room with people puking and bleeding and dying all over the place when you could be on the Left Bank in Paris?'

CM:

No doubt your memories of your father bringing love and healing to people, led you to a belief that doing the same would help heal, not just people but South Africa. You were searching for the answer to your own question. How do you bring about change?

NS:

In Soweto I was dealing with a lot of people the cops would bring in. People they'd beaten to a pulp. I was in a rage about the whole situation. I was also in a place of despair. I thought I was going to do healing and all we were doing was fixing. They'd bring in a broken-down machine and you'd sew it up and patch it up and send it out and three weeks later they would come back. It became a very difficult place for me to go, and instead of feeling like I was doing something positive, I felt like it was a hopeless situation.

But these were subconscious drives. On a conscious level, it was: how do I survive in this environment?

CM:

When did you decide to leave?

NS:

One morning I woke up and there was a voice in my head, and it just said, 'You're out of here.' So I resigned, bought a one-way ticket to London and sold all my furniture. I had a lot of artwork because in my evenings I was an artist. I had my paintings and drawings and sculpture and everything else. I just sold it, got on a plane and went to London for a short while. I very quickly understood that the English were not… Not my cup of tea. It felt oppressive.

CM:

What year was it?

NS:

It was '69, and I was looking for freedom. That was what drove me. I had to find a place where I could be myself.

CM:

After so many years of having an oppressive society around you, I can imagine England didn't have the level of freedom you needed.

NS:

I moved to New York soon after but that wasn't much better. I believed from devouring *Time* magazine from top to bottom every week that everyone had two helicopters in a garage. But when I arrived it was in the middle of the worst snowstorm, and there was a garbage strike. The city was filthy, and there was dog shit everywhere.

I knew one guy in New York and I was illegal, so I couldn't practice medicine. In the end I went underground. The romance of being the artist on the Left Bank with bare-breasted women hanging on your arm very quickly evaporated and became, 'How do I get enough money to buy some food today?' I was 30 and starving, but I learned how to survive. I learned how to say motherfucker and cocksucker – the use of language was so different to home. I couldn't even afford public transport, so I bought myself a bicycle.

One day, I met a very well-known Avedon model, Wally Coover. Irish, spoke out of the side of her mouth and every second word was 'fuck this' and 'fuck that'. I was completely besotted. Avedon had discovered her opening the door of his car and took her under his wing and made her. We would dress up and go out at 10 o'clock, starting with the downtown bars, which would be Max's Kansas City, with Patti Smith. I think Blondie was a waitress and Andy Warhol hung out. Then you'd do the midtown bars at midnight, and after that you'd do the uptown bars at two, and then home at four. I kept saying, 'I've got to work. I've got to create a living.' I was trying to be a photographer during the day. I had made up my mind to try and do a photo session a day.

I became a photographer because there was no way I thought I could make my graphic artwork earn a living. I didn't know that there was a thing called the music business and that there was a graphic arts side to designing album covers. I didn't know. Within a year I started meeting the people who introduced me to the music business. My first job would be as a graphic designer for Columbia Records. I was an album designer. But even before that I started meeting all these people. I remember seeing Patti and Robert Mapplethorpe at a bar, and

I said, 'Hey, can I do a photo session?' They said, 'Great.' Soon after that I started to meet people from Andy Warhol's Factory. Very quickly, I got introduced to the subculture of New York.

CM:

Do you remember what camera you started with?

NS:

I think my father had given me a Pentax, and then later on maybe I could afford a Nikon – but it's not about the camera. It's about the human being.

CM:

Were you shooting 35mm?

NS:

Nothing was fast enough, because I shoot on the emotional moment. I'm not trying to 'take pictures'.

Eventually, I met a guy called Bob Cater; he was the leading graphic designer, art director in the music business. At one point he was the creative director of Columbia and then he was consultant to Time Life. He was a tour de force of a human being: powerful and creative, conscientious, but an artist through and through. He saw the stuff I'd been shooting on the streets of New York. He was looking at my portfolio... And at this point I'm in total despair. Thinking, 'What have I done? I can't go back to South Africa.' Then I see Bob's eyes tear up.

Three months later, he gave me my first shoot, which was to go to Woodstock, meet with The Band behind *Music from Big Pink*. and shoot the liner notes.

CM:

This is when the Famous poster got produced, right?

NS:

Yeah. I was out of money and I borrowed a car. I'd never driven in the States and I had about six or seven rolls of film. I borrowed a strobe and I got lost on the way up to Woodstock. By the time I got there, I was two-and-a-half hours late and Robbie [Robertson] and The Band were absolutely fucking enraged at me.

I did the session with them, which was very fast because very quickly I had no more film. I drove home thinking, 'I have fucked up my life, because this was not fun.' I didn't know how to talk to them. I got back and developed this stuff from Woodstock. I looked at it and I didn't like anything. Everything I was photographing for myself was spontaneous; I was learning to use the photo session as a way to discover the nature of communication and create relationships with people. Not particularly for taking photographs.

CM:

Portrait photography is fundamentally about that personal connection.

NS:

Exactly. So, I didn't like anything. Ten days later, I'm still obsessing, and I feel like I've found one image. I walk across from the West Side through Central Park to Bob's brownstone, which is this four-story building that he owns with a red door. I push the picture under the door and I leave, too nerve-wracked to push the doorbell. Ten days go by.

Finally, I call Bob. The first thing he says is, 'Where the fuck have you been? I don't have your phone number and you just disappeared!' Then he goes, 'Oh, and by the way – good news. Robbie Robertson loves your picture. We've decided that we're not going to use my stuff on the cover. And I've got this great idea, because I think the picture is so fabulous. I'm going to make it a fold-up poster, so that when people pull the shrink wrap off, they open up a poster.'

CM:

How long was it before you realised something career defining had just happened?

NS:

When I used to hang out with Wally, at every bar there was a jukebox and there were always posters of the latest stuff. Dylan and James Taylor and The Rolling Stones. Suddenly, every bar we went to, my picture was up on the wall. I go from not being able to get a meeting with any kind of art director, or have a comment on my portfolio, to people calling me and saying, 'Are you the guy who shot the poster? Do you have any time to come in and see us?' This was Bob's initiation, and then he got me the design job at Columbia.

I shoot on the emotional moment. I'm not trying to 'take pictures'.

About a year or so into that, Bob called me one day and said, 'How would you like to go to Los Angeles and become the creative director of United Artists Records?' And I'm thinking, 'Where's Los Angeles and what's a creative director?' He said, 'Do you want it or not?' I said, 'Yeah, I want it.' And he said, 'Pack your bag. You leave in a week.'

I arrived in LA three years after arriving in America. When I arrived at the airport in New York from London, they gave me about a week to stay and I had one friend. At LAX there was a limo with this blonde girl who, when I got into the car, gave

me a wad of hundred-dollar bills and drove me to the Hyatt House.

CM:

Where all the music industry partied and let loose.

NS:

There was a green convertible Mustang waiting outside for me. My first walk that night was up Sunset Strip. I saw all these billboards and realised they were a kind of societal art gallery. In my mind I wanted to be up there.

So, I had arrived in LA, and I was the creative director of a record company. Everybody in town wanted to meet me because I was going to be the guy to give jobs to designers and photographers. Suddenly, my life was in LA with sun, and I thought I'd arrived in heaven.

CM:

But in the deep end a little?

NS:

When I realised being a creative director is a combination of all my creativity, of photography and being able to design and just sort of conceptualise, it was the easiest thing. And there was a wonderful family there, of people who embraced me.

CM:

At United Artists?

NS:

They were genuine and good, and seemed very grateful and excited to have someone who came in and made the changes they were looking for.

CM:

You were a fresh perspective.

NS:

Completely. I was too stupid to realise all those old album covers that were done for Blue Note, with

I'm a documentarian, waiting for the authentic moment, because it's nothing you can actually create – it has to emerge.

those wonderful black-and-white photographs, were an art form. I looked at them and went, 'That's fucking old'.

[Norman would continue to work at United Artists for several years, during which his team was nominated for several Grammys. He then set up his own photography studio in LA, on Sunset, and began working with the likes of Tina Turner, Joni Mitchell, Stevie Wonder and many more.]

CM:

Can you talk to me about your time filming and shooting in the LA studio?

NS:

I was scraping through, but kept building and building and building this astounding archive. I've got over 500 filmed sessions with artists and creators across disciplines. Directors, actors, writers, dancers, musicians and mavericks like Steve Jobs, and other types of political people. It has all yet to be released.

I started discovering, while working in my own professional platform as an artist and doing all these different things, that there is this incredible archetypal pattern behind the creative process, whether you're a director or a writer or a musician. It follows a certain hero's journey, a map. What happened is, I'd go, 'Gee, I've got Scorsese in my studio for four hours.' He and I would hang out the same way you and I are hanging out, and the conversation was peer-to-peer stuff. I would take him through my process, which was: people walk in and they inhibit in front of the camera. By the time they walk out of my sessions, they don't give a fuck.

CM:

You created a safe space.

NS:

Where you're completely emotionally present and the first one to be emotionally open, they, the subject, get so involved in the communication and the relationship that they forget there are cameras there. I've got people handing me cameras on the still side. I've got three or four cameras going, and some of these cameras go right up – but they're so involved in the excitement of where we're going.

I developed a script I could use when needed. I'd say to someone, 'Look, if you're worried about how you look, I'm just going to get shots of you looking worried.' They'd go, 'Ha, ha, ha.' Then I'd capture that. In the end they'd go, 'Okay, what the fuck, lets go.' I'd say, 'Look, I promise you nothing that we film today will ever be put out without me developing it, cutting it and showing it to you. If you don't like it, we throw it away.'

I knew I could never go to management or record companies and say, 'I want to film,' because I'd get sent right to the lawyers and nothing would ever happen. So I would start a session, get into this wonderful communication with the artist, and once they were going 'Wow, this is great,' I'd say, 'Look, would you mind if I film?' At that point, I thought it was going to be a feature film.

I said [to the artists], 'Look, I will bring you the material. I will be the guardian of the integrity of the material.' I'm not looking for the bullshit. I'm looking for who we are, when we function at the higher reaches of human creativity. There's enough crap out there. In fact, that's mostly what's out there. People are scared to go into the beauty of who we really are.

That's what my relationships are about. That's what my project was going to be about. I put all my money into the studio and filming. From when I first started shooting in 1975 — what I call the early days — to the end of the '80s, I'd spent about three or four million dollars.

It was money here, money there. A studio crew, lights, sound and a 16-millimeter camera. So many artists were coming at me that I couldn't keep pace. I would get Ray Charles at the beginning of the week and Stevie Wonder at the end. People would say to me, mid-week, 'We're out of money. You can't film.' I'd go, 'Okay, I won't film.' Then Stevie Wonder's management would call, so everyone would go, 'Okay, we're going to film.'

I just went down that road of discovering my voice as an artist. Who am I? But also, what am I trying to accomplish in my photographs?

I was looking for images where people looked alive, inspired and in their power. And so for me, to find a way to engage people – not from an intellectual level, which would be about control, but

from the heart and from the emotional experience in the moment – that was the key.

I'm a documentarian, waiting for the authentic moment, because it's nothing you can actually create — it has to emerge.

I always started my sessions by initiating vulnerability, which is always scary. I'd go into this phase of being really nervous, and not knowing where the fuck I was going. Then, ultimately, by [...] being very open and vulnerable and saying to people, 'Hey, I'm scared, I'm nervous' — which is hard — I'd end up connecting with people. We'd end up in a zone with each other, where there was a sense of trust. Suddenly, time seems to stop, and the whole thing seems to flow without doing anything.

Eventually, the artist would say, 'Wow, this is amazing. I thought I was coming to have my photograph taken, and I'm just [...] having a great time.' Then I'd say, 'Okay, now I want to push this. Let's try things we've never done before.'

The next phase in my session was this phase of challenge. If I started too early, people would freak out. I was learning a different kind of art form, and that art form was: what is the nature of human, authentic, vulnerable, intimate communication? That's what I'm interested in. What's the counterpoint to the violence model I had come across in South Africa?

I realised I had to do something with compassion and passion and heart space, and the emotional realness of communication. Then people don't project 'enemy' onto you.

Underneath everything I was doing – playing soccer, doing medicine, graphic design [...] – there was an inner function; an inner drive, an inner motivation. Looking at my father, I can say, 'He's a healer,' but then know the difference between healing and fixing in an intellectual way. Healing is about change. Further from that, it's just discovering. Healing is helping people see that they have options.

What is the option to violence? What is the option to this feeling of powerlessness I have?

I've got this doorway that I've opened, because I'm now a successful, public personality photographer. [...] People say to me, 'How do you get there?' I have no fucking idea. You don't know what you're doing, in the early days. You have to just do things instinctively. You find out afterwards that there was a vision you didn't have words for.

It's a wordless knowingness. I had to fight against myself to overcome my intellectual control, which was cultivated for my safety, in order to allow the possibility of uncertainty and spontaneity.

[...] The biggest source of pain and crisis in the world right now is the separation that people feel, but also separation from self, from our own emotion. When people look different, we project the idea of 'enemy' or 'threat' onto them. I was in Africa, surrounded by Black/white separation, intellectual and medical separation. Doctors would say, 'Oh, what a wonderful case of heart failure,' rather than, 'Here's a human being dying in front of my eyes, who needs love.' The idea that if you get emotionally involved with your patient you can't be objective, is wrong.

CM:

Do you remember the first time when that mode of communicating with your subjects started to happen?

NS:

In the beginning it was something spontaneous, with the thought behind that being, 'How do I get people to give me that eye contact and that vitality?' What I wanted was a sense of aliveness in the photograph. I didn't want to be someone photographing the blights of humanity, the emptiness and the pain. That is the work of documentary guys, and I respect them. I'd seen enough in the hospital in Soweto, and it wasn't...

I was aspiring to who we could be; who we could become if we rise to the challenge of discovering the higher reaches of human integrity, human creativity. None of those words were there, but that was my inner drive.

I was inviting people to my sessions and getting artists to perform spontaneously. It became an actor's studio and an adolescent party work session, all scrunched together. People said to me, 'It's amazing to be in a room with you and Joni Mitchell, and for Joni Mitchell to sing a song that's going to end up on an album. But,' they said, 'there's something else going on that transcends even that. The conversation and the relationship between... we've never seen anything like that.' It opens doors into meeting people at another level, where we realise the humanity.

CM:

Is Joni the person you've photographed the most over the years?

NS:

I did the most sessions with her, but I've shot a lot of other artists multiple times. As time went by at the studio, I thought, 'There's something happening now in this communication.'

Standing six feet away from Ike and Tina Turner — those were the kind of people I was shooting then — there was this incredible dynamic of coming together in a synergy of being artists and creators, where separation goes away. […] You are, almost in your DNA, committed to being creators, beyond anything else. There's a sense of oneness, when you really connect that way.

CM:

It's a wonderful feeling. The hairs go up on the back of your neck.

NS:

I'm addicted to it. Can't put the camera aside.

CM:

Were there tough days in the studio?

NS:

Starting the way I did, everyone got stoned and everyone got loaded. I did my bit. I was so scared in the beginning that before people walked in, I probably had about two double scotches, or three. When they arrived, I was Mister Spontaneity. 'Hey, let's party.' And then I'd smoke a couple of joints to temper it a little bit. I didn't like coke, because it took your heart away.

I'm working with the most standout people on the planet, so I knew how to work... You wouldn't even have known that I was stoned. But I was getting loaded, and at a certain point I went, 'Here I am asking these artists to let go of resistance and be spontaneous, but I'm doing it with a crutch.' As we all are. I decided one day to stop.

The truth is, we're shit scared, and it's our crutch. It's a way to deal with something you don't know how to deal with. Getting to the answer for 'did I have a bad day?' I decided to stop doing drugs, because I wanted to prove to myself I could do it. For a year, it was horrible.

CM:

It took a while to find your feet?

NS:

It took a while for me to believe that I could be spontaneous.

CM:

The lack of self-belief got in the way, more than the fear?

NS:

I knew I had the capacity to be there, and I had to do it by choice, not by chemicals. The first shoots... Actually, I got really good photographs, because I have the discernment: I know when it's real and when it's not real. But it took a long time for me to be able to engage people, because when I got loaded, I'd be a little bit cheeky. I'd push the relationship very quickly.

[…] It's a dance. Sometimes you lead, sometimes you let yourself be led. That's the core of the whole process, it's a collaborative, vulnerable, intimate relationship, and at times very honest.

CM:

What happened at the end of the '80s?

NS:

I stopped being a photographer full time. I was on the cover of all the magazines, and suddenly I disappeared, because I was in debt for a lot of money and getting married.

The top advertising agency in the world, which was Chiat/Day at that point, represented Apple, Steve Jobs and a lot of big corporations. They came to one of my screenings. Every three months I would take film from the sessions that I'd developed, and I'd have screenings at these rooms in Hollywood, and I'd invite producers and all kinds of people, hoping someone would invest in my project, so I wouldn't have to pay for it.

The truth is, we're shit scared, and it's our crutch.

Jay Chiat and a guy called Lee Clow, who was the top art director in the whole graphics world at that point, came to one of my screenings. They contacted me afterwards and said, 'Look, your film is off the charts, it's stunning. Could you make this happen in commercials?' I said, 'No, I can't, and I'm not interested, because it's all scripted, market researched, nothing.' Lee Clow, being the guy with the clout, said, 'I'll come up with a campaign where you'll have no scripts. You can do it spontaneously and we'll throw these millions of dollars at you.'

I took my photography career and I stopped it. I ended it. I became a highly successful commercial director – which for me was high-paid film school – for 15 years.

During the '90s — the second part of the '80s, into the end of the '90s, up until 2000 — I was gone. I put my stuff away. At the time, I didn't like it. I didn't think it was sharp enough. I didn't see what I see now, which is that I was getting the soul of the artist. I was looking at it from, 'Well, I had a two-and-a-quarter, and it was sharper.'

I just thought, 'Okay, photography opened up filmmaking. Commercials opened me up to feature films.' I mean, some of my shoots, the budgets were a couple of a million dollars for commercials. If you're a successful commercial director, an A-director, you made more money than the top feature directors.

I suddenly was successful. I bought a three-storey architect's house with plots of land, and I had a three-storey production company. I had offices in New York and Chicago and Toronto.

Through the commercial jobs, I paid myself back what I'd spent. But when I got to 1999, I thought, 'I can't shoot another fucking commercial.'

CM:

Not enough soul?

NS:

When you do the top commercials, it's an art form, but it had gotten repetitive. Then something really interesting happened. Paul Allen, who had been with Microsoft, was opening up this museum in Seattle called The Experience Museum [now Museum of Pop Culture], dedicated to Jimi Hendrix. They called me and said, 'The first exhibition is on the creative journey, and knowing the work you've done, we would like you to help us put the installation together.'

I came in as their director. The first thing they said is, 'We want to do the story on funk music, and here are 30 artists we want you to photograph and film and interview the way you do...' I had to say, 'It's not interviews, it's a conversation.' But [Paul Allen] has all the money in the world, so suddenly I had five, six cameras. I put my commercial career aside and came back to photography, but photography as a filmmaker/communicator, around the creative process.

This was a corporate project and I cut a documentary film for them on the roots of funk. Right after that, I followed up with all these documentaries for Caltech, California Institute of Technology. They said, 'We've got more Nobel Prize winners here than anyone else; we'd like you to do one of your explorations on the creative process of the Nobel scientists.' Out of that, the jet propulsion lab came and said, 'We'd like you to shoot this.' It was my idea to shoot a documentary on the scientists and engineers who put the rovers up on Mars.

Then Paramount came to me and said, 'We want you to shoot all the stars of our shows.' So instead of shooting individual artists, I'm now moving into multi-disciplinary arenas: sciences and different creative disciplines. That's what I've been doing since 2000. I then went back to shooting photography, but for The Rolling Stones, you know what I mean? I'll shoot the Steve Jobses. People who have a gravitas. I was trying to get my archive funded, to turn it into a TV series, but my dialogue of saying, 'I'm exploring the higher reaches of human potential...'

CM:

Doesn't sell well?

NS:

People are going like, 'What are you on?' I got into a state of despair and I went, 'You know what? This isn't for me. Fuck it. I'm not even going to try.' I'm going to build this body of work up, and I'm going to do workshops — which I'm doing now — and I'm going put out books on the dynamics and archetypes of creativity.

As I stepped out of wanting to hustle, people started coming to me. I'd get, 'What are you doing?' I'd say, 'I'm doing it because I'm impassioned by the great creators, who in their integrated place of being creative are examples of who we really are and who we can become.' Unfortunately a lot of creatives don't take that over into their private lives, but for me it's... How can I take what I'm learning here, and create a platform to show how humanity can take conscious control of writing their own story?

CM:

Big questions. Are there sessions that have stood out for you personally over the years, with certain people?

NS:

There are two ways to answer this. One is, when you work the way that I do and you go deeply into an intimacy with someone, they could be unknown people in terms of public personalities, but you sometimes get the most profound beauty and depth of humanity. Then there are those ones who stand out because they're so fucking powerful

Start to work on your own inner self, because that's what you bring to the table, no matter what you do.

on stage, and in their courage to be who they are. You're just trying to rise to the occasion.

That usually comes down to 'the real'. The real greats are not great by mistake. They're there because they work their fucking asses off, they work hard, they're smart. They know exactly what they're doing. Sometimes they're defensive because the world literally tries to suck the blood out of them, so when they trust you and they open up, it's amazing.

The real greats are not great by mistake. They're there because they work their fucking asses off.

Take the conversation with [Martin] Scorsese. We were talking about, 'can you forgive yourself...?' He's making movies about these, quote unquote, unforgivable people. And we had a conversation about why he does that, and he says, 'I'm in this journey of wanting to forgive myself. I know I have these same feelings.'

At that level, when you hook into some little kid who's a hip hopper from the East side here, and he discovers this guy four times his age... By the time we've had the session, where we tune in at the level of this incredible built-in creativity, there's no separation.

Like this one guy, he's huge... you wouldn't want to meet him on a dark street. At the end [of a session] he says, 'Hey man, you're my dog.' Okay, we're communicating. Yeah, I am his dog, and he'll go anywhere with me.

So the answer at one level is: the depth at which I connect vulnerably with people is always profound. Then there's a Tina Turner, who is just so fucking... every second is so empowering. And Ray Charles – every word that comes out of his mouth is poetic. Some of the newer people that I've worked with... I mean, I'm still shooting now. I'm back shooting people. The current material I'm working on is another octave of where I'm going with the creative process.

But the great artists I'm working with now are the same as the great artists I worked with when I first started. I say to people, 'If Bach or Michelangelo were around, I'd be doing sessions with them.' You can't say at the end of it, 'Oh well, Michelangelo's out of date.' There's no such thing. When you get to the authenticity of the creative process, it's eternal. It's timeless.

CM:

Do you still get the fear? Or do you deal with it now?

NS:

No, no, no. What's happened is, I'm so tuned into the destiny I'm living now, that I can't wait to get in a room with people and go into the beauty of the depth of a relationship. It's an absolute honour. Before, when the ego of 'Am I good enough?' was there, that was part of it. That's no longer... It's not that I can't get into my ego once in a while.

CM:

Sure, but it's not what's driving you.

NS:

I'm functioning in a different octave of who I am, and I know that where I'm going is about healing, which is about change, and is about giving people other options. [...] I'm creating a new map around the creative process, to a new paradigm where you start functioning not out of 'Am I good enough?' and 'Are you going to love me?', but 'How can I take this incredible gift that I'm so grateful about and share it, to counter that feeling of separation in the world?'

It's a different set of motivations. That's the best way I can describe it.

CM:

Your journey's been pretty extraordinary. For people getting into the world of photography and film these days, would you advise anything?

NS:

Start to work on your own inner self, because out of that, discovering who you are, that's what you bring to the table, no matter what you do. If you're a student at photography school, please learn the technical thing in two months. The rest of the time, if you're going to be working with people, or even with the world that you're observing, learn to discover the emotional authenticity and the vulnerability of your experience of who you are.

If you don't have that part, you're not going to be able to communicate. For me everything moved into the nature of communication with oneself, with the different aspects of self. When I was at medical school, I thought human beings were egos. I didn't realise that the ego is the lowest level of human consciousness. There are multiple levels from your subconscious to your unconscious to your higher self to dimensions beyond that, and these are not esoteric concepts. When you actually do the work, you learn how to enter your subconscious and find out what's going on, in the subtext of what's *really* going on.

CM:

Lastly, and I suppose very simply, why does photography matter to you?

NS:

Like any form of creativity, if it's a reflection of the authenticity of the creator, then it's a vehicle of authenticity. That's a very esoteric, but practical and real definition of it.

I can look at photographs and think, 'What was the emotional experience that the person was having when they shot this picture?' Some people are not good at photography, but they see a tree or a sunset, and in that moment they're touched by its beauty, and they pull out their iPhone and take a photo. If I was to ask them [...] 'what was the authenticity of that moment?' and they look at that picture and go, 'It reminds me of that experience,' then that's all that matters.

EVA SERENY

I first met Eva very briefly at an exhibit of her work in London. It was to coincide with her book *Through Her Lens*, showcasing the many years she spent photographing on film sets and creating publicity shots for magazines such as *Paris Match* and *The Sunday Times*. In 2019 I went to her home for coffee. We enjoyed a conversation about her life and extensive career as a photographer, as well as her brief but award-winning stint as a film director. Sadly, Eva Sereny passed away in May, 2021. As the photographer behind so many iconic images, including on-set photography from *Raiders of the Lost Ark*, *Last Tango in Paris*, *Death in Venice*, *Catch-22* and *The Great Gatsby*, her career carried her through Hollywood at its height. As a woman at the top of a profession traditionally dominated by men, Eva was 'humble but fiercely proud of her work' (Carrie Kania, Creative Director of Iconic Images, custodians of Eva's archive). She leaves the world with an incredible legacy of photographs, including her captivating portrait session with Romy Schneider and her work with Harrison Ford, Jane Fonda, Al Pacino, Elizabeth Taylor, Audrey Hepburn and many more.

Eva Sereny, Romy Schneider, 1971
© Iconic images

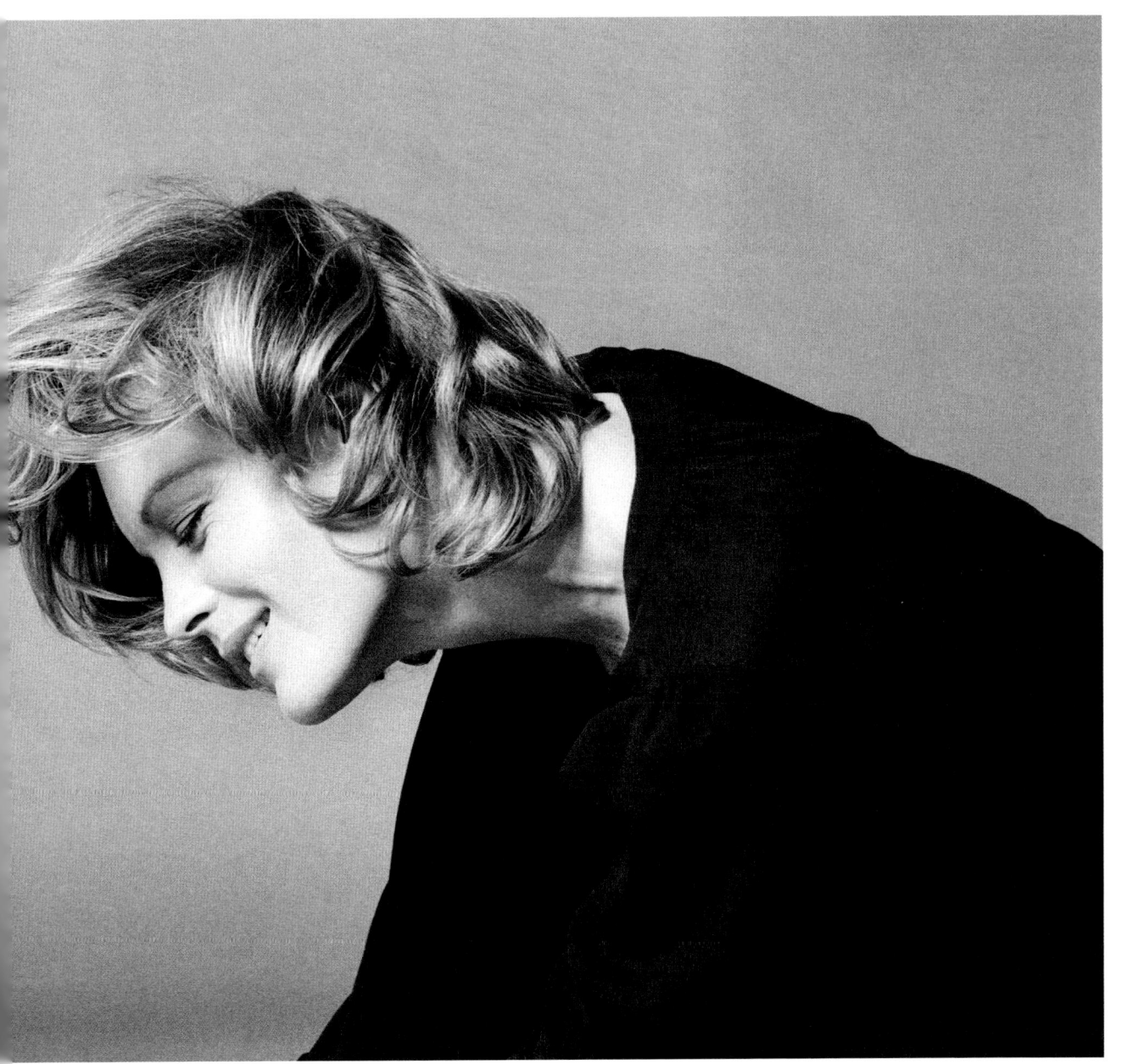

Charles Moriarty:

Where did you grow up?

Eva Sereny:

I was born in Switzerland. I was a child when my father came over to England because of work, and then the war broke out. France became occupied, so I came to England with my mother. Our journey from Zurich was quite extraordinary. We went by bus right through the Pyrenees, the south of France, across Spain, to Portugal, which was a sort-of spy area at that time.

CM:

How did you get to England?

ES:

My parents at that time were quite well off and there were these sea planes that came over to Bournemouth from Lisbon. I remember one of them was shot down. The Germans thought somebody very important was on the plane. And, poor guy, it was Leslie Howard – the actor from *Gone with the Wind*. I can't remember if my mother told me that, but it was just before or after our plane.

When we arrived in England, we became 'enemy aliens', which to me has always seemed an odd way of putting things. [...] Enemy aliens in England, as if we were some kind of criminals. We had to go to England; that's where my father needed to be, because he was a chemist. He had a bit of a factory in Switzerland, and had come over to London to get his patent. I think it was with Monsanto, who actually looked after us during the war. We had a lovely house on the Thames; I mean beautiful. The Thames was literally right at the end of the garden.

It was extraordinary. Oh, how life changes. Then we waited. You couldn't have a car, you couldn't have a camera. We had restrictions, but we were given everything.

CM:

Because you were considered potential enemies of the state?

ES:

Yes. You couldn't go five miles out of town. But it was idyllic. My parents had two Hungarian maids – it was ridiculous.

CM:

Did you get a sense of the war?

ES:

I did; we were bombed out twice. One time we had gone down to Torquay, and the third house from us got completely trashed. Then, when it was the flying bombs, we had gone to Cumberland. We had a very lovely flat in Stanhope Gardens at the time. That got completely destroyed. I was scared, very scared at that time. But then I went to a convent school in Waverley, which I loved. We had such fun, but next door to us there was a farm and there were all the Italian prisoners of war. They used to smile at us through the fence.

When I went home, I used to be so scared. You waited for the whistling to stop.

CM:

The alarms?

ES:

When you don't hear it anymore, you know that they've passed.

CM:

Did you stay at the convent until you were 18?

ES:

Yes. Afterwards, I started to think about what I should do for work. By then my parents were without a penny. Initially, my father brought me into a sort of secretarial thing. But I'm not good at that sort of thing; I can't bear it. […] Shorthand, typing; I wasn't gifted for any of it. But it had its use later on in life.

CM:

What kind of imagery or art were you exposed to, early on in life?

ES:

The education was very normal, basic. I did get a job in the secretarial world for a film distribution place. I was always interested in the arts in that sense.

CM:

You enjoyed the movies?

ES:

I absolutely loved them.

CM:

It must have been a really wonderful thing later in life to find yourself on movie sets.

ES:

Yes, but what I really wanted was to be in front of a camera. […] I went to various places with a group and we were living in digs. I tasted that and it was not going anywhere. I even went to Dublin actually – these are not very photographic stories.

CM:

It all connects to you and your practice.

ES:

I started [in photography] very late in life. I've never been in a photographic…

CM:

Institution or class?

ES:

I'm handmade; we'll put it that way. Years ago, in Rome, Italy, my late husband had a car accident, which he survived. There is an artificial lake just outside of Rome with a bridge over it and he went right into the water. Thankfully, he was totally fine

– he had nine lives, that one. I at that time had two sons, and they were quite young. It was the early '60s. […] I was well into my 30s. I never used to give my age, because I'm much older than I look. And I was trying to keep… to get work.

I was sitting there at the hospital, and I thought to myself, 'I haven't been to university or anything.' […] We went [to Italy] in 1957, and I had been trying to get a career going in England, but I couldn't. I couldn't find what I wanted. That was why my husband and I decided to go to Italy.

When I went home, I used to be so scared. You waited for the whistling to stop.

So, I'm sitting there in the hospital and, luckily, he didn't even have a scratch. He went out through his windscreen to get out of the water. The reason he was in hospital was because he had picked up a bacterial infection from the water. I was sitting there thinking, 'Good God, what am I going to do with my life; what if he'd died?' I had my two sons to think about. I knew I had a creative mind, but I can't draw. And I just thought, *photography*. Just like that.

So, being a very determined person, I got books about everything photography related, and my husband built me a little darkroom, but honestly, I knew nothing. There was nobody to talk to. I did try to be an assistant to some well-known photographers at the time, but they didn't even reply. And I thought, 'My God, I can't even do that'. So, I started using my husband's Rolleiflex, which I still have here.

I was clicking away with this, that and the other. Things somehow started to come together. I started reading things, developing and printing my work. Friends would ask me to photograph their children because it looked like I knew what I was doing. We had a very close friend at the time who was head of the Italian Olympic Committee, which in Italy is like the minister of sport. We went with him to Mexico in 1966 or '67, because it was going to host the next Olympics. And I just took a lot of photos. At the time, he was starting these athletic centres for children. He said, 'Why don't you go around them and take photographs?' They were in various parts of Italy, during the Mussolini era.

CM:

Was it a campaign?

ES:

It was to help children get into athletics. So, I went to these various centres, for swimming and all kinds of things. They loved the work, how I saw it all. People started saying to me, 'This is good'. But I got a little bored with that, because it's so easy to say 'good'. It doesn't mean a thing. I eventually decided to give myself a test, to try and start a career. I came to England, to London – and this is God's truth. Exactly how it happened.

I didn't know anybody. I had nothing to do with journalism. The only thing I knew was which newspapers were important. I liked *The Times* and thought newspapers and I could be a good fit. I didn't make an appointment – I just walked in. There was a guy at the reception desk, and I said, 'I've got some photos I'd like to show,' and he said, 'Oh, go up there, second floor'. I mean, literally. I really didn't look like a photographer. I was…

CM:

An Italian lady?

ES:

Bourgeois completely. Absolute.

CM:

I think you most likely confused them.

ES:

Well, yes, probably. I was lucky, but I was my whole career — so I realise, now more than ever. Even if you're the best person in the world, you have to have luck. My success was down to two things working in tandem. The first thing was that I met this picture editor, and the luck was that it was a quiet day. I didn't see anybody else in the big open-plan office. He took me to the side into a glass cubicle, and started to look through my book. I had handprinted everything at home, and he said, 'Look, do you mind leaving the book with me for a couple of days or so?'

I knew I had a creative mind, but I can't draw. And I just thought, *photography*. Just like that.

'No, absolutely not, goodbye, thank you very much.' So, I left my book and out I went. Within two days, I had a page in *The Times* with my pictures.

The heading was, 'These are the Future' — the sort-of Italian hopefuls of the Munich Olympics. That is how it happened. It really was extraordinary. Somebody told me that I needed an agent, so I went to Camera Press and soon I started working for *Marie Claire* and *Elle*. I was in Paris a lot. It was editorial, fashion editorial. That started things off, and then they said, 'Have you ever thought of doing film?' I hadn't, so I got an agent in Paris for publicity. The work and my career started to build.

CM:

Did you have a style of shooting by then?

ES:

My thing is, I have to feel who I'm shooting. I have to feel it. [...] There has to be empathy; it has to be there. And I know when I've done it — that's the shot. The technical part isn't as important.

CM:

Is that something that took you a little while to find?

ES:

It became automatic. I didn't realise what I was doing. It was only later on that I knew.

CM:

What was the first film you shot publicity for?

ES:

The first one of any importance was *Catch-22*. Somebody told me there was a publicist in Rome and I should go and see him. I still remember his name, Gordon Arnell. I'm sure he's not around anymore. Bertolucci is now lost, too.

CM:

You worked with him on Last Tango in Paris, *with Brando, right?*

ES:

Oh yes, and others. One of the best things when working with Bertolucci on *1900* was his DOP [Director of Photography], Storaro [Vittorio Storaro]. In my opinion, he was one of the best. Even though I did a lot with Dougie [Douglas] Slocombe. who was also incredible, Storaro was incredible with light.

I take most of my stuff always in natural light, because I've never been a technician. Yes, I've done studio stuff, but I never liked it; it's too automatic. And that's why, shall we say, my career stopped – because I was never happy with digital. I couldn't feel anything.

CM:

When you were working on films, did you ever shoot unit, or was it always behind the scenes for promotional purposes?

ES:

Always behind the scenes. [...] You couldn't shoot when they were shooting at all. Even in rehearsals you can't; they don't want to hear the click. Then the unit photographers had this kind of...

CM:

The box?

ES:

I think I used it once and then I threw it away. I was never the unit photographer. Whether I'm being commissioned or not commissioned, I abided by the magazines. I worked an awful lot for *The Sunday Times* magazine and *Paris Match*, and a whole lot of others.

CM:

Which photographers inspired you?

ES:

There were so many. Cartier-Bresson was the first. I've always loved that one with the boy and the baguette, and more generally his images of people. He felt those people. But I didn't used to think of it that way. Getting older [...] there's so much more clarity and understanding. Taking a photo really does something to me. And that's really the sign. I'm terribly sensitive and I don't always know how to process that sensitivity.

I always worked quite quickly. For instance, Audrey Hepburn, I didn't know her; she just came back from filming on set, we had a little talk, nothing much, and then while she was sitting down, I took some shots. I had very few shots and then she left. That's the thing, you know. [...] The more I speak to you, the more I realise that it really is probably my sensitivity which is a little bit overboard.

You know, for the actual photography, I was always so nervous. I had sleepless nights. It wasn't a joy to do it; it was a joy to get it and see what I had done.

[...] I did a publicity shoot once, and I knew I wasn't getting anywhere. I started adding stupid things, like getting a bunch of grapes and making her [the model] look up... Oh, it was awful! I can't even remember her, but I remember those bloody grapes. I just couldn't get into her. I couldn't find it.

I had one disaster as well, which I paid for in a way, although it wasn't my fault. I was hired to photograph Karl Lagerfeld, and at the time I was living up in the mountains, Chamonix. My publicity agent, who was a friend of mine, she rang and said 'American Express wants you to do this lovely publicity shot.' So, I booked my place to Paris and the flight was going to leave about three o'clock in the afternoon.

When I woke in the morning, the snow was so high. I got to the airport but there were no flights. I rang my agent and she nearly went berserk. It was then organised for the next day. Eventually, I got to Paris, to Karl's apartment. When I arrived, he said, 'It would never have happened to me.' And I said, 'Well, there was nothing I could do. Even by train I wouldn't have made it.' And he says, 'Well, I would have swam the Atlantic and got there.' I felt very small. He was all right, but that was my big disaster: Karl Lagerfeld.

CM:

Did you have a strong community of photographers around you, who became friends?

ES:

No, because I've always been alone. You know I've travelled, number one. Number two, most of the photographers were men, with their group. The one who was very good to me, was Douglas Kirkland. But apart from Douglas there was never a group

– maybe one or two unit photographers who were lovely. One or two that weren't.

CM:

What was it like, working in this industry as a woman?

ES:

This is all wrapped up in a longer story. I had worked with the greats – I'm talking about Truffaut, Fellini, Bertolucci, Pollack, Spielberg; there is a list. Eventually, I decided I really wanted to direct. So, I went to a friend of mine, a producer, and he said, 'Well, you know, you haven't been to film school.' 'Yes, I know, but I've been on many sets with the greats.' We were joking, but he said, 'Look, what you've got to do is find a subject and do a short film.' I wrote a treatment from an idea, and someone else wrote the script.

I had a young producer who was trying to promote herself and her work. We worked out something and I got Michael Palin to star, which wasn't a little thing in the end. Shorts are normally about five, ten minutes, but mine was half an hour. During production, [George] Lucas asked me to come over to San Francisco, because he wanted me to take pictures of his daughter. While I was there, I decided to visit friends in Los Angeles. [...] So I met Frank [Marshall] and Kathy [Kennedy], and I just said, 'Will you help; can you do me a favour?' I showed the script to Kathy. I said, 'I'm not asking for the world, just open the door for me.' Because we did have a bit of money, but it wasn't enough.

Kathy loved it. I met with Robin Benson, who was the focus puller for Dougie Slocombe. I said to Robin, 'Would you like to be the director of photography on this little piece that I'm doing?' And he did, and he did a great job. And I won the BAFTA.

> I was lucky, but I was my whole career – so I realise, now more than ever. Even if you're the best person in the world, you have to have luck.

CM:

That must have been pretty thrilling.
[The BAFTA sits across the room, proudly presented, as it should be.]

ES:

Extraordinary. Now we get to women in the industry. [...] I thought the world was at my feet, but it wasn't. A girl from *The Sunday Times* came to interview me in London, and she started to ask questions, but she didn't know much about the film. I don't think she'd even seen it. She started by saying, and I was terribly naïve, 'How do you feel about being a female director?'

I thought to myself, 'What the heck are you talking about?' It's not a question of lifting bricks or something. It's the same thing: a woman or a man could do it.

'But how do you feel about that?' And I said, 'Well, I can't answer you. It's just a piece of work that I did; one is a director and they direct and work things out.' I don't even know if the [article] came out. It annoyed me.

After winning the BAFTA, it was decided that I needed an agent in LA, otherwise it was all pointless. I got to LA, and a lady from an agency met me at some café, for a salad or whatever. I was feeling pretty good. I was looking good and I felt energetic.

'Hello, nice to meet you,' she says. 'Sit down and order whatever; tell me a little bit about you.' So, I talk a lot, and she just keeps eating, eating, eating. And I didn't touch the food because I didn't have time. Until I got bored of talking and watching this woman eat. So I said, 'Look, I think I've covered a good bit. I can send the film to you if you like.' She looks at me and she sort-of says, 'Yes, very interesting,' and eats some more.

I thought the world was at my feet, but it wasn't.

Eventually I tire of this and ask her what she thinks about it all. She says, 'Well, you know, there are two problems.' And I say, 'Okay, what are the problems?' 'You're not 25.' I say, 'No.' 'And you're a woman.' I swear to God.

I was terribly upset and, I swear, those were her words, verbatim. I was in shock. Because I thought when she said there was a problem –

CM:

That it would be something you could fix, and instead it was two things you had no control over.

ES:

That was it. And that was what it was like, being a woman in the industry.

CM:

Is there a body of your work or a series that you're particularly proud of?

ES:

Do you know Romy Schneider? I have a book I made called *I Met Romy Schneider*. We shot it when we were working on *Trotsky* [*The Assassination of Trotsky*, 1972] with Burton. I didn't know her, but she rang me up at home; must have gotten my number from the publicist. It was about nine thirty, ten o'clock at night. 'This is Romy, would you like to take some pictures tonight?' Of course, I said yes. It was pouring with rain, I remember that. But then I thought – how the hell, I haven't got a studio. I rang up a friend who had a little place, but as I told you, I don't know anything technical for studio work.

Romy came in, I put on some music, we had a bit of champagne I had brought, and we started to shoot. But I had no assistant and didn't really know studio equipment, so I can't believe that I did it, to this day.

I showed [the pictures] to her and she seemed very happy, which was the major point. Sadly, I made the mistake of showing them to someone from one of the major German magazines. I said, 'You must promise me you won't print it until she accepts it. You must promise.' 'Oh, of course." Bastard went and printed them.

The next day I was very upset because I was being commissioned by *The Sunday Times* magazine to do her costumes for *Ludwig* and then Romy called me absolutely outraged. I tried to explain that I shouldn't have gone to him, that he had promised me. I thought I'd lost the job for *The Sunday Times* magazine – but it worked out okay. I spoke to Michael Rand at *The Sunday Times* and he wasn't very happy, but in the end, I took the pictures and they got the cover. I think the reason she was so angry with the leak was because she didn't get the cover.

CM:

I'm sure you have quite a few stories. How about the leading men? Paul Newman?

ES:

That shoot was one of my favourites. My other was Jack Lemon. He was such a lovely, funny guy and so much fun. So was Newman.

CM:

One of the last films you worked on was part of the Bourne series. Was that the end for you and photography?

ES:

It was the end. Matt Damon almost got me fired; apparently my camera's click distracted him. I spoke to my close friend Frank Marshall about it, as this had never happened before in my short career. Anyway, yes, it was the end.

CM:

Do you think much about photography now?

ES:

I don't want to do it; I'm just too tired. Your whole outlook at a certain age is completely different.

CM:

Did it bring you joy?

ES:

You know, for the actual photography, I was always so nervous. I had sleepless nights. It wasn't a joy to do it; it was a joy to get it and see what I had done. That was the only real moment that gave me satisfaction; shooting was full of anxiety.

CM:

You were happier in a darkroom.

ES:

Oh, to print was my joy. I loved it – and to see [the photograph] on a shelf. The first time it happened, in *The Times*, I was on the train and there was my work, in the paper, and I thought to myself, 'That's me! That's mine!'

HANNAH STARKEY

Northern Irish artist Hannah Starkey and I talked over Zoom in August 2020 about her work, feminine perspectives, the future and #MeToo. I've been a fan of Hannah's work for many years. Ever since I saw her piece *Untitled – October 1998*, I've been caught up by the dialogues at work within her photographs.

Hannah Starkey, Untitled, January 2001
© Hannah Starkey

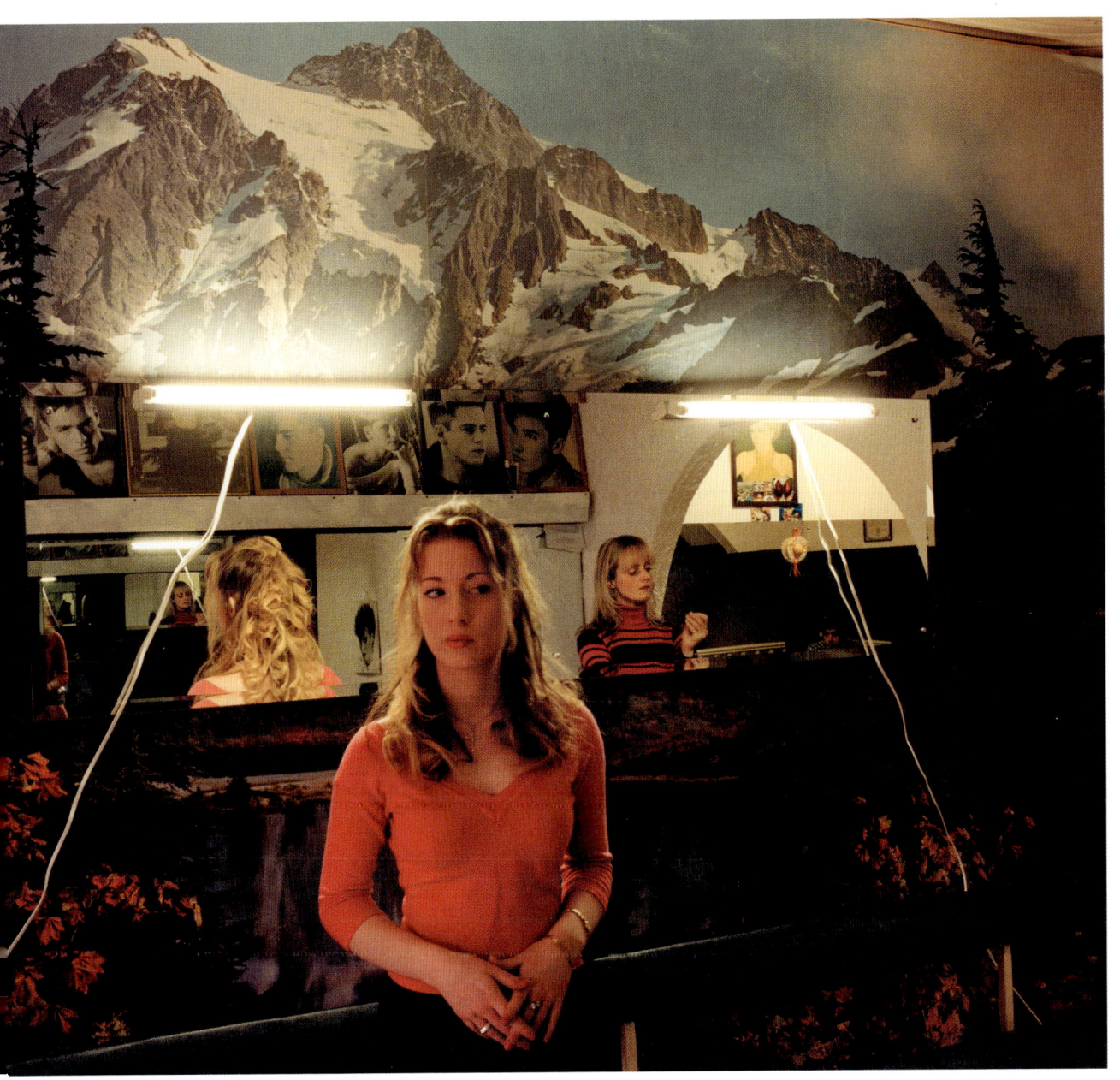

Charles Moriarty:

You were born in Belfast. Did you grow up there?

Hannah Starkey:

I left to go to university, but up until that time, I lived in North Belfast. I used to get asked the whole time about the IRA and the UDA. It was almost like a pick up line: 'So where are you from?' And then it was, 'Can you explain to me what is going on there?' It's like… Jesus, nobody understands what's going on there. I'm not going to be able to explain it to you.

But it's a funny thing, when you're born into a place like that, because it's all you know. I didn't really think it was abnormal. I mean, [the Troubles] didn't affect my daily life in any way. I was very lucky; I never saw any atrocities. But because you didn't know anything else, you didn't question it so much; you just got used to the normality of it. And because Northern Ireland was a very low-grade conflict, it went on for 30 years. I suppose it was something people lived with. They didn't know any different. Well, actually, it depends when you were born – but if you were born in the '70s, you went straight into the thick of it.

For me, it was a really good place to grow up because I didn't have any negative memories from it. I enjoyed the type of place Belfast was. It's actually a very friendly place; you can't stop people from talking to you. You'll never be alone. I also like its sense of humour, which was very dark. It was a coping mechanism, of course. It's very particular to a place like the North of Ireland, and sometimes it doesn't translate very well in England.

They take [humour] a little bit too literally. They don't realise that you're just messing with them.

That's another thing I loved about Belfast, with all the shit that was going on: people's behaviour – day-to-day behaviour, their normality – was heightened, in a way. I remember Northern Ireland as a place where you learned things like justice very early on. How important that was to people. You learned to get out of your comfort zone and mix, because otherwise…

I was known as a Catholic. You could just end up never knowing what it actually was that you were conditioned to be frightened of or intimidated by. It was very important to my mam that I didn't get stuck in the hate, so she made an effort to take me to places that were mixed religion. The youth club that I went to was mixed religion, and that kind of thing.

CM:

That was a great thing your mam gave you.

HS:

I think it's always stayed with me. When you walk in somebody else's shoes, when you actually understand where they're coming from, you can be a lot more compassionate, and a lot more open to communication, and to understanding each other.

CM:

I'm jumping ahead, but it feels like that idea permeates your work.

HS:

Yeah.

CM:

Did you have a big family?

HS:

No, I was an only child. I think I was a little bit of a miracle birth, because my mam couldn't have any other children after me. But she did go out of her way to make sure I wasn't a spoilt, can't-share-my-

For me, if a picture I'm working on looks like one of my pictures, that's very important to me. I'm not even sure if it's possible, because there's so much photography in the world. But I do think that my pictures look like my pictures.

toys kind of kid; she knew what the assumptions were about only-children. It was also very unusual in Northern Ireland.

What is interesting now, is that there are so many only-children, particularly within creative homes. Women are choosing to have only one child, and much later in life. I remember, when I sent my girls to school, that there were a lot of only-children. It means you've got a lot of chiefs, really.

CM:

You hope everyone learns to get along.

HS:

I don't know if you come from a really big family, but I love my own social time. That's really important to me, and I can feel myself getting irritated if I haven't had any time alone.

As an only child, you escape. Your fantasy play, your imaginative play, is very heightened because you disappear into that internal world, which is a place I really like being. So effectively... I was thinking about this the other day: how I was as a child, and my experiences with life. I'm still doing the same thing.

This job gets very lonesome. I suppose it depends on the kind of photography you do, but for me it's a way of life. Because you are an observer in the world, when you go out it's really hard not to think about how things look – and if they look that way, what do they mean? Photography is a perfect medium in which to propose those questions, not necessarily to answer them.

CM:

Did photography and art feature much at home when you were young?

HS:

No. But, when I was 14, I had a head injury, which resulted in a stroke about three months later. I lost my speech and was paralysed down the right side of my body for a while. I found it really hard to keep up in school. My language processing wasn't very good, and this was when we were starting GCSEs.

I ended up doing photography as one of my subjects, as the school was smart enough to see that I could probably communicate visually. I was

As an only child, you escape. Your fantasy play, your imaginative play, is very heightened because you disappear into that internal world, which is a place I really like being. [...] I'm still doing the same thing.

kind of interested in it, but I was also 15, 16, so I wasn't really interested in much, apart from having a lot of fun. I liked photography, but I didn't think about it much. We had a project to do from school, and I did it on the streets of Belfast, and showed it to my mam. I remember her saying to me, 'There you go, you've found your calling.' I remember her saying that, and where we were when she said it, and how she said it. I know it didn't mean much to me then, but it's exactly what photography became for me.

[...] The work that I produce has always resonated with people; there's always been a good response. So

I suppose in a way, I can say that photography carried me for the rest of my life. It's quite strange, but... It's my life, being a photographer. I'm glad that I accidentally fell into it. I then did a photography A-Level, a degree, and an MA at the Royal College, I graduated in '97, which was a good year to graduate.

CM:

I really enjoy the continuity in your work. Each piece is different, but throughout the body of your work, the same conversations seem to be happening. Did you start working with specific themes at university? Or was that something that came along later?

HS:

I think I've always been interested in documentary photography. But when I was studying photography, I found that categorisation had a very strict approach in its application. I found it was really too limiting. Also, I didn't want to be labelled as a fashion photographer. Because I had studied all the different applications, I thought that there must be a hybrid. The work that I produced at the Royal College started when I did my degree at Napier University in Edinburgh, but it didn't really come out until the last year of my MA. I think that's the beauty about an MA. You've done all this studying while you're growing. You're studying as a teenager, and then by the time you get to your MA it's such a lovely release to work on what you've already learned, but on your own work too, and to find your own signature style.

For me, if a picture I'm working on looks like one of my pictures, that's very important to me. I'm not even sure if it's possible, because there's so much photography in the world. But I do think that my pictures look like my pictures.

CM:

There's a definite dialogue that I associate with your work, within the images. I can almost always tell that it's yours, sometimes just from the positioning of the subjects. You only put women in your work; what's the reasoning behind that?

HS:

When I was a young woman, I found that a lot of the images I was seeing of other women were very narrow in their aspect, very one-dimensional ideas of what it means to be female. So I started photographing my own female subjects, to see the images that I wanted to see in the world. At the time, it was the mid to late '90s. There was still – how can I say this – a kind of conscious bias against female photographers... well, female anything. The idea that they weren't as good as their male counterparts had been going on for a long time, and feminism had a bad name.

As a female artist who was working with feminist subject matter, as the 20th century has shown us, it was really tricky. Your work could be dismissed, or seen as something that wasn't as important as the hard, gritty, realist, male documentary that was going on around the time. Things have changed a lot, but in the '90s, peoples' ideas about women were still, especially in this country, pretty backward.

When I photograph women, particularly young women, they tell me the same things that I was talking about, when I was their age. Of course, there have been steps toward equality, but there are some still to go. I think the society, and the patriarchal system we live under, is still really hard on women. I just find it extraordinary, after

20 years, to be hearing that women still face the same problems in terms of child care, in terms of domestic violence, in terms of sexual assault.

CM:

Is that something you try to represent in your work?

HS:

No; what I want is to produce images of women that are representative of them. But they're not specific portraits about women or their struggles. They're just, in a way, a female form in whatever the scenario or background or location that I'm using.

But in saying that, because I've been doing this for almost 25 years, my process keeps changing. [...] I used to be much closer, around more people. Then I distanced, and I constructed the photograph in a different way to slow down the eye. It's instinct and it seems to be a reflection of what I'm experiencing, and my perspective, and that's obviously going to change throughout the years. You start off as a young woman, then a mother of small children, then a mother of teenage daughters, and then middle aged – all those sorts of things. So, what I'm interested in and the perspective is slightly different, but it is a continuum producing these images. I think it's a bit like Hokusai Katsushika's wave, and the fact that all of his paintings from that series were about Mount Fuji. Women are my Mount Fuji.

Maybe I'm obsessed with doing the same work, I'm not sure. But there's so much rich material in it. My experience of bringing it together and making a picture... it helps me figure out what it means to be female. I find it hard to make work about people in an area that I don't know about. I'm just really careful of ever being opportunistic, or exploitative.

I photograph what I feel a real connection to, When working it can get confusing, because [the models are] actors, or people I've cast from the streets. I go from having no relationship with them to something quite intense during the creation of the picture. And it's very important for me that it's a collaborative process. You can do this much better with digital now, where you can show who you're photographing the picture. Which I always do, because I always think it's really important for them to see that it's not about them, and it's not judgmental and it's not scrutinising in any way.

So the process of taking the picture is very collaborative, and I like that a lot. And we talk about everything, from menopause, to childbirth, to employment in the city... Going back to Belfast, my mam was a talker. I think it is just that warmth and the connection you can have with a person, particularly a stranger, where you talk about things, and then probably won't see each other again, or not very often. So that's the thing.

CM:

I find that, as a photographer, you can have very singular moments with a person, full of connection, and then never meet or see them again. There's something in the act of two strangers conversing deeply that's very freeing.

HS:

For me to make the picture, it has to feel authentic or sincere. There has to be a sincere reason for doing it. My honesty and openness with the person I'm photographing is part of that transaction. I've asked if I could have their image, effectively, and I have to be respectful and responsible about that.

But it's great. I would hate to have to do anything else.

Photographing real women is really interesting, and it's become harder. Since the arrival of Photoshop, people are obsessed with perfection. Women are way more critical of their image now than I've ever experienced before.

CM:

When I look at one of your photos, the scenes are very momentary, mere seconds. But when you

What I want is to produce images of women that are representative of them. But they're not specific portraits about women or their struggles. They're just, in a way, a female form in whatever the scenario or background or location that I'm using.

create those pieces, do you do it over a long period of time? Is it something you set up over a whole day?

HS:

Generally, I've observed something that I want to recreate. I like giving people a chance to think about whether they want to be photographed or not, so that's why I set them up.

It's kind of an intuitive response; sometimes a woman can walk past me, or I see her getting off the bus or something, and she just has this energy about her that I want to communicate to other women, particularly younger women, about how being attractive is also about your confidence and how you carry yourself. It's as much about all of that as how you look. These little gestures and postures, the spring in your step, that kind of thing.

If I walk past a woman and I feel that energy, I will ask her if she'll be in the picture. To try and capture that energy is a different way of photographing women that would hopefully communicate to my daughters that it's really about loving yourself and not being self critical, and thinking about the real value of being you.

In a way, I'm also looking for role models who I can put out in the world. Sometimes I find myself running after women, and I tell them what I do, and I give them my card. I feel like I go around giving women compliments, because that's effectively what I do in my work. It's very nice to tell a woman that she's beautiful, or that she has a great presence or strength about her. As an artist, it's legitimately hard, otherwise I wouldn't have asked her. It's part of my job to communicate this, so she

I do find with digital, you can be a bit trigger happy. You can over-shoot, and then looking at the edit of the shoot after is torturous because you've got too many choices.

can decide what she's getting into, if you know what I mean.

That's really where the work comes from. It's either the inspiration that I've had on the street, an idea, or something that's affecting me a lot if I'm thinking about the environment and the planet. I try and make a picture that's female-based about those issues, but also an image that's constructed in a way that means anyone can access it.

What I love about photography is that it's still and it's mute. It's only you and the picture.

CM:

It's your private conversation.

HS:

It's nothing else. There's no music, no sound. It's just you. It's a very internal conversation you have. It's really interesting to construct photography – the cues and signifiers you put into an image. What I find fascinating about an image is how you can make it both universal, but very specific to the viewer. And that specific aspect – that's a bit out of my control. That's what they project into the picture. There's no more information I lay down than what's in the picture. I like the ambiguity of that, because walking in [the model's] shoes, or maybe just taking the time to think about other people's experience in the world, is kind of what these pictures are about.

Since the arrival of Photoshop, people are obsessed with perfection.

CM:

Do you have any major influencers?

HS:

Philip-Lorca diCorcia. I came up in the '90s, and it was a really interesting time. Photography was making its way into the art world – not necessarily through artists who used photography, but through photographers like Gorsky and Struth and Jeff Wall. Cindy Sherman is always a firm favourite.

I bought a book yesterday by Mary Ellen Mark. I love that I haven't opened it yet, and there's a whole experience in there that I haven't seen for a very long time. She photographed Tiny, the girl Tiny, for about 30 years. It goes through Tiny's life. I have such deep respect for – female photographers, but I know it's not specific to being female – but photographers who really invest their time in...

CM:

Stories and narratives?

HS:

Photographing somebody's life. That's not what I do. I photograph people, women, almost as they're passing. It's just a quick engagement that takes the energy from the excitement of meeting up, doing the photograph, talking. That's the energy I'm looking for in my work.

CM:

The power within that singular moment. Are your tools important to you? Do you shoot digital now, or still film?

HS:

I shoot digital now. Film was a pain in the ass, but it's so much better than digital. What was interesting was coming from analogue and then moving into digital. I don't have a romanticism about analogue. I embrace digital, because it helped me. You're not working blind. Especially if you're working with someone and you're working in a collaborative sense, to have a digital back is fantastic.

I do find with digital, you can be a bit trigger happy. You can over-shoot, and then looking at the edit of the shoot after is torturous because you've got too many choices. Whereas with film, because you're limited to 12 frames, there's something about those 12 frames that really make you get the picture in a different way.

Digital has changed how I work as a photographer, and how I see the world as a photographer. I do curse digital sometimes, for being so easy. But that sounds like a contradiction, and it is a contradiction.

CM:

I think there are lots of contradicting things about digital. What are you currently working on?

HS:

I have a show coming up at the Hepworth Gallery. It was supposed to open soon, but due to Covid, they have postponed it until 2022. I've got two years now to work on that show, and it's such a luxury to go through all my writing, sketches and location shots, and all of that sort of thing. It's a real privilege to be able to re-evaluate at this stage, so I'm glad I've got the time for that.

Then there are a few more commissions that I'm working on. Prior to lockdown, I was a Guildhall, City of London Artist in Residence – the first one – and that was brilliant. I was commissioned to celebrate women working in the city. I have a little dog who I like to take with me. […] He's almost my first assistant, and probably a casting agent, because he'll be like, 'Oh, look at me, I'm amazing, you just want to stroke me, don't you?' And then, invariably, it's always women who stop and say, 'Oh my God, can I touch your dog?' And then that's that.

It allows the process of selection to be random, because I do think about my own unconscious bias when I am looking at people or thinking of casting for a picture. Why would I choose them? Identity is really important at the minute,

and working in photography you kind of have a responsibility to represent every women, which is impossible. But for there to be women in the pictures who other women feel a connection to, is really important for me.

CM:

Do you find, with the emergence of things like #MeToo, that the dialogue surrounding women in the workplace is finally, if slowly, changing?

HS:

Yeah, I do.

CM:

Is that an interesting subject for you to then narrate in your work?

HS:

It's very interesting, because when I'm talking to other women in these kinds of contexts, you talk about really deep stuff. I'm always amazed at how many women I meet who have had a bad experience somewhere along the line. But with #MeToo, everyone now knows. I think that's kind of amazing, how the movement has put a stop to those guys getting away with it.

TOM STODDART

After a few false starts in 2020, Tom and I got to chat at length over Zoom about his incredible career as a photographer. Tom is very modest when it comes to his work, but he has a wonderful archive, and his journey with photography is full of insight.

Tom Stoddart, Sarajevo, 1992
© Tom Stoddart

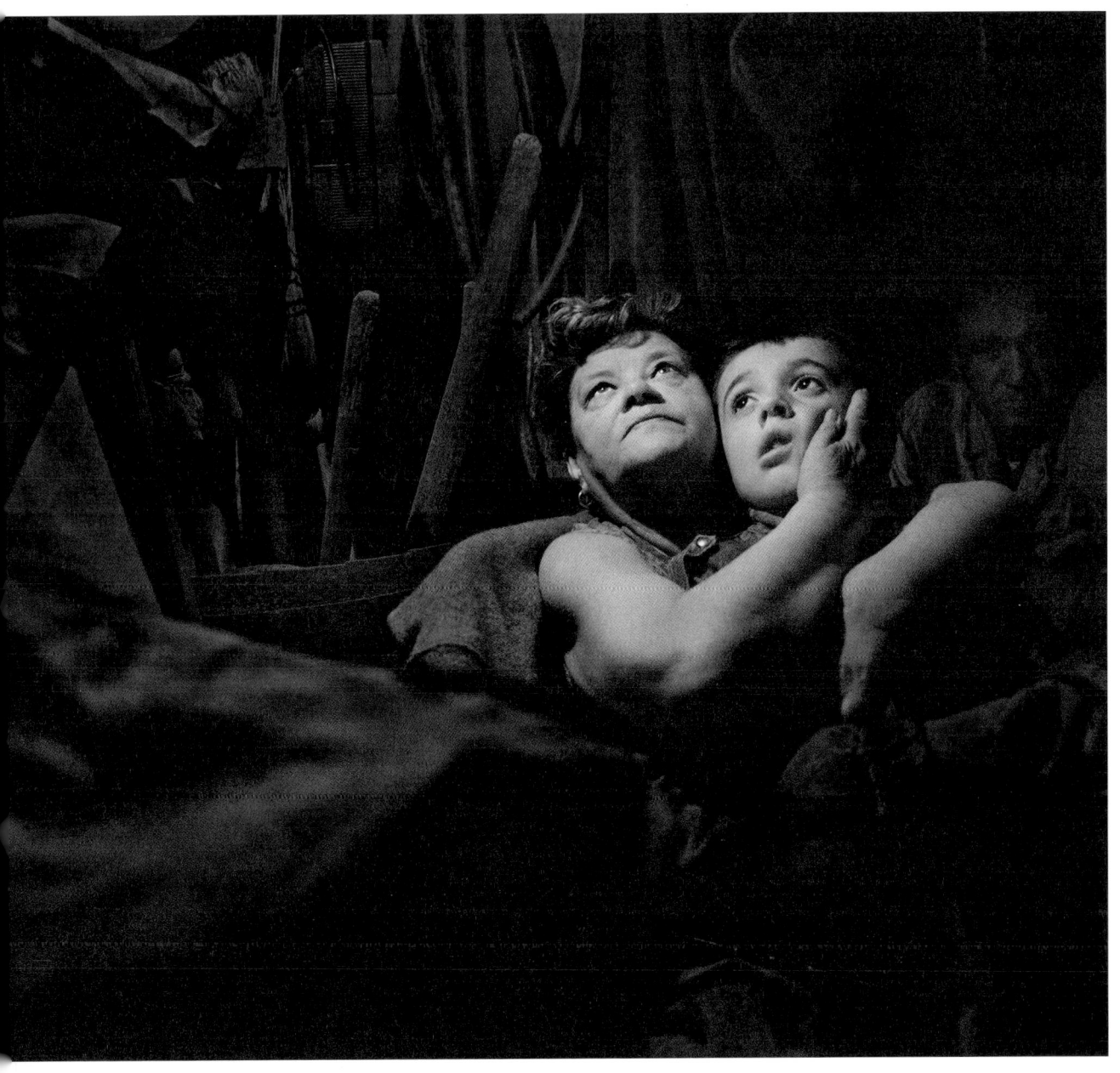

Charles Moriarty:

When did you start getting into photography?

Tom Stoddart:

I come from the north east of England. My upbringing was poor; my dad was a farm worker and my mother had been a nurse. There wasn't a lot of money around, which resulted in me never having a camera, or any access to photography as a kid. In secondary school, there was no equipment.

At school I was quite good at writing, so I had the idea that I would like to be a reporter, and the local newspaper in our area were asking for an apprentice photographer. I thought if I could get that job, I could then move into reporting. I was only 17 at the time. I got that job, mostly because I lived in the right place, as they wanted someone who could cover that area. On the first day – and I always think it's worth repeating this – the senior photographer/picture editor said, 'You'll have a champagne lifestyle on a beer salary,' and it's kind of been like that ever since.

What I noticed quite quickly, even in those days, was that the reporters never went anywhere. Most of their work was quite boring, on the phone to people. Whereas on my first day I was in the back of car, charging about the countryside meeting people, and I really enjoyed that. I quickly realised I didn't want to be a reporter.

I spent five years working, doing hatches, matches and dispatches. Everything you do with local newspapers. I really enjoyed it. It wasn't very well paid, and it wasn't very creative at all. It was very much, 'put a group together, take as many pictures as you can, hopefully everyone in the group will buy a picture so the proprietor will be pleased'. It was really low-level community stuff. But as we know, that's very important.

CM:

It was an education.

TS:

Definitely. Learning how to talk to various groups and how to behave in front of people, some arrogant, some humble; how to gauge the situation both in terms of how you speak to people and getting them to do things quickly when you've got 20 people together at a dinner dance who are pissed…

It was a time of local adventures, and at that time I had no understanding of photojournalism, or any idea of wanting to better myself. Gradually, as I got older, I thought, 'This is an enjoyable way to make a living, and I would like to try and be better at it'. So, after about 5 years — I think I was 22 — I decided to try and move up.

At that time, you had the great papers. *The Daily Express* was a great broadsheet, and *The Sunday Times* was producing amazing things. It was then that I had an awakening. I joined a local picture agency in York and the guy who ran it was a classic kind of ogre, but he knew everything about the industry and the currency of ideas. How to turn one line in a local paper into a national story – he was brilliant at that. I spent three years working with him and various reporters as well. That was when I really started to learn about taking pictures commercially, because if you didn't sell in the very competitive market, you didn't get paid. It was as simple as that.

CM:

Was there a particular moment or story you were covering that gave you that push to progress?

TS:

I think it was the excitement of realising the

photographs you took were going to be viewed by millions of people, and also just the broad spectrum. One day you'd be shooting in the style of *The Guardian* and *The Times*, and the next day it would be pretty girls down by the canal with ice cream for *Heat* magazine or something. You didn't really earn any money, but it was very exciting, charging around. That was when you begin to think 'I can do this': when you open the *Daily Express* and see a picture of racehorses charging along a beach – a classic *Irish Times* picture, silhouettes, seagulls taking off and all that. And it's your picture, being viewed by millions of people. That was a really big buzz.

CM:

Did that then lead you to London? Your time in York must have given you a strong portfolio.

TS:

It wasn't quite like that. I think it's better to be lucky than good in our game, a lot of the time. I remember, I was working in this small agency, and all the other photographers ahead of me had gone on to really good jobs – like Don McPhee, three *Daily Express* staff photographers and a guy called Eddie Sanderson, who […] went on to be John Wayne's photographer.

I wanted this adventure, travel and all of that. The way it happened for me was, a *Daily Mail* feature writer came to the area to write a story and I was assigned to go out with him. He bought dinner. He had expenses, which we did not, and he mentioned that the *Mail* had just lost a photographer to freelance. He said, 'Why don't you

call the picture editor?' — a man who I knew of, but had never met.

The first mistake I made was to call about ten in the morning. He was well known as being the toughest picture editor in Fleet street. I called him and I said, 'I'm Tom Stoddart, and I work for [company] in York'. There was a long silence, so I said, 'I hear you've lost one of your staffers, and I wonder if I could apply for the job'. I was totally naïve. There was another long silence. Then he said, 'I've never heard of you. If you were any good, I'd have heard of you'. He crushed me in about two seconds flat. But he said, 'If you're ever in London, come and see me, but I know I'll never see you,' and hung up the phone.

So, there I was: stood in a phone box, because I couldn't call from the office. I just thought, 'Okay'. I'd never been to London, but the next day I got on a train with a poxy little book of pictures. I arrived at King's Cross, asked the taxi to take me to the *Mail*, went to the news floor and asked someone where the picture editor was. I went in and I said, 'I spoke to you yesterday; you were very abrupt with me. I'm here now, and I'd like you to take a look at my pictures'. He didn't say a word, just flipped through the book. Finally, he asked, 'How much is he paying you?' I told him some miniscule amount, and it started there: he gave me a short-term contract. I moved to London, and that's where the next step in my ladder started.

CM:

Did you work specifically for the Mail, *or did you bounce about?*

I had a contract with the *Mail*; freelance came later. But shortly after the *Mail*, I moved to the *Daily Star* as a full staff photographer. I went back up north and was paid very well to be on staff. But it wasn't enough. I sat in the Manchester office of the *Star/ Express* and watched the Iranian embassy siege, with the SAS storming through the windows. I'd been out taking pictures of little old ladies making jumpers out of their dogs' hair. In many ways, things hadn't changed. There was more money, but I needed to be where the action was happening; that was what I wanted. So, I asked for a transfer to London,

I was at the *Star* five years in total, but then the real job was to go freelance. There are only so many images you want to take of Diana, etc. So, I left. I went straight from the *Daily Star* to *The Sunday Times*, which was a culture shock. I was freelance and didn't expect to get any jobs, but the phone rang one morning; they had a guy who'd done something wrong, and they needed a photo of him. So, I found his address and waited outside. When I saw some movements inside the house, in the morning, I went to knock on the door. He answered. I said, 'Are you Mr. Smith?' He said, 'Yes,' and I whipped out a small canon camera, *bosh*, right between the eyes, classic *Daily Star* training.

I set off down the path. But he ran out the front door after me with a screwdriver. So, we had a battle in the front garden, and eventually we ended up back in the house. He was very angry. He called the picture editor, who he spoke with, and then put the editor on to me, who checked that I was okay. He said he had negotiated with him so I could get out. I went back to the office. I developed the

film, which was perfect and pin sharp, but when I brought it to the picture desk, the editor said, 'This is great, but I'm afraid we can't use it.' 'What do you mean?' I asked, and he said, 'I gave him my word we wouldn't run it.' At the *Star* it would have been page one, but not at *The Sunday Times*. He did then ask me to follow the guy to try and get another picture, so I then had a week of following this guy when he knew I was about.

I see myself as a decent photographer, who's tried hard at every level that I've worked at.

I learnt so much from these people about ethics and trying to do the right thing. There were two amazing sports photographers, Chris Smith and Aidan McCabe. Seeing their work coming in on a Saturday morning when they had five minutes to get a first edition image sorted, was when I really began to get a love for excellent photography.

I'd just sit quietly in the corner, listening to them, learning from them. Through simple things like looking at their contact sheets, they taught me how a photographer moves and thinks when he's got only 36 frames instead of 3,600.

Photographers will nearly always get their best

shot in the first seven frames. Some would peak around 15 or 20, by the time they'd really figured out their angle and everything. Then some, like Robert Frank, would just do the one frame. It was that kind of learning curve.

I also learnt about how they worked with light. When working in black and white you have to have a good understanding of light and treat it as a friend, which sounds corny and clichéd, but not for me. They taught me how to think about the image.

CM:

Do you always shoot black and white?

TS:

This is my 50th year as a photographer. I've got plenty of cameras but no work [laughs]. But never mind.

In my early days, at the little paper, you learnt to be in the darkroom and tap glass plates on your teeth to decide which was the gloss and which was the matte in the dark. To piss in the developer to warm it up, for that extra bit of warmth. Working with chemicals, etc. From there to the 2 ¼ square. Learning how to turn a Rolliflex over your head in a crowd, and how to shoot from the waist in a difficult situation. At every stage, every generation of photographer would say, 'You'll never work with that.'

In Fleet Street, it was pretty much the same as now: two zooms, because it's all well and good wanting to be arty, but if you're 20 meters away standing on a ladder, or you're on the other side of the world photographing a royal, you can't do much with a 35mm. That changed when I started doing more serious stuff. I found my style, is the best way of putting it. I stripped away all the excess, I stopped carrying so much, I changed to two Leicas and three lenses.

CM:

Was Sarajevo your first big freelance story?

TS:

The picture editor at *The Sunday Times* knew I wanted to do that kind of stuff, so I'd been given Beirut in 1992 for one of the tabloids when the Israeli forces were bombing Yasser Arafat's PLO [Palestine Liberation Organisation] out of west Beirut. It gave me a taste to see whether I could deal with stuff like that: more serious and certainly more dangerous.

Then for *The Sunday Times* I'd been fortunate enough to get in and out of a camp with Marie Colvin, which is still the most important set of photos I've ever taken, because they actually stopped something. When we got the material out, the reaction in the world was huge. The images were splashed all over *The Sunday Times*, which is read in the White House and the Kremlin, so it actually made a big difference and saved peoples' lives.

CM:

Were there certain reporters you really enjoyed working with?

TS:

When you find a good reporter to work with — who are as rare as rocking horse shit — it's a joy. They understand what you need and give you the time. You're a team. I always enjoyed working with good foreign correspondents.

I love photographers, and it's a tragedy that the high street photographer has disappeared. Photography is a very broad church and coming from a small local newspaper I respect all photographers who are making a living — and even now, the ones who are just doing it for pleasure. But when you're working for a newspaper at that level, you have to produce; you can't just spend thousands of pounds and go off and not get something. When you're working with a very good correspondent…

I worked with a guy called David Blundy, who was sadly killed. I don't have a very good track record with foreign correspondents. He was killed in El Salvador. We worked on the TWA hostage, when the plane was taken hostage. I worked with lots of really great [reporters], but mainly I would work on my own. I wanted to move away from filling holes. In the end of the day, when you work for a paper, that's what you're doing. I wanted to have a voice and tell my own stories.

CM:

When you worked in a place like Sarajevo, did it affect your mental health?

TS:

I'm not a war photographer or a conflict photographer. That's one of those things there are very few of. The people who focus purely on war end up chasing it and become quite unwell. You want to be on the biggest story in the world. If you look at any conflict – take, for instance, Rwanda – and look around the room, it's the same 20 or 30 photographers every time. James Nachtwey, David and Peter Turnley – great guys. I could go through a list.

It was always the same photographers who would travel, because at that time, *Time* magazine was very strong and you had Newsweek, US News and [World] Report, *Paris Match, Stern, Life, Le Figaro, The Sunday Times…* All these guys had budgets to send wonderful photographers to the biggest stories in the world. I would sit around, maybe in a hotel in Jo'burg, for Mandela's election and think 'This is what I was put on earth for. This is where I want to be.'

We realised it was quite a special time. It wasn't Vietnam, where you had Larry Burrows; we were the generation after. But we knew it was a special time, and that if you put the time and effort in you could make photo essays to be proud of, and if they were good enough, they would get run by the papers and the magazines. […] I think the difference now is, you can't aim to have a cover and ten or twelve pages in a major magazine.

I understood the importance of photojournalism, and that a great still photo was incredibly important. If you look at some of the anti-Vietnam images […] they resonated with people. You saw them carried on signs, and you realised a great still image in a magazine stays in your head. You can look at something, put it down, go make a cup of tea, pick it up again, and see something else in that same image. Whereas television visuals flash in front of your eyes and don't embed; they're gone. Obviously, things like 9/11 are different. But by and large, TV news goes straight out of the brain.

CM:

Images like 'the falling man' that were replayed over and over, stay with you. I'm sure that particular image has stuck with the majority of us who watched that day.

TS:

In many ways, that's what we are all aiming for; pictures of our time, the picture of Liam Gallagher with the union Jack; great portraiture, John Lennon and Yoko, goofing around on a bed. There are pictures that resonate throughout history, and if you're lucky you might get one or two that stand the test of time. I think one of the things with black and white, certainly one of the things I've realised now, is that by shooting in black and white, and shooting the way I did…

In Bosnia, […] all the other guys were working for the big magazines, so they had armoured cars, and they had massive day rates because they were in danger and all of that. But they were all crammed in together, shooting the exact same story, getting the same shots each week, whereas I could basically walk down the street and maybe see a lady

You need to start at the end. You need to make money out of your work.

cooking or arguing about buying some leaves from a seller, because there was no food. And that to me was a more valuable scene. I was building a jigsaw, whereas the other guys were just trying to get their ten rolls and then have them shipped to New York or whatever. So, I think the pictures that were shot of everyday life, certainly have a longer lifetime.

CM:

When you take these photographs, what's your level of interaction with the subject?

TS:

At that time I'd stripped away all the telephoto lenses. In the *iWitness* book, I think there are maybe two from Bosnia that were… You know, it was dangerous, so you had to…

Most of the time I was lying on the ground, waiting for people to run to me. But I tried to interact with people as much as possible. The images I'm most proud of are ones where I stood in front of someone, four or five feet, took the shot and then left. There's an image of a lady crying in Sarajevo, when she's about to put her boy on a bus. That's the kind of thing I was trying to do; tell a story but through them.

When I want to wind up my art photographer friends, I always say art photography is about 'look at me', whereas photojournalism is about 'look at this'. They get pissed off about it, but I'm really just teasing them as I love photography and creativity in all its forms. Photojournalism for me is about having the privilege to go somewhere that millions of others can't and having the experience, and through that, bringing back images that are truthful, informative, educational. They can be entertaining as well, because not everything is bad.

That's really why I push back on this idea against war photography. You have someone like Don McCullin, who's a good friend of mine, and James Nachtwey especially, and a lot of their pictures take you in one direction: down, down, down. But in extreme situations you see great love, you see great humanity. Things go on: love, sex, generosity. People adapt, and I think it's just as important to show that side of it whenever you can.

CM:

Are there images you've taken that still give you a thrill, that transport you?

TS:

I've got about six where I think, 'I couldn't do better than that'. I see myself as a decent photographer, who's tried hard at every level that I've worked at, but I don't think of myself as a great. People like Eugene Richards – any of his work, even now, is just unbelievable photojournalism. The word 'genius' is bandied around by a lot of people, but in my opinion there are very few who deserve that title. He consistently produces amazing documentary work, and he does it with empathy. He works so close to people, and you don't get that access without people understanding you're a force for good, and that you're not there to take away from them.

[Photography] is a lifelong occupation.

James Nachtwey is another of them. He has a book called *Inferno*, and it really does take you to hell. James is a genius with a camera, even now. In his book, *Inferno* – a huge tome that he sent to, I think, every world leader – he talks about working during the cholera epidemic in Goma, Zaire. He describes it as being in an escalator to hell. Some of the things we've seen have been awful, but then you contrast that with… You know, I was lucky to be at the Berlin Wall the night it came down, just by pure luck. To be there on the day that 22 million South Africans voted for their first Black president. Six weeks travelling around with Mandela. These are incredible, privileged things to have witnessed.

But – like you – you know your work, the access you've had and the trust you've had from the people you've photographed. These people are heroes and icons to millions of people. I was looking at your work and it jogged a memory when an agency got in touch to say there was a guy called Timberlake, and he wanted me to go on the road with him. I said, 'No, you mean Timberland,' as I'd never heard of Justin Timberlake. I ended up doing three weeks on the road with him.

I was looking at your behind-the-scenes stuff on tour. People think that stuff's easy. It's absolute shit, with the strobes and lights, and with film as well. You really have to figure out how you're going to do it – but I love that challenge. It's great to be working on the big international stories, earthquakes and famines and conflicts, but it's also nice to have something where you can be in the bubble. That's why I started doing politics.

I managed to get inside Tony Blair's campaign in 1997. It took two years for them to allow me to go in, because we don't have a culture the same as in America, where they have about seven staff photographers covering the president. To go to them and say 'I want to follow you every second,' with the first Labour Prime Minister in 18 years – they don't trust you, and that's the bottom line. You can earn that trust, but those photographs are very seldom used.

Right now, I'm freelance; I'm a commercial photographer. It's no good for me to be standing outside a bus trying to shoot pictures of Tony Blair or David Cameron with everybody else from *The Guardian*, Reuters or Getty. I need to be on the bus.

CM:

You've been doing this for 50 years. How do you feel about photography now? It's changed a lot.

TS:

It has, and a lot of my colleagues are pretty down about it. I'm talking about professionals who make a living out of it full time. I always say to them, 'You know if you're on a bus in Dublin, and you look down and along the streets there are all these people with instruments, busking, this is where we are now.' We've had it so good for so long. If you think pretty much everybody can write English, but how many people get paid for writing, how many paint and get paid money? Musicians who've been playing for years and never get recognised – that's where photography is now at.

If you want to be a professional now, you have to be very good and you have to be very, very lucky. You have to understand the business side as well as how to make photos. A lot of courses are designed where students are paying a lot of money to go to lectures, but when I go there and do a talk, the students don't know the first thing about business or about the currency of ideas. They just get told how wonderful they are. They're unprepared for the real world.

CM:

Is there a method or pathway to shooting the kind of work you did in Sarajevo?

TS:

You need to start at the end. You need to make money out of your work. People think it's shameful to make money out of your work. Magnum was set up in order for those guys to protect their copyright and make money. They morphed into an agency that did wonderful photojournalism, where people got paid well for their work.

But going back to what you said, there are so many guys who get on a plane and they shoot something, a famine or an earthquake, but then they come back and they don't know what to do with the work. They think they can just call up *The Guardian* or *The Independent*: 'I've been to Ethiopia.' If you're going to do this kind of stuff you need good people around you. If you want to be a photojournalist you need distribution. You don't have to be with the big agencies like Getty or whatever, but you have to know that somebody is going to work for you.

I don't mean to be a downer, but young photographers have no idea of the dedication needed for this kind of thing. This is a lifelong occupation. The amount of yourself that you have to give to be working at a decent level leads to divorce. People have no idea.

CM:

Any major regrets?

TS:

I regret having to find it all on my own and not having a mentor. With photography, a camera is just a box with a hole in it, and once you strip away all the bullshit, it really all comes down to who you are and how you see the world

ACKNOWLEDGEMENTS

This book came together with the help of many hands.

Thank you to all of my interviewees for their candour and time, and to all of their assistants who helped make these interviews a reality.

To everyone at ACC Art Books, thank you for your patience. I know this took much longer than anticipated – first ones always do, I suspect.

Last but not least, thank you to my brilliant literary agent, Carrie Kania of C&W.